Creation and Abortion

CREATION

═══ AND ═══

ABORTION

A Study in Moral
and Legal Philosophy

F. M. KAMM

New York   Oxford
OXFORD UNIVERSITY PRESS
1992

Oxford University Press

Oxford   New York   Toronto
Delhi   Bombay   Calcutta   Madras   Karachi
Petaling Jaya   Singapore   Hong Kong   Tokyo
Nairobi   Dar es Salaam   Cape Town
Melbourne   Auckland

and associated companies in
Berlin   Ibadan

Copyright © 1992 by F. M. Kamm

Published by Oxford University Press, Inc.
200 Madison Avenue, New York, NY 10016

Oxford is a registered trademark of Oxford University Press

Library of Congress Cataloging-in-Publication Data
Kamm, Frances Myrna.
Creation and abortion : a study in moral
and legal philosophy / Frances Myrna Kamm.
p. cm.   Includes bibliographical references and index.
ISBN 0–19–507283–9.
ISBN 0–19–507284–7 (pbk.)
1. Abortion—Moral and ethical aspects.
2. Abortion—Law and legislation.
3. Abortion—Law and legislation—United States.
I. Title.   HQ767.15.K36
1992   363.4'6—dc20
91–22932

2 4 6 8 9 7 5 3 1

Printed in the United States of America
on acid-free paper

To my mother and the memory of my father

Preface

This is a philosophical examination of certain issues of applied ethics, based on my more theoretical work *Morality, Mortality*. Here I deal primarily with the moral issue of abortion, as well as self-defense, euthanasia, and pregnancy. This book began as a relatively short section of *Morality, Mortality,* but when that book grew beyond a reasonable size, the short section was cut and became this book. Derek Parfit, the editor of the series in which *Morality, Mortality* is to appear, kindly permitted me to publish the material separately.

This book was prompted by my attempt to understand and modify Judith Thomson's most important discussion of abortion, "A Defense of Abortion." Her discussion is irreplaceable and unique. It was kind of her to encourage my project.

I have benefited from the helpful suggestions regarding recent versions of this book given to me by Derek Parfit, Thomas Scanlon, Judith Thomson, Shelly Kagan, Dennis Thompson, Bruce Ackerman, Jonathen Bennett, Tony Kronman, Michael Stocker, Owen Fiss, Richard Fallon, Seana Shiffrin, and those others who are credited in footnotes. Kagan made especially detailed remarks on organization. I thank Ronald Dworkin and Lawrence Sager for insightful discussions. Many years ago I wrote a paper on abortion for a class of Robert Nozick's, whose help I then greatly appreciated.

I am indebted to Thomas Nagel for his continuing support and encouragement and the intellectual standards he sets.

I also would like to thank Drs. Kenneth Ryan and Rapin Osathanondh, as well as the staff and patients, for making possible my observation of abortions at Boston's Brigham and Women's Hospital.

I am grateful to my typists, Nerssa Miller, Marie Palumbo, and Helen Snively, to Lynn Gay for help indexing, and to Cynthia Read, Jeffrey Gordon, and Ann Wald for their support and advice.

My efforts have been supported most recently by a New York University Presidential Fellowship (1985), an American Association of University Women Fellowship (1985–86), a Silver Fellowship in Law, Science, and Technology at Columbia University Law School (1986), and a Fellowship in Ethics and the Professions at Harvard University (1989–90).

Shorter versions of all the chapters were presented as public lectures: a Silver Lecture in Law, Science, and Technology at the Columbia University Law School (January 1987) and a Faculty Colloquium public lecture at the New York University Law School (April 1987). In addition, an earlier version of some of the chapters was presented at a New York University Law and Philosophy Colloquium Meeting, Fall 1986, and in 1984 in Ronald Dworkin's seminar in political theory at the New York University Law School. I am grateful to these audiences for their comments, and to members of the Society for Ethical and Legal Philosophy for discussion in Fall 1989.

New York   F. M. K.
August 1991

Contents

Creation and Abortion

Introduction

It is widely assumed that if a fetus[1] were acknowledged to have the rights of a person, abortions (and many other reproductive freedoms) would not be permissible. This prohibition would perhaps seem even more justified if the fetus were accorded the rights of an infant, as we tend to be more protective of them than of adults.[2]

In this book, I shall examine arguments favoring the permissibility of abortion even if the fetus is considered to be a person (or infant). I shall focus on those cases in which this approach is thought least likely to succeed, namely, nonrape cases. In the first chapter I consider a general argument for permitting the taking of a life in nonabortion contexts. In addition, I also consider the moral distinction between killing someone and letting someone die, and I briefly discuss euthanasia. In the second chapter I apply this argument to specific cases. In the third chapter I discuss variations of these cases and alternative ways of dealing with them. In these chapters I develop elements of a theory of self-defense. I employ some farfetched hypothetical cases in the hope that we can then reason without preconceived commitments and emotional responses. The results should be relevant to abortion. In the fourth chapter I consider an analogous argument for the moral permissibility of aborting a fetus, the cutoff abortion argument. In the second part of Chapter 4, I turn to significant differences between the analogous cases and abortion, those factors that many people consider crucial to understanding the problem of abortion, for example, equality of the sexes and the naturalness of pregnancy. One reason for not presenting these factors earlier is that, I believe, they can be used in arguments for or against the permissibility of abortion only as supplements to the argument first considered in the analogous cases. In particular, I contend, it makes sense to consider these factors only once an argument based on bodily autonomy is already in place. In the fifth chapter I criticize the cut off abortion argument and consider two alternative approaches to abortions, the benefit–burden approach and the immigration argument. This chapter covers additional differences between abortion and analogous cases, in particular, that pregnancy involves creating a new person, that people desire to have children, and that sexual relations play an important role in many people's lives. I shall try to develop a theory of what we owe to the people we create and to relate this to both abortion and the creation of people for the sake of helping others. In the sixth chapter, I explore the implications of the benefit–burden approach for requiring "informed" consent for an abortion, the implications of abortion for the responsibilities that women who continue their pregnancies would have to their fetus, and the effect that mechanical means of gestation outside the human womb would have on the permissibility of abortion. Some of the points I shall make are implicitly critical of other philosophical and legal discussions, but I shall limit my explicit criticism of the literature.

My aim is not to conclude that abortion should be permissible even if the fetus is a person (or infant) but to see what premises would have to be true in order to reach this conclusion and whether we could argue for these premises. By inquiring into the moral permissibility of abortion, we shall try to determine whether those who would have abortions if the fetus were a person would violate some basic moral requirements, so that we would be justified in referring to them as murderers, or if they are acting in an exceptionally insensitive and selfish manner, or on the other hand if they are acting reasonably from a moral point of view. Deciding whether an act is morally permissible and within the bounds of ordinary sensitivity is an important decision when judging other people and also ourselves, as it limits reproach, self-castigation, and guilt. It is, however, less relevant to limiting regret, for example, for lost opportunities. It also can never completely be the basis for our deciding what to do, for we may wish to go beyond these minimal moral standards. This distinction between moral guilt and regret should be kept in mind in reading this book. Notice that I am here discussing both moral permissibility (e.g., one is within one's rights to do something) and ordinary moral sensitivity (e.g., it may be insensitive to exercise moral rights). Both these are distinct from legal permissibility, and ordinarily more demanding. The moral discussion is relevant to the issue of legal permissibility insofar as the legal discussion of the impermissibility of killing must mimic the moral discussion. For example, the legal and moral discussions must both consider what losses someone will suffer if they are not permitted to kill.

Considering the problem of abortion from the viewpoint that the fetus is a person is a fascinating intellectual exercise. But it may also be useful for public policy purposes, as many people do consider the fetus to be a person. Further, with the increasing use of such technology as sonograms, people claim to "bond" to fetuses as they do to infants. Pregnant women thus are encouraged to think of themselves as already being mothers—in part because they are then more likely to take care of themselves in pregnancy—even though technically only someone who has given birth is a mother. Such attitudes may then make abortion more difficult if the fetus to whom one is "bonded" or of whom one thinks of oneself as "mother" is found to be defective. Indeed, people may be involved in inconsistencies, if they believe that the fetus is a person and yet want to abort it because it is defective.

Bonding and maternal attitudes, of course, cannot and do not establish that a fetus is a person. The fact that someone comes to care for a fetus no more shows that it is a person than does the fact that animal lovers come to care for cats means that cats are persons. Nor does the fact that the fetus in some physical respects resembles a human person mean that it has capacities for consciousness, for example, that may be necessary to be deemed a person. It is ironic that if a fetus developed from the brain outward, so that the mental capacities most likely to qualify it for personhood were present even when a sonogram did not yet show any physical likeness to a baby, there would probably be less bonding to it.

In any case, if an argument did morally justify abortion even if the fetus were a person, or if it showed it to be impermissible, this finding would be significant to those who think the fetus is a person. I shall assume that the fetus is a person merely for the sake of argument, but I recognize that this may be a false assumption.

For purposes of argument, should we assume that the fetus is not only a person but an infant? If the greater care we show infants is based on their being incapable of helping themselves, then this will not distinguish them from adult persons who are helpless. Suppose we are more likely to help them because they are the future generation and we are biologically programmed to take extra care of them. This need not necessarily have moral weight, unless not blunting these instincts deserves moral weight because survival of the species might be affected. Do we think that we should help the younger rather than the older person because the younger has had less life so far? We do not usually give greater weight to not killing twenty-year-olds than we give to not killing fifty-year-olds.

These points are meant to suggest that we must be careful as we assume the fetus to be not only a person but an infant. We should be on guard that we are then not more resistant to killing it from merely biological or sentimental motives, if there are insufficient reasons from a moral point of view for not killing.

Methodology Employed or Presupposed[3]

Some philosophers begin with a theory—prominent concepts, principles, or procedures—whose correctness is either immediately clear to them or has been argued for; in either case, they accept the theory to be logically prior to consideration of its application to specific cases. If they are convinced of the theory's correctness, they will accept any implications it might have for particular cases. For example, they may believe that happiness maximized is the most important goal, no matter how it is achieved. Although such philosophers may sometimes feel uncomfortable with the results of their theory, they do not allow their intuitive responses to cases to overrule the theory. (They may, however, expect their theory to give an account of why they have such intuitive responses that diverge from the theory. This is like the scientist who must account for our seeing the world as colored, though our color perceptions do not negate atomic theory which tells us that objects are fundamentally uncolored.)

A Second Method

Other philosophers may begin in the same way but are not so firmly committed to their initial theory. Instead, they examine its implications for various cases, and if the implications conflict with their pretheoretical judgments, they sometimes use this conflict as a reason for altering either their theory or their pretheoretical judgments. What is it about such judgments that enables them to sometimes overrule a theory? The same mind that initially accepted a theory as plausible also finds the implications of that theory to be unreasonable. That is, a pretheoretical response to the moral significance of general principles or ideas was necessary to accept a theory; the same type of response, only more of them, is called forth by cases.

How a Theory May Change

How does a theory change? Consider a theorist who is committed to maximizing happiness. Suppose he is confronted with cases in which there are no actual harms (in the form of diminished utility) but he agrees nevertheless that there is wrongdoing. An example is someone who has been treated paternalistically. His utility may be enhanced but his will has been violated, and this is a wrong. The theorist, despite his theory, may agree that it is right that a person direct his own life, even if his utility is diminished. The theorist may also agree that it is right to evaluate and revise desires one has in the light of something other than higher-order desires one actually has.

Our theorist would here be conceiving of a case involving factors that he may never have thought of before, that is, a case that distinguishes wrongs from harms or one that involves goods other than the satisfaction of desires taken as givens. He then responds to this case in ways that imply that he is rejecting as a standard for evaluating its outcome the maximization of utility or the satisfaction of given desires. He may then shift to another standard for evaluating outcomes, for example, a Kantian one.

No doubt, the theorist already holds some views that allow him to conceive of such new factors and also to respond to them in such a way that he will judge his utilitarian theory to be inadequate. These views which are used to judge the adequacy of his theory may not change. But a rather significantly deep principle—his principle of utility maximization has been jettisoned or revised.

A Third Method

The third philosophical method begins with responses to cases—either detailed practical cases or hypothetical cases with just enough detail for philosophical purposes—rather than with a total or even a tentative commitment to a theory. This procedure is attractive because it permits recognition of new factors that may be morally relevant in certain cases, factors that no theory yet developed emphasizes. Philosophers using this method try to unearth the reasons for a particular response to a case and to construct more general principles from these data. They then evaluate these principles in three ways: Do they fit the intuitive responses; are their basic concepts coherent and distinct from one another; and are the principles or basic concepts in them morally plausible and significant, or even rationally demanded? The attempt to determine whether the concepts and the principles are morally significant and even required by reason is necessary in order to understand why the principles derived from cases should be endorsed.[4]

The Method Used or Presupposed in This Book

The method used or presupposed in this book is closer to the third method than to the first two. We present hypothetical cases for consideration and seek judgments about what may and may not be done in them. The fact that these cases are hypothetical and often fantastic distinguishes this enterprise from straightforward applied ethics, in which the primary aim is to give definite answers to real-life dilemmas. Real-life cases often do not contain the relevant—or solely the relevant—characteristics to help in our search for principles. If our aim is to discover the relative weight of, say, two factors, we should consider them alone, perhaps artificially, rather than distract ourselves with other factors and options. For example, if we wish to consider the importance of property rights relative to that of saving a life, we should not consider cases in which we can avoid violating a property right in order to save a life.

Some people have difficulty considering cases in which the factors and alternatives are purposely limited and thus are different from those of the real world in which other alternatives are possible. This tendency may simply reflect the fear of having to make hard decisions; therefore, to test this hypothesis, one must find out whether such people are afraid to make decisions in real life cases in which the alternatives are limited. Furthermore, the tendency in itself to introduce other options into a hypothetical case reveals something about a person's judgment concerning the relative weight of the original alternatives. For example, it is probably only because someone believes that it would be wrong to violate a property right in order to save a life that he feels the need to consider ways of saving the life without violating this right. If cases are sufficiently unlike real ones, can we have responses to them? Or do our responses reflect carryover from real-life cases that are similar but also crucially different, with the crucial differences responsible for our responses? I believe we are capable of explicitly excluding certain real-life factors and conceiving of and responding to cases with only the factors we wish to attend to at the time.

The responses to the cases with which I am concerned are not emotional responses but are judgments about the permissibility or impermissibility of certain acts. These judgments are not guaranteed to be correct, and one must give one's reasons for making them. These reasons, in turn, are not personal emotional responses to the acts but point to properties of the acts themselves.

Responding definitively to a case does not necessarily mean responding quickly. But the fact that a response takes time to make does not mean that it is being deliberately constructed. Having responses to complex and unfamiliar cases requires that one see a whole complex landscape at once, rather than piecemeal. This often requires deep concentration. Only a few people may be able to respond to a complex case with a firm response. If "Goldilocks" is the fairy tale best associated with Aristotle's doctrine of the mean, then the "Princess and the Pea" is the fairy tale best associated with the method I describe: someone, despite much interference, cannot ignore a slight difference that others may never sense. Because even slight differences can make a moral difference, it may be necessary to consider a large variety of cases with only slight differences among them. This approach gives the impression of thoroughly working over a small area with the result of greater depth. Sometimes, however, a detail interesting in its own right is omitted for the sake of better exhibiting the final result.

Those who have definite responses are the natural sources of data from which we can isolate the reasons and principles underlying their responses. The idea here is that the responses come from and reveal some underlying psychologically real structure, a structure that was always (unconsciously) part of the thought processes of some people. Such people embody the reasoning and principles (which may be thought of as an internal program) that generate these responses. The point is to make the reasons and principles explicit. Because we do not begin with an awareness of the principles, it is less likely that the responses to cases are the results of a *conscious* application of principles to which one is already committed. An alternative model is that certain concepts that people have always worked with (even consciously) commit them—without their having realized it, consciously or unconsciously—to other concepts. The responses to cases reveal that one set of concepts and principles commit us to others, and these concepts and principles can then be added on to the description of the underlying structure of the responses, but the structure was not always psychologically real.

We are not arguing that such principles are correct simply because they generate responses in some people. Rather, to be plausible, such principles must be related to morally significant ideas. It would be ideal if we could show that the concepts and principles that generate or account for the responses in cases are required by reason. Furthermore, it is not assumed that the role of principles, if they are discovered, is to help us decide cases to which our responses are not clear. It is quite possible for someone to have clear, pretheoretical judgments about every case, without being able to articulate their principles. (Indeed, because the principles to be discovered are likely to be correctly formulated only if they are derived from all the types of data, using a principle based on only one type of case in order to decide another type of case may lead to the wrong answer regarding the latter case.)

What would be the purpose of making principles clear and explicit if we did not need them to settle cases about which we are uncertain? Perhaps it is simply to attain a greater understanding of what underlies our responses; perhaps it is to help us organize our moral thinking. Having our principles in hand may also make it easier for us to point out crucial factors in cases to those people who do not share our responses. Furthermore, it is possible to acquire a deeper understanding of our pretheoretical judgments by way of principles or theories which explain them, even though we are less certain of those principles and theories than we are of the judgments themselves. That is, our certainty about our pretheoretical judgments is different from, and not necessarily increased by, a deeper understanding of them.

Finally, we should not expect such principles to be simple or singular. Many of their components may prove to be irreducibly important. We may expect, however, a continuity in content between the factors we point to in certain cases and the components of the most general principles derived from those cases. In moving from cases to principles, one is less likely to find the same discontinuity in content that marks a theory whose principles are essentially utilitarian but that commend deontological responses to cases as a way of maximizing utility in the long view.

Note, however, that in this book, as opposed to *Morality, Mortality,* I am not so strongly concerned with isolating deep principles and fundamental reasons. I shall stop at what I consider a more superficial level than I do there in drawing conclusions from cases. Furthermore, many of the proposals that I consider here are merely intended to be reasonable views for one to hold, rather than shown to be necessary views that one must hold. How does this relate to the claim that ethics is an a priori rather than an empirical discipline, given that some think that only necessary truths are known a priori? We can know a priori that something is a reasonable (if not a necessary) view, without having to perform empirical investigations to discover this.

A Moral Theory

It will help to understand the discussion of cases in this book for the reader to have some idea of the type of moral theory I believe can be derived from the method of cases used generally: we discover that common-sense morality has a nonconsequentialist structure. Consequentialism is, very roughly, the view that acts (or rules or institutions) are morally right if they maximize overall good consequences. Nonconsequentialism does not ignore consequences when evaluating the moral permissibility of acts, it merely claims that factors other than consequences matter. Nonconsequentialism has two important components: (1) permission not to maximize the overall best consequences, sometimes referred to as an option or prerogative, for example, the option not to make large personal sacrifices to produce the best state of affairs as an outcome; (2) constraints on promoting the best consequences, for example, not killing one innocent, nonthreatening person—threatening persons are treated differently—in order to save five others, even if those five will die because someone has threatened them to save yet others.

How can we justify options? Samuel Scheffler has argued that an option (which he refers to as a prerogative) can be justified because we have the capacity and strong natural tendency to see things from a personal point of view. This leads us to value things out of proportion to their value from an impartial point of view.[5] (The latter point of view takes into account everyone's point of view and perhaps more in order to determine what is the best state of affairs.) He thinks moral theory should endorse to some degree our natural tendency to be motivated to act from a personal point of view, rather than making it wrong to act unless this promotes an impartial point of view.

In my view, options do pertain to a person's capacity and tendency to act from a personal point of view. This is only a tendency, of course, as someone may choose to act from an impartial point of view. However, options are not responsive to whatever we care about out of proportion to its value from an impartial point of view. For example, suppose that from my personal point of view, I care more about someone else's life than is merited by its value from the impartial point of view, or even from his own personal point of view. This does not mean that ethical theory should grant me an option to do what I want with what I care about so much, namely, that other person's life.

With this proviso, can we justify options, understood as morally permissible choices between acting from an impartial point of view and acting from a personal point of view? They are justified, I believe, by concern for individual autonomy, in the sense of concern for an autonomous individual who is not a mere means to the end of the best state of affairs. Some argue that to try to justify options by means of concern for autonomy is merely to assert again what they are by definition: We should give people a choice (option) because then they have a choice (autonomy).[6] But the idea of persons who are not mere means to the end of the best state of affairs but are ends in themselves, having a point even if they do not serve the best consequences, goes beyond and helps ground the idea of autonomy as mere choice or control. It is this idea of persons that options (and constraints) help capture.

By contrast, finding something good about acting from a personal point of view that cannot be achieved in acting from an impartial perspective is only a partial defense of options. To justify options positively, we do not want to defend acting from the personal point of view, but to defend having the choice of whether to act from a personal point of view or an impartial point of view.

How can we justify constraints? First, what form should constraints have, to fit intuitions about cases? Traditionally, two have been proposed. One is built around the do harm–allow harm distinction (recently discussed mostly as the killing–letting die distinction). The other is the intend harm–forsee harm distinction, otherwise known as the doctrine of double effect (DDE). If not harming in certain ways or not intending harm is a constraint and more important than doing good, should not an agent minimize the occurrences of harm or the intention to harm, rather than abide by a constraint that prevents an agent's doing harm to someone even if it will prevent a similar harm to many others?

Suppose our moral system gave us permission to minimize violations of persons by causing a lesser number of comparable violations rather than imposing a constraint. This would be incompatible with our moral system's endorsing as high a degree of inviolability of persons. Suppose there were a constraint. Then each person who dies as a victim of a violation of a constraint because we do not minimize violations, nevertheless dies recognized as an inviolable person, harm to whom our moral system has not endorsed. If our moral system permitted minimizing violations of persons by violating other persons, it would not recognize the inviolability of those saved anymore than of those persons used to save others. (It is important to see that it is the permission to kill not the actual killing that has this effect.) If we permit the violation of one, we endorse a different conception of every person, including ourselves. By contrast, if more violations of constraints occur because we do not permit violations, that is, we abide by a constraint, this does not mean that we endorse the correctness of these violations. More people die, but the conception of each person that we endorse remains that with a high degree of inviolability. If this is what people are in reality, then our moral system will reflect the truth. It would even be contradictory to endorse minimizing violations of some types of prohibitions for the sake of showing respect for constraints. For example, to endorse minimizing violations of the prohibition "do not harm to prevent comparable harm to a greater number" by endorsing some such violations, would simply eliminate the prohibition from the moral system. Indeed, it would make more sense formally to transgress such a constraint for the sake of maximizing utility, than for the sake of showing respect for the constraint.

These points support an agent-neutral account of a constraint. That is, the constraint need not be based on an agent's perception that harm to his potential victim has an agent-relative magnified value. It can be wrong for the agent to harm someone, not only to save the potential victims of others, but also to save more numerous potential victims of his own earlier or future acts. The reason is that a moral system that permitted him to harm the one would defeat a value that should concern all agents, the inviolability of any potential victims. His victim is special only in that he, the agent, will face that particular potential victim.

Despite the constraints against harming innocent bystanders, such harm sometimes is morally permissible. And defense against morally innocent people who are threats is permitted. One interesting possibility is that there is some connection between the option not to promote the best consequences, in particular the option not to make certain large sacrifices to aid someone, and the permissibility of harming someone. It is essentially an instance of this possibility that we shall investigate in this book.[7]

Roe v. Wade and Privacy

Before beginning the substance of my argument, I shall briefly consider the U.S. Supreme Court's *Roe v. Wade* decision from a philosophic point of view.

In that decision, the Supreme Court said that if a fetus were a person, abortion would be impermissible. Still, it agreed that there was a right to privacy implied in the Constitution (especially in the Fourteenth Amendment) and concluded that abortion fell under that right. It has been argued that in this and other cases, the Court failed to clarify the idea of privacy and to distinguish it from the right to autonomy. That is, it failed to distinguish the right not to have things known about one (privacy) from the right not to be imposed upon. But (as we shall argue further) the notion of autonomy may also not properly capture what is at stake in an abortion, as it does not distinguish between requiring a woman to work to support a fetus and requiring her to keep a fetus in her body. That is, the prohibition of abortion may be a concern because it interferes with bodily autonomy and integrity (the right not to have one's body imposed upon), rather than because it limits autonomy in general. Abortion cases, therefore, are related to cases involving the forced use of bone marrow or human experimentation.

Constitutional and Philosophical Persons

The Court was convinced that the right to abortion as an instance of the right to privacy could be outweighed if the fetus were considered to be a person. Indeed, given that the Court used the notion of privacy as something like a right to be left alone, its concern was that as the fetus developed, the woman would not be alone. That is, she would affect not only herself but also another person in her womb. The right to an abortion could not then be based on a right to privacy. The Court, therefore, first explored whether the fetus was a person according to the Constitution. This is not a philosophical but, rather, a constitutional idea of the person. To do this, the Court first used a method typically employed by strict constructionists in judicial review. It investigated, for example, whether those who passed the Fourteenth Amendment intended it to cover the fetus, by looking at legislation on abortion at the time the amendment was passed. Legislation was lax then, and so the theory is that those who proposed the Fourteenth Amendment, citizens of their times, would not have intended it to cover fetuses.

A more liberal approach to discovering whether the Fourteenth Amendment protected the fetus presumably would not only rely on what was in the minds of its framers (as evidenced by their culture's contemporary views). Instead, it would consider other parts of the Constitution, the basic values of the country as exhibited in its entire history of legal decision making and the like, and on these grounds decided whether the Fourteenth Amendment should apply to fetuses.[8] In fact, this approach might be a more promising route to determining whether the fetus is a constitutional person.

In this vein, the Court interpreted other laws and court decisions as giving rights to the fetus only on the assumption that it will be born and become a person. Therefore, interfering with its being born would not be contrary to the spirit of these decisions.

The Court found itself unable to decide between conflicting religious and philosophical views of when human life begins. Presumably it meant here by "human life" not just the presence of genetically human material, as the fetus is clearly that, but human being (a collection of human organ systems directed toward self-sustenance) or, distinct from this, a person understood philosophically. These two notions differ: A Martian might be a person but not a human being, and some human beings may not be persons. (For example, if self-consciousness were necessary in order to be a person, then those without any self-consciousness would not be persons.) Or perhaps the Court just meant by human life a human creature worthy of the same protection given to those who clearly are persons. In any case, it also argued that no state may choose a contested theory of human life as the one on which it will act.

Viability and Potential Human Life

Despite its inability to decide the philosophical question, the Court believed that the state has a compelling interest in protecting potential human life at viability. (Viability is not chosen as the point at which human life is present, but only as the point at which the potential for human life gives the state a compelling interest. In turn, compelling interest signifies that a woman's interest in having an abortion can sometimes be overridden.) Viability is the capacity of a fetus to live outside the womb, albeit with mechanical support. The question then arises of whether each one of a set of fetuses that could survive on a machine outside the womb would be viable if there were only one machine available to support only one of the fetuses.[9] Or would the fetus be viable if it could live in a machine once out of the womb but it could not in fact be removed from the womb alive? It has been pointed out that viability is a function of technology and so, theoretically, could be pushed back to very early in pregnancy. It is, therefore, not clear why, in the Court's view, viability is indeed such a crucial point if it is not necessarily correlated with a later stage of the fetus's development, let alone a stage in which it assumes the characteristics of a person rather than merely those of a potential person.[10]

Indeed, the whole question is problematic, whether concern for potential human life (at viability or earlier) should have the power to override a woman's interest in aborting a nonperson. Consider the following argument: (1) The potential for human life can exist when a sperm is headed toward an egg and will join it to form a conceptus that will develop into a person. But presumably, we may interfere with this potential by introducing a contraceptive barrier that prevents the sperm and the egg from meeting. The potential in itself does not have the right not to be interfered with. (2) Consider a fetus, at any given stage of its development from conception onward, though independent of its potential for further development. Does the state have a compelling interest in protecting it, in virtue of the properties it has at that stage? That is, imagine that, at any given stage (e.g., a one-cell conceptus, a zygote, a three-month fetus, a viable fetus), the fetus will remain at that stage for one hundred years and then die. In other words, it will not die soon, but because of some nutrient that was missing in its environment at the appropriate time it is no longer capable of developing. Would we have the right to dispose of such fetuses?[11] I suggest the answer is yes, as they are not rights bearers. (3) Assume that potential returns to any or all of the fetuses that we imagined in Point 2. The question is whether at those stages at which the fetuses' properties minus their potential gave them no rights, they could have rights because they had these properties plus potential. That is, does the combination of two factors that separately confer no rights—that is, potential alone, as described in Point 1, and properties alone minus potential, as described in Point 2—generate a right not to be destroyed? Only if this is possible should the fetus as a potential human life be protected.

An argument that this is not possible is as follows: If, in virtue of its occurrent (potential–independent) properties, the fetus at this stage does not have a right to life, can it have a different right, namely, the right to maintain its potential for further development? It would be wrong to take away the potential for life from a creature that has, because of its occurrent properties, a right to life, which is understood here as the right not to be destroyed. But if a creature's occurrent properties do not give it the right not to be destroyed, could it have the right not to be deprived of its potential to develop into a creature that will have such a right not to be destroyed? Is there any creature that does not possess the right not to be killed (e.g., a paramecium, a hamster) that does indeed have the right not to be deprived of the potential to develop into a person, assuming that we can give it such a potential by injecting it with a chemical?[12]

Suppose that a creature that lacks the right not to be killed also lacks the right not to be deprived of its potential to be a person possessing the right not to be killed. Would we nevertheless have to consider that such a creature's best interest lay in developing into something better than it is now before we took away its potential (by killing it)? Thus is the fetus at any stage—considered without regard to its potential—a creature whose best interests in any matter (let alone retention of its potential to be a person) we should consider? Furthermore, what in fact is in its interests? If the creature that it will become will be radically different from what it is now, is it in its interest to become that radically different creature. Might it be in the fetus's interest when it is at time 1 ($t1$) to survive only until $t20$ (a few weeks), as $t1$ and $t20$ are reasonably similar? But, it may also be true that at $t3$ the fetus has an interest in surviving until $t30$, for similar reasons. On this view, if we destroy the fetus at either stage, it will lose only the few weeks of life that it is in its interest to maintain. That is, if very little is in its interest, killing it will deprive it of very little and so is of less significance.

We may be tempted to say that the rights and interests that must be considered are not the fetus's but, rather, those of the person who will exist if we do not destroy it in its fetus stage. But if this person does not yet exist and we can prevent its existing, how can it have rights? (Future generations, those who will definitely exist, may have the right that we consider their interests, but this is different.)

By contrast, it may be argued[13] that although the fetus changes significantly over time, it is the same being as the later person. Either it and the later person are stages of a single human organism, or the fetus is already the human being in development. As such, it is in the interest of that single being not to lose its future, even if it changes radically.

Whatever the right answer is to the significance of potential, there is no doubt that we may feel that we are wasting potential and acting against nature and life when we destroy a fetus with potential, though we do not believe it is a person. But this feeling may have much in common with the feeling that we waste and resist nature and life when we use contraception or even when we refuse the occasions on which sexual attraction presents an opportunity for relationships. Yet repression and control and the rejection of opportunities are commonly invoked in the service of duty, fidelity, and work.

A final puzzling matter in connection with viability: In *Roe v. Wade,* the Court said that the state may prohibit some abortions in order to protect potential human life at viability; it did not say that it must do so. But it might be argued that only a factor that gave rise to a state's duty to prohibit abortions could override the factors supporting a woman's right to have an abortion. For how could a factor that is so weak that the state may choose whether or not to act on it still override a right?

Notes

1. I shall use the word *fetus* to refer to the developing being in the womb at all stages of its development, from earliest to latest.
2. I use the word *infant* rather than *children,* as it is possible that children,

who are more firmly embedded in human networks or whose future has more psychological continuity with who they are currently, should be protected even more than infants. We may, of course, be more protective of infants than older persons because of (biologically programmed) concern with genetic continuation.

3. This discussion is taken from the introduction to *Morality, Mortality,* vol. 1.

4. For some discussion of the ways of relating ethical theories and judgments of cases, see my "Ethics, Applied Ethics, and Applying Applied Ethics," in D. Rosenthal and F. Shehadi, *Applied Ethics and Ethical Theory* (Salt Lake City: University of Utah Press, 1988), pp. 162–87.

5. Samuel Scheffler, *The Rejection of Consequentialism* (Oxford, England: Oxford University Press, 1982).

6. Shelly Kagan, *The Limits of Morality* (Oxford, England: Oxford University Press, 1989).

7. I discuss all the issues of this section in more detail in *Morality, Mortality,* vol. II; "Harming Some to Save Others," in *Philosophical Studies* 57 (1989): 227–60; and in a discussion of Kagan's book in *Philosophy and Phenomenological Research,* December 1991.

8. Such an alternative approach to constitutional interpretation is described by Ronald Dworkin in *Law's Empire* (Cambridge, MA: Harvard Univeristy Press, 1986).

9. I owe this point to Jeffrey Gordon and Jessica Lane.

10. Later I shall offer one reason why viability matters.

11. By their lacking potential, these fetuses are unlike frozen embryos, which do possess potential.

12. Michael Tooley, "Abortion and Infanticide," *Philosophy and Public Affairs* 2(1972):37–65; and Paul Bassan, "Present Sakes and Future Prospects," *Philosophy and Public Affairs,* 11(1982):314–37.

13. As Warren Quinn does in "Abortion: Identity and Loss," *Philosophy and Public Affairs,* 13(1984):24–54.

1

May We Kill
in Nonabortion Cases?

The Violinist Case

In 1971 Judith Thomson[1] suggested that it would be helpful when discussing abortion to consider the following analogy: Imagine, she said, that you have been kidnapped by a group of people who want to save a dying violinist. The only way to save him is to plug him into your kidneys for nine months. (No one else is available for use.) You have nothing to do with the fact that he is dying or that he needs your kidneys; nevertheless, the group plugs him in to you. In order for you to be freed from the violinist before the nine months are over, he must die, either because he will die without support from you or because we must actively kill him in the process of, or even as a means of, detaching him from you. Thomson concluded that it would be morally permissible to kill the innocent violinist in any of these ways.[2]

Variations

Expanding on Thomson's analogy, also consider cases in which you were attached to the violinist voluntarily with the intention of helping him, or as a foreseen result of your voluntary act. Is it permissible to kill him or to have him killed in order to free yourself?[3] In particular, consider the following variations on becoming attached to an unconscious violinist: (1) Someone puts the violinist inside your body against your will. (The costs involved in keeping him are similar to those of pregnancy, labor, and delivery.[4]) (2) You perform some action in the normal course of your life that has the consequence, without anyone's deliberately arranging it, of the person's materializing inside your body. Although you knew that this might happen, you did not plan it to occur. As two subdivisions of Case 2, we may imagine that either you took precautions to prevent this attachment from occurring but that your precautions failed or that you did not take any precautions. (3) You voluntarily place the violinist inside your body in order to help him, but without actually promising anyone to keep him there until he is saved.

The question to be answered about these cases is if you decide that you no longer want to support this person because you object to having him in your body, whether it is morally permissible for you to have this person—who is completely passive, unconscious, and not morally responsible for being inside you—painlessly removed by a third party acting on your behalf, before the nine months are over. We must answer this question in such a way that if your positions were reversed, you, as the dependent, would accept it as morally permissible to be treated as you intend to treat the person dependent on you.

The question introduces the role of a third party, as we are interested in the analogy to abortion. Most abortions today are performed by doctors rather than by the pregnant woman herself.

The Removal Procedure

What does the removal procedure do to the violinist? Because we are using this case to help our thinking about abortion, we should consider at least four procedures: (1) The violinist is removed from you, without directly attacking him, by severing the link between you and him. Although he emerges whole, he dies without your support. This is comparable to one type of induced labor.[5] (2) A solution is injected into you, the supporter, causing the ejection of the violinist, the dependent. This solution is caustic, and it interferes with the dependent's respiration and damages his organs, thereby killing him. In this case, the dependent is killed in the process of removing him. There thus is some sort of direct attack on him, even though it is not intentional, and so it is comparable to a saline abortion. (3) The dependent is removed by directly attacking him, for example, by crushing his skull. The attack on him is intended, even though his death is not, strictly speaking. This is comparable to a craniotomy. (4) The violinist is attacked with the intention of causing his death, because suppose (for the sake of argument) unless he dies it will not be possible to remove him.

If we can justify Procedure 4, which seems the most difficult to justify, we can also justify the other three. The distinctions between these procedures is drawn keeping in mind the Doctrine of Double Effect. We do not necessarily accept its view that intending death is impermissible.[6]

Ending a Life in Order to Stop Supporting It

What follows is a possible general argument for the moral permissibility of a third party's killing the violinist in order to detach him from you, a different argument from the one Thomson presents. It has five steps:

1. The need to have your body, and only your body, provide support in the mannner of pregnancy does not confer the right to have such aid begun nor to have it continue. Nor does it give you a duty to aid.

2. You have no special obligation to give such aid per se (e.g., because of voluntary acts performed, considered alone or in combination with need).

3. Killing the violinist means his losing only what is provided (life) by the support that neither his need nor any special obligation requires you to give; it does not harm him relative to his preattachment opportunities and does not cause him to lose anything that you are causally responsible for his having that he would retain independently of you. (I use "not harm him relative to" to point to a comparison between preattachment opportunities and the condition he will be in if killed.)

4. The costs of supporting the violinist are significant enough so that in conjunction with the truth of the other premises, they can justify our killing him to stop them.

5. To end the imposition, killing the dependent is the only way that is not excessively costly to the supporter.

This argument is not meant to justify destroying the violinist as an end in itself. But it does aim to justify using his death as a means of ending his attachment to you, should this be necessary.

Now let us consider the steps of this argument and their validity:

1a. *Need alone confers no right or duty: Letting the person die is permissible.*

It is assumed that you have no obligation to put the person into your body for the sole reason of saving his life, even though it may be commendable of you to do this. If this person has a "right to life," it nonetheless does not include the right to use your body solely in order to save his life. Therefore, it would have been permissible to let him die in the first place rather than attach him to you. (Any "Good Samaritan" laws that require a person to come to the assistance of another do not require such bodily aid.) It also is inappropriate to refer to the refusal to undergo a large imposition as "selfish." Rather, it may be self-interested to refuse to undergo such an imposition; that is, one acts out of concern for oneself, but not all self-concern is selfish, as the latter phrase implies inappropriate self-concern. For example, to refuse to give up one's life for a cause may be self-interested, even unwise, but it is not necessarily selfish. Making the sacrifice may be morally commendable but still supererogatory (i.e., beyond the call of duty), and the failure to make it need not be morally wrong. Note that it is possible to care about the fate of the violinist and be willing to make some efforts to help, while still permissibly putting one's own interests ahead of his when there is a significant conflict of interests. It may even be morally permissible to require large social sacrifices to prevent death, where the burden on no one person is too large.

1b. *Need alone confers no right to continued aid or duty to give aid.*

Just as he has no right to the initial use of your body merely because he needs it, the violinist has no right to the continued use of your body merely in order to save his life, even if there are no further negative effects on you other than the use of your body. You also have no duty to give continuing aid just because he needs it. That is, the violinist's need is not a sufficient reason for either the initial or the continued use of your body. If you are required to let him stay once he is in it, it must be for some other reason.

2. *No special obligation to give aid.*

a. A commitment by you to keep the violinist in your body could give him a right to stay. But even your voluntarily attaching him to you with the intent of helping him does not by itself constitute a commitment to allow him the continued use of your body. Analogously, if you voluntarily bring someone into your home, he does not have a right to stay longer than you want him to, simply because you brought him in. If his removal were safe for him, you could have him removed even if he wanted to stay.

Further, assume that you voluntarily attach a person to you, knowing that your aid will have to be provided in installments. That is, after a short while inside you, he will drop out alive and have to be reattached. The reattachment itself is not a burdensome procedure for you. But suppose that you decided the effort of helping him was becoming too much for you. Even though you began with the intention of finishing the project and were aware of its requirements, it would be permissible not to put the person back inside you if he then would be no worse off than he would have been if you had not supported him in the first place. That is, you are not committed to support him merely because you began, knowing what would be needed from you.

In sum, we often are allowed the option of voluntarily trying to do something for someone without thereby being committed to continue. Voluntarily beginning a project, even with the intention of completing it, does not in itself constitute a promise to continue. The permissibility of stopping often depends on whether the person that we are helping will be no worse off if we stop than he would have been if we had not started.

In contrast, however, a contract might indeed bind one to continue. I say *might* because a contract by itself might not be sufficient if it were not morally permissible to allocate the sole use of one's body before the time at which it is to be used. If this were the case, those who relied on such contracts would not have a right to have them enforced.

It may be relevant to Step 2 that the violinist is unconscious, and so he does not form any expectations that are then disappointed. But even a declared intention to carry through a project that does raise expectations is not the same as a promise to continue it (i.e., a promise is an invitation to rely on one's intention). And if someone's expectations are not truly justified, should their mere psychological presence alter the permissibility of what we may do?[7] It is hard to believe that anyone's expectation should be enough added reason to require significant efforts, if need plus voluntary acts do not suffice.

All that I have said is consistent, I believe, with the following: (1) Once one starts to help someone, if one is willing to continue making such efforts, one can give as a reason for continuing this project—rather than turning to a new one—that one had already begun this (first) project. (2) Having worked already on a project need not reduce the obligation to give more to it than to other projects that one has done nothing to support, on the grounds that one has already given something to the (first) project. (3) Giving a lot, if one chooses to, creates a sense that one is heavily involved in a project, and so the upper limits on further efforts that one will feel it appropriate to make will rise, as involvements generate psychological pressures for their continuation. But all this is different from a moral obligation to continue. (4) If you interfered with someone else aiding the violinist, you may have to continue on pain of making him worse off than he might have been.

b. Suppose that you do not volunteer to support the violinist but that his attachment to you is the unintended, though foreseen, possible consequence of some voluntary action by you (minus any good intention to help him). There is also no reason to think that what you have done, by itself gives him the right to the continued use of your body or gives you a duty to continue.

Assume that the continuing presence of the dependent violinist in your body against your wishes is not required merely because he needs your help or merely because of your voluntary actions (or your actions in conjunction with that need); that is, the two do not create a special obligation. Then a reason for requiring that he remain could be that he would have to be killed in order to be removed, not merely allowed to die. That is, one would have to interfere fatally with either him or a life-saving procedure that is already in process.

It might then be said that the violinist's continued use of your body is not required except if the killing itself were not permissible. That is, the objection being raised to terminating the person's residence in your body is that it means killing him, and he has a right not to be killed. Furthermore, killing him involves harming him, and he has a right not to be harmed. No other reason requires his continued use of your body. Because we are deciding whether such a killing is permissible, the objection that it is not permissible to remove him because this will kill him—and hence it is required that he stay in your body against your will—is still only a suggestion. It cannot be assumed to be correct.

Another reason for requiring the violinist's remaining could be that not continuing to support him would put him in a worse position than he would rightfully have been in, had he not been attached to you. This objection would hold even if the stopping of aid did not mean killing him. So, if your support stopped spontaneously and had to be restarted in order to save him, perhaps it should be restarted for this reason.

The next step in the argument considers these two possibilities:

3. *The violinist loses only what he has gained by your support; he is*

not harmed relative to preattachment opportunities, and he loses noth-
ing you are causally responsible for his having which he would retain
independently of you.

If your support stops and/or the violinist is killed, he will lose no more than the benefit of continued life that comes from using your body.[8] I use the word *benefit* because even though the violinist receives nothing he did not have all along (his life), he is benefited by keeping it rather than losing it, as he would have without your support. But keeping his life need not be a benefit because of the time he spent attached to you. For example, if this time period offers none of the goods of life, by itself it would not be an improvement over death. But, it may be a necessary step to a future life that does offer such goods. The violinist's future life thus is a benefit of his attachment to you even if such a benefit will also require the later support of others.

One implication of this point is that the violinist would be no worse off if the support stopped and/or he were killed than he would be if he had never been attached to you in the first place (because he would be dead).[9] A second implication is that he would be losing only the benefit that he gained from using a body to which he had no right merely because he needed it to stay alive (as argued in Steps 1a and 1b) and no right because of a special obligation (as argued in Step 2) or because of these two factors together. Nevertheless, the violinist is harmed by being killed because of the future opportunities he might have had, as he would have gone on living if he had not been killed.

We may summarize Step 3 as follows:[10] We need not deny that we harm the violinist in killing him relative to (i.e., in comparison with) the condition he would have been in if you had continued support. But it may not be wrong to harm him in this way, because we may be obliged only not to harm him relative to the condition he would have been in if he had not been attached. Why? Because if you have no duty to aid him because of his need or other grounds of special obligation, any condition he is in as a result of your aid is not something he has a claim to keep, at least as long as he continues to need your support to maintain it. There-fore, his being in that improved condition once attached cannot be the base line relative to which we must not harm him. The base line is, rather, how he would have been if never attached to you.

Things might be different if he could retain what he had gotten from your support without you, even if not without the aid of others. (This is the point of the last clause of (3).) For example, suppose we find some-

one who is dying. We give him a medicine and he is much impr
no longer needs our help. We may not kill him simply becau:
not be harmed relative to the condition he would have been in (dead) if
he had never gotten aid.

The Tentative Output Cutoff Principle

One tentative principle that might be suggested on the basis of Steps 1
through 3 is as follows: It is permissible and not unjust to kill when
killing is nothing but eliminating a life produced by the use of your
body—a use not required by need or special obligation—in order to end
that use, so long as the person killed is no worse off without the benefit
resulting from this use than he would have been if he had not gained this
benefit and, in addition, he does not thereby lose anything that you are
causally responsible for his having that he could retain independently of
your further support. I shall call this the *tentative output cutoff principle*
(because we cut off the output—the benefit of life—of support). It is
supposed to explain why the fact that we would kill and harm does not
imply an obligation to continue support when no other factors imply it.

The tentative output cutoff principle allows you to kill someone in
order to end losses to yourself that are as great as those that you need not
have suffered in order to save his life initially. It seems most natural to
use this principle when we take away from someone something that is
not his, as, for example, when someone obtains something that was
never his by means of an improper use of someone else. Yet here we use
this principle to deal with something that belongs to someone (his life)
yet is retained by improper means.

However, the fact that someone is retaining something that is his can
make a difference, as it can determine which reasons can justify destroying this something, this benefit. That is, it is because someone has a
prior claim to his life that we can take it away only in order to stop the
efforts that preserve it. But assume that we do not conceive of someone's life as his possession or analogous to it. Then the tentative output
cutoff principle would maintain that it is wrong for someone to continue
to live when his life has been enabled by improper means, even if his
death is not necessary to stop the use of those means. This is analogous
to what can be done if someone receives by improper means property
that is not his: Corrective justice allows us to take it away simply to undo

his wrongful gain. But when someone improperly retains what is in fact his, we do not seek to prevent his keeping it because the means to his gaining it are improper, unless we can thereby correct for the use of those improper means.

It is also true that it is not only by way of your bodily support that the violinist retains his life. His own bodily processes play some role. Is the benefit, then, a joint product that one party cannot destroy without the other's permission? The claim is that if one party—who is necessary to the joint product—continues to be used for its production when such use cannot be required except, possibly, because we must destroy its product in order to stop the use, then we may destroy the product. To summarize, according to this position, the violinist—who benefits from an otherwise morally unrequired use of another person—cannot protest the ending of this use simply because it means that he will lose what he has gained from it. To put it another way, we cannot say that an otherwise unrequired use of your body becomes morally required simply because the violinist who benefits from it will lose this benefit if his use of your body is ended.

We shall turn next to the problems with this tentative output cutoff principle.

First Problem

In general, the fact that we do not make someone any worse off than he otherwise would have been does not necessarily make our act permissible. For example, if a second murderer will shoot someone even if the first murderer does not, the fact that the first murderer does not make his victim any worse off than he otherwise would have been does not mean that he has done no wrong. Indeed, the first murderer is the one who harms the victim and, in this case, wrongfully harms him.[11]

Let us return to our analogy and suppose that the dying violinist is about to be aided by someone other than you and that this someone will complete the task. Before this can happen, however, a villain appears and is about to interfere with this aid. But before the villain can act, you attach the violinist to yourself and then later kill him in order to detach him. The violinist is thus no worse off than he otherwise would have been had he not been attached to you. Nevertheless, you have actually made him worse off, because by interfering with the other person's efforts to save him, you—instead of the villain—have deprived the violinist of the opportunity to be much better off than dead, as he will be when you kill him. By attaching him and then not continuing this support—whether by killing him outright or simply not reattaching him if he falls out—you have wrongfully harmed him. This is true even though the villain would also have interfered with the other person's aid.[12]

This shows that not making someone any worse off than he otherwise would have been is not sufficient to prove that you have not harmed him relative to the opportunities he rightfully had before being attached to you or to show the permissibility of your conduct.

Note that Step (3), unlike the tentative output cutoff principle, does not itself use "no worse off." It uses "not harmed relative to opportunities had prior to attachment." We now understand better why it does this. It focuses on what you do to the violinist, rather than merely on his condition.[13]

Second Problem

The tentative output cutoff principle implies that the support that you are not required to provide in order to save the violinist's life is also the support in whose name you may kill him in order to stop providing it. This implication holds as long as the violinist thereby loses only the life that he gains from your support and is no worse off than he would have been without your support. But taking away this benefit from the violinist still means harming him relative to the possibility of his continuing to live, even if it does not mean harming relative to opportunities he had before being attached to you, since no one would have helped him if you had not. Due to this, it is possible that the efforts you should make in order not to harm the violinist may be higher than those you are obliged to make in order to prevent his dying. The full causal responsibility for a person's death seems to have additional weight. We thus need to show that bodily imposition is significant enough to permit killing someone in order to avoid this imposition, that is, when Step 3 also holds.[14]

It may be helpful to digress briefly to the general problem of the moral significance of killing someone versus letting someone die.[15] Step 1 states that you may let the violinist die rather than have him put into your body. The objection was raised that ending such support necessitates killing the violinist and that killing someone may not be permissible even if letting someone die is permissible. I believe that killing someone may sometimes be impermissible even when letting that person die is not. For example, suppose that I am driving five critically ill friends to a hospital. On the way I hear a cry from a drowning person. In this case I may allow this person to die rather than fail to get the five to the hospital. However, suppose that I see someone pinned to the road in front of my car on my way to the hospital. I may not run over him even if I know that stopping would result in my not getting to the hospital in time to save my five friends. That is, I must tolerate a greater loss in order not to kill someone than I have to in order not to let someone die.

(Perhaps, however, these are not the best cases to show that we must sometimes tolerate a greater loss to avoid killing someone than to save a life. In the letting-die case, if we do not save one person, we shall be saving five, thereby fulfilling whatever duty we have to aid. By contrast, in the killing case, we shall let some die rather than kill someone else. An alternative set of cases are the following: I should swerve into a tree to avoid running over someone, but I need not swerve into a tree if this alone will make it fall into the water, thereby providing a rescue plank for a drowning person.)

The N.Y.U. Law Cat

To clarify this conclusion, consider the case of the ledge cat. Passing by the New York University Law School one day, I saw a cat walking on a ledge high above some construction work. The cat was looking with curiosity at what was going on beneath it. If the cat jumped, it probably would have been killed, as the ground was hard and full of pointed rocks. Should I call out in the hope that this would make it come to me instead of jumping down? But perhaps my call would startle the cat and cause it to topple over onto the construction when it might not otherwise have jumped at all. Here, as I saw it, the chances were equal that by calling out I would either save the cat or kill it when it otherwise would not have died. Would it be worse, then, to kill the cat when it otherwise would not have died or to let it die if it decided to jump? I decided that I would rather take the chance of letting the cat die than be directly responsible for its death. But if the probability of saving the cat were greater than the risk of killing it, then I should risk killing it in order to save it. Analogously, doctors sometimes operate to increase the odds for someone who might live without the surgery, while taking the risk that the patient might die because of the surgery. This is permissible because the odds of killing the patient are smaller than the odds of saving him by the surgery.

A Morally Significant Distinction

One fact that distinguishes morally between many of the cases of killing someone and letting someone die is that it is conceptually true of letting someone die that the person we do not aid and thus allow to die, loses only what he would have had with our help. But often when we actively kill someone, he loses what he would have had independently of us.

Sometimes, however, a killing case, in fact, has this property which is conceptually true of letting someone die. This is so in the case of the violinist, for when he is killed, the violinist loses only what he would have had with your support. It is this similarity between killing someone and letting that person die in this case, that, it is claimed, helps make killing him permissible if letting him die is.

What hampers this conclusion is that even when it shares this conceptual property of letting someone die, actively killing someone is still an interference with him as letting die is not. This difference, however, may not make the killing impermissible; it may only increase the amount of effort deemed sufficient to make killing him permissible in order to avoid the effort.

The $100,000 Case

As an example of this statement, suppose that it is neither unjust nor indecent to refuse to save someone's life at the cost to you of $100,000 when handing over the money will lower your economic status from upper- to lower-middle class. Despite your refusal, someone else has illegitimately taken your $100,000 and is using it to save the first person's life. Is it permissible to kill the first person, the beneficiary of your money, in order to get your money back? Consider alternative ways in which you could cause the beneficiary's death: (1) You could take your money back, with the result that he dies. This may be neither indecent nor unjust, though it may be psychologically more difficult to do than would refusing aid in the first place. (2) Perhaps you cannot retrieve your money directly, but not because the beneficiary is preventing your taking it. He remains faultless. The only way that you can retrieve your money is to kill the beneficiary directly. But in this case, killing him seems not only indecent but also unjust. This is so even though the person whose life you would take is alive only because of your $100,000.

What is the difference between Alternative 1 and Alternative 2? In Alternative 1 you directly take away your money, but in Alternative 2 you directly attack someone else's body. The fact that you must attack and destroy what is his inhibits you, I believe. If Alternative 2, killing someone, is inhibiting, then this raises problems for the tentative output cutoff principle.

Suppose that you were planning to use the $100,000 for surgery to free yourself from the violinist who is attached to your body and that this surgery will not harm the violinist. If you do not have this surgery, however, he will be attached to you for nine months. May we directly kill the beneficiary (in our previous example), who is illegitimately using your money, if this is the only way for you to get your money back? In this case there is hardly less resistance to killing someone, perhaps because the beneficiary of the money does not himself pose the threat to your body and the violinist's imposing on you is not related to saving the life of the beneficiary of your money.

These cases suggest that we would fatally attack someone only in order to preserve another person's physical (rather than financial) integrity, even though we may let someone die in order to preserve financial integrity. It is also easier to justify killing someone when he himself is a threat to your physical integrity by his imposing himself on you and/or when he benefits from such imposition on you.

Our discussion of the $100,000 case affirms that at least sometimes you must suffer greater losses rather than have us kill a person whose life is being saved by your aid than you would have to suffer just to save a person. It also suggests that if we directly attack the violinist attached to you, it must be in order to maintain your physical independence and integrity. Some people may reject a fatal attack on the violinist's body if the violinist *himself* is not imposing on your body as a result of the benefit of life he is receiving from you. I believe that this is a stricter condition than is necessary to justify killing the violinist. Still, this condition is met in the cases of concern to us now.

The $100,000 case itself does not demonstrate directly that you must tolerate a greater imposition on your body before we kill the person who is imposing than you must in order to avoid letting someone die. The $100,000 case does, however, suggest a difference between letting someone die and killing that person to cease supplying life-saving aid, and it also warns us not to assume that because Step 1 is true, we are permitted to kill someone.

Euthanasia

It is interesting that killing someone may make a difference even in cases in which that person's death is agreed to be in his interest and the issue of justice has been resolved. For example, in the case of voluntary euthanasia, the person in whose interest it is to die gives someone else the permission to kill him, intending his death, rather than merely to let him die. Here, it seems, there is no injustice in killing. If someone waives his right not to be killed and we also do not act against his interest but, rather, in his interest, the killing seems justified.

It is sometimes said (by proponents of the doctrine of double effect) that it is permissible for a doctor to give a pain killer to a terminally ill patient foreseeing that it will lead to a quicker death, but not to give a lethal injection with the intention to cause death. The doctrine says that it is permissible to do this if we do not give the drug in order to bring about the death and also if the loss of life is the lesser evil relative to the cessation of pain, which is the greater good. (It is important to emphasize that the permissibility of giving the drug depends on the latter proportionality clause.) By contrast, suppose that the pain killer no longer has its pain-killing properties, but it still slows the heartbeat and so is now a "death drug." In this case, we may not give the drug in order to bring on death, according to the doctrine, even if the patient requests it.

But the doctrine of double effect analysis has problems, as there does seem to be an argument for the permissibility of intending someone's death in order to relieve his or her own suffering. My version of this argument is as follows:[16] The permissibility of giving the pain killer depends on death's being the lesser evil and the relief of suffering's being the greater good. In other medical cases, it is thought to be permissible to intend a lesser evil to achieve a greater good. For example, we may decide that in order to reach and remove a tumor, we must amputate a healthy leg. That is, the amputation is the lesser evil intended to bring about the greater good of life unthreatened by a tumor. If we may intentionally amputate the healthy leg, why may we not intentionally deprive someone of life, when it is already granted as a premise of the doctrine's argument for the permissibility of bringing about death as a side effect, that death is the lesser evil?

Consider an objection to this argument: There are cases in which what is granted to be the lesser evil may permissibly be brought about as a side effect, yet may not be intended. For example, in the course of giving a lecture, along with many new true beliefs that come to be had by the hearers, it is foreseeable that some new false beliefs will also arise as a side effect. These false beliefs as a side effect are a price worth paying for the greater good of more true beliefs. Now suppose that on one occasion the only way for me to achieve the goal of giving an audience many new true beliefs is to do something with the intention that they form a false belief. It may well be morally impermissible for me to do this (e.g., lie) to achieve the greater good, even though it would be permissible to tolerate the generation of the false belief as a side effect of the informative lecture. Intending the false belief makes a moral difference.

This objection implies that we must decide whether killing a terminally ill patient is more like amputating a leg—which is not intrinsically morally wrong and may be done for his own good—or more like doing something with the intention that someone have a false belief, which is intrinsically morally wrong and may often not be done even for someone's own good. Note however, that if the greater good becomes great enough, even a means that has something intrinsically wrong with it, like a lie, may come to be justified. So, if the lie may sometimes be justified, we must decide whether intentionally depriving someone who is terminally ill of some life (or intentionally attacking life itself, as I believe some people see this) at his request could be significantly worse than a lie, that is, deliberately manipulating someone's mind. Others have argued that if his life is his to control, it is a good thing if he gets to do with it as he wishes for his greater good. If this is so, the amputation model will hold.

This pro-euthanasia argument requires the consent of the person to be killed. It does not only rely on showing that we would do him a greater good, and so does not justify paternalism. It may well be permissible not to aid someone when we control what that person needs—though perhaps it is not permissible for doctors who have a duty to aid—if we believe it is in his best interest not to receive what we control, even if he wants aid. Yet it may not be permissible to intrude on what is his (e.g., his body) to achieve his own greater good when he does not wish this to be done. (Here the difference between killing and letting someone die also comes out.[17]) When the double effect doctrine endorses giving the pain killer that, as a side effect, causes death, does it mean that we do not need consent from the patient? Patient consent seems to be required both when death will be a side effect and when it is intended, if there is intrusion into someone's body.

Yet even if it is permissible to perform voluntary active euthanasia, we are not obligated to do so, and so even the person who requests it does not have a right to active euthanasia. And even though many people are willing to kill someone for his own good, many others are not. Their resistance stems from their concern with being responsible for ending a life. People, however, do often have a right to refuse treatment, and we do have a duty not to interfere with this right. Therefore, people do have a right to be allowed to die. (This is not necessarily a right to passive euthanasia, as we may not be intending the death; only letting someone die with the intent that death come is passive euthanasia.) This distinction in the realm of rights may be important when deciding public policy. Although many people who wish to be actively euthanized may not get their wish if we do not permit active euthanasia, they also will not have their rights violated, nor will we fail in our duties to them if there is a law prohibiting active euthanasia. But we will violate both people's rights and our duties to them if we do not allow for at least the possibility of passive euthanasia, by discontinuing unwanted treatment.

Our discussion of the difference killing makes suggests two more Steps for our argument:

4. *The efforts to support someone are significant enough that in conjunction with the truth of the other premises of the argument, they can justify (specifically) killing someone in order to stop the efforts.*

We now need a positive argument showing what bodily efforts we may permissibly kill someone in order to avoid. (I shall postpone stating this argument, however, as part of it is most appropriately explored in the specific case of forced attachment, described in Chapter 2.)

5. *Killing someone is the only way that is not excessively costly to end that person's imposition on you.*

That is, it is the only way that does not require more effort from you, the supporter, than you would have to make solely in order to avoid our killing him in a situation in which the other premises hold.

The Output Cutoff Principle

With these additional premises we can revise our output cutoff principle, and summarize the five steps of the output cutoff argument to permit killing someone. We should emphasize, however, that these five steps are presented as sufficient—not as necessary—conditions for permissibly killing someone, even in the case of the violinist. That is, it is permissible to end a life that is maintained by the use of your body, in order to stop that use, if the use is not required by need or special obligation, so long as the person killed is not harmed relative to the opportunities he would have had if he had never been attached, and he does not lose anything you are causally responsible for his having that he could retain without you, given that the loss you seek to avoid is large enough to justify killing, and there is no other way to end the efforts which does not require more of you than you must give rather than have us kill him. This principle explains why, though the person killed is harmed relative to his improved condition in your body, he is not wronged in being harmed.

The five-step argument which this principle summarizes is nonconsequentialist. That is, whether the violinist should be saved or killed cannot be decided by determining who will suffer the greater loss, the violinist if he is killed or you if his attachment to you continues. Rather, our analysis is rights-based; that is, you have a right not to maximize overall good consequences by suffering a loss that is less than the one that your suffering will prevent. Yet its being rights-based does not imply that what, in some intuitive sense, is the more important right will take precedence. That is, if asked whom to save, a person being imposed on, as you are in the violinist's case, or another person in a different situation who is being threatened with being killed, you would probably save the second rather than the first person. Here you would be protecting the more important right. This is quite consistent with its being true that when your right not to have your body used conflicts with someone's remaining alive by the use of your body, you may refuse to save him, we may kill him to protect your bodily integrity, and no one ought to stop this. The output cutoff argument explains why.

A Possible Omission

Suppose directly killing someone is morally more serious than letting someone die and the relationship established between people when one kills another should be avoided. Then perhaps we should avoid getting ourselves into situations where we will be making such large bodily efforts that killing to stop them is permissible according to conditions 1 through 5. And if we get ourselves into such a situation for no good reason, perhaps we should not be allowed to kill, despite satisfying conditions 1 through 5. Consider an analogy: Suppose it is permissible to punish someone for performing a wrong act. If we had the opportunity to prevent him from doing the wrong act should we do so, in order to avoid being in the situation where we have to legitimately punish him? If we do not do what we could to avoid being in the situation, would it be harder to justify punishing him? That is, will the justification for punishing him depend, in part, on whether we could have prevented the situation in which the question of punishment arises? Since we are concerned with moral permissibility and ordinary sensitivity, we must decide whether concern for these factors implies that we should prevent the situation from arising, or whether preventing the situation is supererogatory beyond ordinary sensitivity.

As things stand, conditions 1 through 5 imply that it is permissible to kill in order to stop support in the violinist case, so long as nothing we do leads to an obligation to give or to continue to give aid per se (i.e., if it stopped spontaneously one would not have to restart it), and the efforts are sufficiently large to merit killing. This is independent of whether we could have avoided being in this situation. We could have an obligation not to kill only if we either had an obligation to continue aid per se, or the efforts were too low to justify killing to end them. This all suggests that we could be indifferent between not starting aid and killing to stop it, when the efforts are high enough to satisfy conditions 1 through 5.

But it is possible that even if voluntary acts do not lead to a commitment to keep giving aid when condition 3 holds, they may lead to an obligation not to kill because one had reason to avoid being in a situation where one might kill, even in accord with conditions 1 to 5, and because one did not do what one should have to avoid being in the situation.

These considerations suggest that we might also have to show that:
6. You have no special obligation not to kill in accord with 1 to 5,

because there was sufficient reason for your being in the situation where you would kill.

Since we are concerned with permissibility and ordinary sensitivity, we must ask what these factors would have required of you in order to avoid being in the situation where you would make use of 1 to 5 to justify killing the violinist. Perhaps when attachment is intentional, it is required that there have been some probability of completing aid. When attachment is the unintended, but foreseen result of a voluntary act, the costs of avoiding the act should be sufficient reason for being in a situation where one justifies killing by conditions 1 to 5. It is important to note that the probability of successfully aiding which is required, as well as the cost of avoiding the act which leads to attachment, may be quite low, just because killing in this case does meet conditions 1 to 5.

I shall not include this extra step in the argument, since it may in fact not be necessary, although it is worth keeping in mind as the concern it addresses eventually will play a part in the discussion of abortion.

Another View

There is an alternative perspective on killing: Situations in which others impose on us are opportunities for self-restraint. No doubt we would be acting within reason if we complained or objected, took matters in our own hands, or directed others to act on our behalf. Still, not doing what is morally permissible, and even morally justified, will bring better results in the long run if it saves a life. According to this view, to act on one's rights is to succumb to temptation, and different people succumb at different points. In the particular case of killing another person, performing the act or directing that it be done will make one's life worse than if one had suffered large losses that could nevertheless have justified the killing. Sacrifices whose burden will pass are more wisely endured rather than performing or directing the performance of a killing.

Yet, for better or worse, we are concerned in this book with moral permissibility and adequate sensitivity. Recall that deciding whether an act is morally permissible and morally adequate is important when we judge other people and when we judge ourselves. It limits our reproach of others, self-castigation, and guilt. It is, however, less relevant to limiting regret, for example, over lost opportunities, and can never completely decide for us what we should do. The distinction between moral guilt and regret should be kept in mind.

It is also worth noting that in the discussion of abortion we will consider the social effects of an individual's not exercising her right and also the affect on her self-concept. Then we will introduce other reasons for action besides an individual's concern for avoiding a physical burden, and these reasons may fit the alternative view we are now considering more satisfactorily as justifications for a killing than does the simple avoidance of physical burdens.

Summary: The Basic Strategy of the Output Cutoff Argument

The basic strategy of the output cutoff argument is to show, first, that it is permissible to let the violinist die and, second, that his being killed by a third party also is permissible, in part because letting him die is permissible. This killing is shown to be permissible because one does not have an obligation to stay attached to someone rather than have him killed, when the killing involves only taking away a benefit (i.e., continued life) the victim need not have been given, and does not involve the victim's being harmed relative to opportunities he had prior to attachment, or his losing what you are causally responsible for his having and that he could retain without the use of your body, and when your efforts are large enough to merit a defense involving killing, there being no other way of stopping the efforts that is not too costly to you.

If the violinist had the right to only a short stay in your body or if (as Thomson puts it) it would be indecent to refuse him a short stay, it would not be permissible to kill him in order to end such a brief stay. Nonetheless, you might still want to end residence even if only a short period remained before he could be naturally and safely detached, if this short period were particularly burdensome, perhaps because a long period of attachment had preceded it or in virtue of its coming to a very painful end.

Notes

1. Judith Thomson, "A Defense of Abortion" and "Rights and Deaths," in M. Cohen et al., eds., *The Rights and Wrongs of Abortion* (Princeton, NJ: Princeton University Press, 1974).

2. In "A Defense of Abortion" Thomson speaks of unplugging the violinist and his dying as a consequence, but in "Rights and Deaths" she allows for intentionally killing him as a means of detaching him.

3. I first discussed these questions in Frances M. Kamm, "Abortion: A Philosophical Analysis," *Feminist Studies* 1(1972):49–64. and Frances M. Kamm, "The Problem of Abortion," in Raziel Abelson and Marie Friquenon, eds., *Ethics for Modern Life,* 2nd ed. (New York: St. Martin's Press, 1981).

4. Susan Estrich and Kathleen Sullivan write, in "Abortion Politics: Writing for an Audience of One," University of Pennsylvania Law Review 138(1989): 119, 126–27, ". . . pregnancy increases a woman's uterine size 500–1000 times, her pulse rate by ten to fifteen beats a minute, and her body weight by 25 pounds or more. Even the healthiest pregnancy can entail nausea, vomiting, more frequent urination, fatigue, back pain, labored breathing, or water retention. There are also numerous medical risks involved in carrying pregnancy to term: Of every ten women who experience pregnancy and childbirth, six need treatment for some medical complication, and three need treatment for major complications. In addition, labor and delivery impose extraordinary physical demands, whether over the six- to twelve-hour or longer course of vaginal delivery, or during the highly invasive surgery involved in a cesarean section, which accounts for one out of four deliveries.

"By compelling pregnancy to term and delivery even where they are unwanted, abortion restrictions thus exert far more profound intrusions into bodily integrity than the stomach-pumping the Court invalidated in *Rochin v. California,* or the surgical removal of a bullet from a shoulder that the Court invalidated in *Winston v. Lee.*"

5. The drug used in most of the induced-labor abortions does kill the fetus.

6. I discuss the doctrine in "The Doctrine of Double Effect: Reflections on Theoretical and Practical Issues," *Journal of Medicine and Philosophy*, October 1991.

7. I owe this point to Arthur Applebaum. A weaker position than that of Step 3 argues that sometimes voluntarily beginning aid can, by itself, lead to a commitment to continue that aid. Examples are cases in which the efforts are sufficiently low, though more than one is required to begin to make. But, voluntarily initiating (sufficiently) greater efforts—such as those involved in our case—cannot by itself result in a commitment to continue. This weaker view implies that voluntarily beginning in itself leads to a commitment that can outweigh the countervailing force of some efforts. Tort law agrees.

8. I emphasized the considerations in condition 3 in "Abortion: A Philosophical Analysis," and "The Problem of Abortion." A similar factor is used in Donald Regan, "Rewriting *Roe v. Wade,*" in *Michigan Law Review,* 77(1979):1569. For a refusal to use the word *benefit* in this way, see Joel Feinberg, *Harm to Others* (Oxford: Oxford University Press, 1984). I discuss

his views in *Morality, Mortality*. We can understand Feinberg's reasons by acknowledging that although it is a benefit to retain something good, we tend to think of someone's life as something that is already his and so not as an additional good conferred on him.

9. Is it worse to be killed than to die a natural death? It does not seem so if the killing is morally permissible. But we cannot assume that it is not—and include this in our reasoning—as we are in the midst of deciding whether it is permitted.

10. I am grateful to William Ruddick for suggesting this clarificatory passage.

11. This was emphasized to me by Judith Thomson and Alan Wertheimer.

12. Our intuitions about this case and the previous one may differ: It may matter whether we do what someone else would have done because he would have done it or we act independently of whether he would have done it.

13. I am indebted to Leigh Cauman here.

14. It is worth clarifying the locution employed here. We speak of efforts we should make in order not to harm (or in order to avoid harming). This should be understood to cover two types of cases: (1) where we will kill unless we make efforts, and (2) where we will wind up making efforts unless we kill. The second type of case is the one we are most often concerned with. It could also be described as a case in which we kill (or have someone killed) rather than make efforts.

15. For a detailed discussion of this issue, see my two articles, "Killing and Letting Die: Methodology and Substance," *Pacific Philosophical Quarterly* (Winter 1983):297–312, and "Harming, Not Aiding and Positive Rights," *Philosophy and Public Affairs* (Winter 1986):3–32.

16. Warren Quinn has made a similar argument in "Actions, Intentions, and Consequences: The Doctrine of Double Effect," *Philosophy and Public Affairs* (Fall 1989):317–33.

17. This point is made by Philippa Foot in "Euthanasia," *Philosophy and Public Affairs* (Winter 1977):85–112.

2

Applying the Argument to Specific Nonabortion Cases

Having constructed the general framework of the argument, we will now examine in more detail how its steps apply to three different situations. In general, the different ways in which attachment occurs may be thought to affect whether there is a special obligation to aid, and what the appropriate baseline is with which to compare the fate of the person killed. We shall also discuss which efforts may permissibly be avoided by killing. In addition, in each case we shall consider an alternative to the output cutoff argument, namely self-and-assisted defense.

Forced Attachment

In the first situation, forced attachment, the following conditions hold:

1. The violinist's need to survive does not, by itself, give him the right to begin using, or to continue using, your body, nor does it give you a duty to start or to continue to aid.

2. You have no special obligations to permit your body to be used when such an attachment has been forced on you.

It might be argued that the violinist has a right to remain in your body because someone must kill him in order to remove him, and he will be harmed if removed. In addition, he might have such a right because if you cease your support of him, he will be worse off than he would have been if he had never been attached to you in the first place. In response to these observations, note the third condition:

3. By being killed and harmed, the violinist loses only what he has

gained by your support, support which has not yet been shown to be required; he is not harmed relative to opportunities that he would have had if he had not been attached to you; and he does not lose anything that you are causally responsible for his having that he would retain independently of you.

Baseline

In the case in which the violinist is forcibly attached to you, the baseline that should be used for deciding whether killing him leaves him worse off than he would have been if not attached or whether he has been harmed relative to (i.e., in comparison with) opportunities before his attachment is not (1) his being alive and on the way to death, the state he was in before being placed inside your body, but (2) his being dead, which is what he would have been if he had not been placed inside your body. We shall compare the consequences of killing the violinist with what would have happened to him if only legitimate means (see Figure 1) had been used to keep him alive.[1]

It is worth repeating what was said above about (3): We need not deny that we harm the violinist in killing him, relative to the condition he would have been in if support continued. But it may not be wrong to harm him in this way. Why? Because we may be obliged only not to harm him relative to the condition he would have been in if he had not been attached. Why? Because if you have no duty to aid him because of his need or other grounds of special obligation, any condition he is in as a result of the aid is not something he has a claim to keep, at least as long as he continues to need your support to maintain it. Therefore, his

Figure 1.

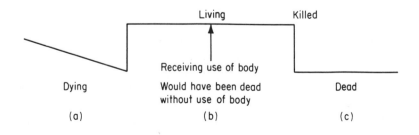

being in that improved condition once attached cannot be the baseline relative to which we must not harm him.

Things might be different if he could retain what he had gotten from your support independently of you, even if not independently of the aid of others. (This is the point of the last clause of (3).) For example, suppose we find someone who is dying. We give him a medicine and he is much improved and no longer needs our help. We may not kill him simply because he will not be harmed relative to the condition he would have been in, i.e., dead, if he had never gotten aid.

Note also that if the violinist's friends attach him to you without your permission, your rights will have been violated. But this violation by people is not crucial to the argument. Suppose the wind lifted up the violinist and blew him into your body. No person would have violated your rights, yet all the premises of the argument are still satisfied. I shall, therefore, include such attachments involving no voluntary act by you in the class of forced attachment.

Is Condition 3 Necessary?

In the case of forcible attachment it may seem that killing the violinist would be permissible even if killing him made him worse off relative to the position he would have been in, and would have had the right not to be deprived of, had he never been attached to you. That is, suppose that the violinist had not been dying and so had no need to be attached to you. Nevertheless, a villain (or the wind) attached him to you anyway, and the only way for you to be free before nine months is to kill him. The violinist gains nothing good from being attached to you, yet perhaps it is permissible to kill him in this case as well.

Furthermore, in the case of forcible attachment, making someone worse off than he would have been if he had never been attached need not involve you or your agent's harming him relative to the opportunities he would have had. That is, killing a person who is forcibly attached obviously harms him, if it deprives him of good opportunities he would have in the future if he had not been killed. But in this case, if the person who kills the violinist is not the person who attached him to you, then by killing him he does not harm the violinist relative to better opportunities he had before being attached. Rather, it is the villain who is responsible for that. In the case of forced attachment, then, it does not seem to matter whether the violinist loses only the benefit of attachment or more than that. As long as he is a burden on your body, it seems permissible to kill him in order to remove him.

How can we argue for this intuitive claim—that one may kill the violinist even if he is made worse off than he would have been if he had never been attached and even if he loses more than he gained from the attachment? One might try arguing for the permissibility of killing on grounds of both simple self-defense and the right of third parties to assist those who cannot defend themselves. My goal is to examine how far one can go with such a simple self- and assisted-defense argument, as an alternative to the output cutoff argument in the case of forced attachment. I believe that it may have some limitations. If it does, then contrary to the self- and assisted-defense argument, the fact that the violinist would lose only the benefit of residence and would not be made worse off than he would have been had he not been attached will help justify the permissibility of killing him even in cases of forced attachment. Furthermore, the fact that the violinist's killer—who did not attach him in the first place—would not deprive him of opportunities he had before being attached may also not be crucial. Rather, it may simply be significant whether or not the violinist is harmed by someone (anyone) relevant to any opportunities for life he had before being attached.

Self-Defense Against Innocent Threats

An argument based on self-defense that would apply to the violinist who is forcibly attached must state that it is permissible to kill even nonactive innocent threats. That is, sometimes people do things that may harm others, but they are not morally to blame for doing so. For example, if a young child fires a loaded gun at someone, she is morally innocent but (indeed) active. One can defend oneself against such a threat, even by killing the child if necessary to prevent one's own death. But people may also be made into nonactive, morally innocent threats. For example, a villain or even a natural force (e.g., a gust of wind) might make a person into a human missile, hurtling at someone with deadly force.[2] (The output cutoff argument, of course, is also concerned with killing innocent nonactive threats, but those who receive life from their imposition and are not harmed relative to preattachment prospects.) One question is whether a potential victim can defend himself against such an innocent threat by killing it. Another question is how great the threatened harm to the victim must be in order for killing to be a permissible response. The third question is whether a third party may do what the potential victim himself may do to combat the innocent threat. (This last question is important to the abortion discussion, as women cannot now abort themselves; they require the assistance of doctors. Of course, this question would be less important to the abortion debate if self-abortion devices were perfected.)

Fatal, Innocent, Nonactive Threats

Let us begin with a case in which the innocent presents a fatal threat, unlike the violinist case. Nancy Davis addressed this issue.[3] She believes that when the threatening party (e.g., a woman) and the person threatened (e.g., a man) are morally innocent (there is no malicious or even negligent aggressor), a third party has no impartial reason for taking sides. Each of the first two parties has a prerogative to defend himself or herself against the other. That is, the person threatened may try to kill the threat in order to save his life, but the threat in turn may try to ward off the attack on her. Each has a prerogative to do so, according to Davis, because each cares more about himself or herself than about the other. This does not mean, however, that right is truly on the side of one person rather than the other, and only a preponderance of right on one side would justify a third party's taking sides.

Perhaps we should distinguish here between justification and excuse: We excuse someone, for example, when under constant duress he acts improperly, but his act is still not justified, as the emotional duress does not provide an adequate reason for committing the act; it would have been better if the emotion had been controlled and not caused the act in the first place. If the potential victim himself were fully justified in killing the threat (because the reasons to do so were on his side), the third party should be able to take his side. If the victim is merely excused, however, then a third party may not take his side. The ordinary notion of excuse includes the idea that reason would have recommended a different course of action. However, it is not clear that someone's exercising his prerogative to defend himself carries the same implication, that is, that reason would have recommended a different course of action. Therefore the distinction between excuse and justification does not, after all, quite explain why Davis thinks that an agent may exercise his prerogative but a third party should not help him.

Third Parties and Self-Defense Against
Innocent Threats

My own view is that a third party may sometimes be permitted to side with the person initially threatened, even though the person threatening him is not acting and is morally innocent. The reason is that the individual who is a nonactive threat and without fault is in a position where she should not be first. For example, she is on another person or on a physical threat coming at a nonthreatening person.[4] She should bear a relatively greater burden for correcting this inappropriate position.[5]

The position of this threat is different from that of a natural object—for example, a stone that the wind hurls at a person—because she is not a stone but, rather, a person who should not be in an inappropriate position relative to others. One person's inappropriate location vis-à-vis another raises moral questions no matter how it comes about, whereas the unfortunate location of objects does not. I take this view in contrast to those who would argue that there is no moral problem unless some agent is morally responsible for causing the threat to be where it is: One simply has a right not to have someone on the body or property to which one is entitled, even if the wind put them there.[6]

Redirection: First and Third Parties

To support the claim that the threat bears greater responsibility for correcting the situation, suppose that a button is attached to a moral innocent who has been made into a human missile. She can press that button and so redirect herself away from the person whose life she is threatening. Redirecting herself, however, will cost her a broken leg, because she will crash into a wall instead. I believe that the innocent threat should press the button and so redirect herself.[7] Suppose that this innocent's potential victim also is equipped with a button that he can press to move him away from the innocent threat, but at the cost of his leg being broken. The claim is that the innocent threat has a greater responsibility to bear this cost, because she is headed to where she should not be, on the victim, who has a right not to be occupied. We prefer to make the situation here one in which the potential victim remains without interference at no cost to him.

Suppose that the potential threatener would break her leg if she redirected herself and that the potential victim would only break his left arm if he pressed his button. I believe that the innocent threat's added responsibility for extricating herself from a position in which she will harm someone else is sufficiently great that she should bear the somewhat greater cost, rather than have the potential victim bear the somewhat lesser cost.

Now suppose that neither of the two parties has a button that will redirect him or her. That the innocent threat would be responsible for redirecting herself if she had a button suggests that if she physically cannot redirect herself, a third party may be permitted to do so at the same cost to her. It is not only in the situation in which she is at fault for failing to press the button to redirect herself that a third party may act. If she should, if she could, then another can impose the cost if she cannot.

Even if all this is true, however, it does not imply that when the cost to the innocent fatal threat is very great, she should redirect herself. Nor does it imply that a third party is permitted to cause her such a great loss in order to save the potential victim. Assume, for example, that to avoid landing on and killing her victim, the innocent threat must press a button that will fatally swerve her into a wall. It would be quite appropriate to require this of a guilty threat (e.g., a malicious aggressor) and to permit a third party to impose such a loss on her in order to save her victim. I believe, however, that it is not appropriate to require an innocent threat to do this. Because she is morally innocent of threatening her victim, she does not owe it to him to give up her life in order to save him. The losses she must sustain to save him should be limited in their severity. A guilty aggressor, by contrast, does owe her victim whatever is necessary to prevent the fatal harm with which she threatens him.

Perhaps the potential victim sees the innocent threat coming at him and knows that she will not fatally deflect herself. He can physically respond in one of only two ways: To save his own life he can either kill the threat or press his button, thereby moving himself away from the innocent threat but breaking his leg. The claim is that the innocent threat should not have to pay with the loss of her life, but if nothing significantly less from the threat will save the victim, then he, the victim, should bear some of the cost rather than kill the threat. We could say he should "pick up the slack." He should do this rather than impose a loss on the threat for greater than the threat owes it to him to suffer. That is, he should suffer a broken leg rather than kill the innocent threat to protect himself. The cost he should absorb is a combination of what he should do simply to save someone's life and what he should do instead of killing someone who will thereby be worse off than she would have been if she had not become a threat.

There are two steps here: (1) deciding what the threat owes and (2) deciding whether the potential victim should assume some of the difference between the severity of their two losses. If he should do this, then a third party should not attack the threat.

Suppose that the threat did not owe it to the victim to suffer more than a broken leg to prevent her harming him. Suppose also that the victim did not have to do more than suffer a broken leg. What should each one do if the victim would suffer permanent paralysis of both legs if he were to move aside rather than kill the innocent threat? (We can refer to such a case in which neither party clearly owes something as a *no-owe case*.)

One solution is that the victim may kill the threat (assuming that this is necessary to stop her), even though this extracts more from the threat than she owes. Because it does this, the threat may resist and defend herself, even by killing the victim if this is necessary to save herself. In this legitimate battle of innocents, third parties should remain neutral. I mean to suggest that each acts permissibly, not just excusably. This is true even though when the innocent threat resists he helps to maintain an inappropriate situation, that is, his imposing on someone else. My view is that this battle of innocents represents a compromise: The victim is permitted to attack because the imposition on him is wrong. The threat is permitted to defend himself because he is morally innocent and so, even though he is where he ought not to be, it is not his responsibility to accept the full high cost of seeing to it that he is not there.

We have now derived the result for some cases which Davis argued for in all cases of defense against innocent threats. However, we reached it by a different route than Davis took, as we assumed that the innocent threat sometimes has a greater responsibility to bear the costs than does her potential victim.

A second solution is to suppose that the innocent threat is not obligated to choose to suffer an overwhelming loss in order to prevent harming her victim, but that this does not mean that others who tried to extract this loss from her would not be in a morally favored position. That is, the victim may kill the threat in order to save his life; a third party may kill the threat in order to save the victim; and the threat may not resist the attack on her. An analogy here is the military draft: We are under no obligation to go into the army until we are called. (We do not have to be the one to initiate service.) But if our number comes up, we must not resist the call, and in addition, third parties can force us to go.

Only the second solution defends both the first and third parties' right to kill an innocent fatal threat and also denies the threat's right to resist. This second solution does not deny that if the loss to the innocent threat's victim were less than a certain crucial amount, he should pick up some of the slack.

Self-Defense Against Nonfatal Threats

The violinist case assumes that there is no fatal threat to you. This prompts the question whether in innocent threat cases where Condition 3 does not hold the victim should pick up prolonged imposition on his body as slack, rather than kill the threat. If he need not pick it up, the second question is whether a third party may kill the threat on his behalf or whether this is a permissible battle of innocents in which a third party should remain neutral. It is not surprising that these questions are difficult to answer, and so I will not here attempt to answer either question, although our discussion of Step (4) will be relevant.

Not Harmed Relative To
Preattachment Prospects

The question to which we shall turn now is whether focusing on an element present in the violinist case but not in most standard self- and assisted-defense cases makes it easier to justify a third-party killing. That is, in ordinary self-defense cases, when an innocent threat is killed, he is made worse off than he would have been if he had never been a threat to someone in the first place. By being killed, he is deprived of those opportunities he had before becoming a threat, as he had the opportunity to be perfectly all right if he had not been put in this position. It is true that if the person who kills him was not the one to make him a threat, the killer will not be depriving him of those opportunities. Nonetheless, if he is killed, circumstances will have deprived the innocent threat of the opportunities he had earlier. This is true even if the innocent threat begins receiving life support if he is attached to you. That is, suppose that once attached, his life immediately becomes dependent on your body, and so if you kill him, he will lose only the life he has because of your body's support. But he did not need to be attached to you. Thus if he is killed, he is harmed relative to opportunities he had before his attachment to you.

In the forced attachment violinist case, killing the violinist makes him no worse off than he would have been if he had not been attached to you, as he was dying and had no other opportunities for aid. In addition, he is not harmed by the killer or anyone else, relative to the position he would have been in if he had not received support.

I suggest that this characteristic of the case is morally significant, for the following reason: We have difficulty supporting a third party's killing a nonfatal innocent threat whose predicament is being made worse off than he would have been if not made into a threat. We can understand why the threat could permissibly refuse to allow himself to be made worse off than he would have been had he not become a threat (beyond what he owes in order to correct his inappropriate position). But what if he is already threatened with death and if being hurled at his victim can save him from his original predicament? As much as his original predicament was undeserved, we still think it inappropriate of him to escape from it by means of an unacceptable (even if nonvoluntary) imposition on another person.

From the threat's point of view, his victim will be part of the solution if being a threat will rescue him from his original predicament. But if the threat did not face a threat to himself before being hurled at his victim, his victim will be more like part of the problem than part of the solution.

In the violinist case, the violinist's current situation is his attachment to you. His rescue from a fatal end to this attachment will also be a rescue from his previous predicament, facing an inevitable death. This, I believe, permits a third party to kill him. To be prevented from gaining over his original position, rather than just to suffer a loss, is a significant factor. Refusing to be someone's refuge and returning him to the fate that he faced before the possibility of refuge was presented is significantly different from playing a role in framing a new and worse fate for someone.

Let us expand on this a bit. I am making two claims. One is that we should be more reluctant to kill the violinist when he did not face a threat of death before his attachment to you, than we should be to kill him if he did face such a threat before his attachment. (All this assumes you did not owe him rescue.) The second claim helps defend the first, given that what a third party may do is in some way related to what the innocent threat himself must do. The second claim (put forth more hesitantly) is that what the innocent threat himself must do to stop his being a threat varies depending on whether or not he was already facing a threat of death before being a threat to you. That is, suppose that our innocent threat has a button attached to her. She is permitted to make less of a sacrifice to avoid hitting her victim and to do more to defend herself from your deadly attack on her, if her being a threat did not save her from a prior death threat rather than if it did. If she did face death before becoming a threat to her victim, she should make more of a sacrifice to avoid hitting him and do less to defend herself, as she should not try to extract herself from her first predicament at a steep cost to her victim.

Having said all this, I believe we can understand the opposite view. That is, one might think that we should be more reluctant to kill someone who would thereby be put back in the position he would have been in anyway. What underlies this opposite view, I believe, is the sense that it is worse to interfere with a good thing that has happened, that is, the rescue from the first fatal threat (even though it comes along with a bad event, your being imposed on), than it is to do harm in stopping what is an unadulterated bad event, someone's coming at you as a threat. Nevertheless, not being harmed relative to preattachment opportunities dominates, I suggest.

I conclude that even in cases of involuntary attachment, Condition 3 should emphasize that the violinist loses the benefit of his attachment, is not made worse off than he would have been if he had never been attached, and is not harmed relative to preattachment opportunities. This means that a third party would be permitted to kill him in order to help a victim avoid losses that are less than would be required in standard self-defense cases to justify the third party's killing. (This is consistent with the losses for which one may permissibly kill being higher than those one need not make to save someone's life.)

Efforts That May Justifiably Be Avoided

The next two conditions are as follows:

4. The efforts to support the violinist are great enough so that in conjunction with the truth of the other conditions, they would justify our killing him in order to stop them.

5. There are no other means of removing the violinist that do not require more from you than you would have to suffer in order to avoid having him killed in the circumstances.

To determine whether these conditions are satisfied, we must return to the issue of what efforts we are justified in avoiding by killing. Our discussion of the self- and assisted-defense argument will help.

The Malicious Aggressor

Suppose that a malicious aggressor deliberately attached himself to you for no reason but to impose on your body for nine months. Would it be permissible to kill him, purely on grounds of self-defense if this were the only way to free yourself? Presumably, it would be. Furthermore, the imposition with which he threatens you is not the minimal imposition for which one could permissibly kill someone. That is, he could threaten to remain for three months in your body, or he might offer a less strenuous imposition than your carrying him in your body; for example, he might be dragged along beside you. It would still be permissible for you to kill him in order to stop him from deliberately imposing on you in these ways.

The Innocent Threat

If one is imposed on by a morally innocent nonactive threat, even when nature (e.g., the wind) rather than a person makes him a threat, one is still subject to an imposition to which one should not be subject, and the innocent threat is still where a person should not be vis-à-vis another person (e.g., in another, without his consent). Therefore, in our discussion of the innocent threat who would be worse off if she were killed than if she had never been a threat in the first place, I argued that it would be right to impose burdens on the threat rather than on the potential victim to stop the bodily imposition. That is, in order to stop the threat, a third party should impose a loss on her before imposing a somewhat lesser loss on the potential victim if the loss to the threat were not excessive. This is the first difference from the case of the malicious aggressor: There are greater limits to what may be done to the innocent threat, who would be worse off if a third party attacked her than if she had never been a threat, than what may be done to the malicious aggressor.

The second difference is that if the loss to this threat in order to stop her would be excessive, the person threatened should absorb some of this excess, "pick up the slack," and suffer some loss rather than impose that excessive sacrifice. But this consideration need not be extended to a malicious aggressor.

The third difference is that once the loss extends beyond what should be picked up, and neither the threat nor the threatener is responsible for bearing it, it is not so clear that a third party should impose a cost on the threat that the threat need not impose on herself. Yet I believe it is not unreasonable to think that the third party should sometimes act to favor the threat's victim: Suppose that the innocent threat would paralyze her victim and could be stopped only by being killed. Although the threat would not need to press her button and fatally redirect herself, and she would be worse off if killed than if never made into a threat, I believe that a third party may permissibly kill.

A question more pertinent to our violinist case is whether carrying someone in one's body for nine months represents a burden that must be borne if being killed is an excessive loss to require an innocent threat to choose, if she would be worse off if killed than if she had never been a threat. (In this latter respect, the innocent threat is unlike the violinist.) One indication that it is not part of a required burden is that it is more than what would be required to justify killing a malicious aggressor. A burden which was the minimum we could help you to avoid by killing a malicious aggressor, might have to be borne in regard to certain innocent threats in order to avoid killing them. But perhaps what is securely beyond the minimum is not part of what the victim of a threat must pick up.

To this we can add the fact that in the violinist case, the violinist will be no worse off and will not be harmed (by anyone) relative to his preattachment prospects (Condition 3). Further, he will have been rescued from his earlier predicament if he is allowed to remain in your body. This will reduce the slack you must pick up, and it will increase what the violinist should be willing to lose in order to end his imposition on you: He should not want to escape from an earlier threat to his life by using you beyond the help you would owe him in order to save his life, although the general concern over killing him (versus letting him die) may increase the efforts you should make. Condition 3 holding, therefore, the way is opened for a third party to side with you when your loss would be the use of your body for nine months (in a fashion similar to that of pregnancy and labor), a use that is securely beyond the minimum necessary to justify killing a malicious aggressor, even if the innocent violinist would not have to kill himself to stop imposing on you. If all this were true, then we would have satisfied Condition 4 for the violinist case. However, more may have to be said.

In sum, we have considered attacks on malicious aggressors, innocents who are threats due to natural forces or due to aggressors, those who will and will not be harmed relative to preattachment opportunities, and those who present fatal and non-fatal threats.

Further Thoughts

When we consider carrying someone in one's body (and going through a painful removal process), is it just the strenuousness of the imposition with which we are concerned? That is, do we think we may kill to avoid a quantitatively large imposition, or may we kill because it is, rather, a qualitatively significant imposition? How do we measure and compare impositions or deprivations? For example, someone may find it much more onerous to be without a new car than to be without a constitutional protection of his free speech. Yet it is debatable whether a system that exchanges basic liberties for economic status (once a certain level of economic security has been achieved) can be morally justified. Likewise, working forty hours a week may be more burdensome to someone than having his body examined. Yet we think we have a right to sentence a criminal to hard labor (or service to the community) but not to physical testing or involvement in (even nonrisky) research experiments involving intrusion into his body.

These analogies suggest that the distinction between the use of someone's body and other losses must be drawn qualitatively, in terms of privacy or integrity of the body. It cannot be drawn in terms of degree of strenuousness alone. But, further, bodily invasions themselves can differ qualitatively. A forced bone marrow transplant may be strenuous, if not very damaging in the long run. But a nonvoluntary rectal exam, which causes less damage and is not strenuous, may be humiliating. Sexualized bodily impositions may be humiliating if nonvoluntary, and real pregnancy (if not the ersatz one in the violinist case) is a sexualized imposition, as well as a strenuous use of a body.

Finally, we can satisfy Condition 5 if there is no other way to stop the nine months of support besides killing the intruder. Let us assume that this is true. This concludes the argument for the permissibility of killing in a forced attachment case.[8]

Voluntary Attachment

Voluntary attachment refers to the case in which you volunteer to help the violinist survive, and no one else can. The conditions are these:

1. The violinist's need to survive does not, by itself, give him a right to begin or to continue using your body, nor does it give you a duty to start or to continue aid.

2. You have no special obligation to let him use your body, because even voluntarily offering support does not, by itself, obligate you to continue offering it. It is not itself a promise to continue, and it does not in itself grant a right to stay. The violinist's need in conjunction with your voluntarily beginning aid also does not lead to such an obligation. If someone will not be harmed relative to preattachment options, if you stop supporting him, this is a point in favor of your feeling free both to start and to stop. That is, we may sometimes try to help someone without committing ourselves to continuing if we find the effort too great. For example, if the violinist fell out of your body, you would not have to put him back in just because he needs aid and you voluntarily began. Here your continuing to carry someone is really providing support in continuing installments. You could simply stop making the next installment. The absence of expectations reinforces this.

Perhaps it is impermissible to remove the violinist because he will be worse off as a result of losing your support than if he had never received it at all, because he would be harmed relative to prospects he had before being attached to you, and/or because we must kill and harm him in order to remove him.

In response to these suggestions, we note that it is permissible to directly kill the violinist in order to stop your support of him, though this will harm him relative to the future he might have had, in part because of Condition 3:

3. By being killed and harmed, the violinist loses only the life that he gains from your support, which support has not yet been shown to be required; he is not harmed relative to his preattachment opportunities; and he loses nothing that you are causally responsible for his gaining and that he could retain independently of your further bodily support.

Why is Condition 3 relevant? If you volunteered to attach the violinist to yourself, it would seem that what he gains from the voluntarily donated use of your body is his by right and that it should not be taken away. For example, perhaps he was dying and would have died if he had not been attached to you; your voluntarily attaching him rescued him and so improved his condition. Killing him now would return him to the condition he would have been in if you had not begun rescue (see Figure 2). This is below his improved condition. Why may you do what will harm him relative to the condition you voluntarily put him into, even if he is not harmed relative to the condition he would have been in if never attached to you? Is this not taking away what you voluntarily gave him? In this case, at least, is not his condition once he is in your body the proper baseline with which to compare his fate if killed?

One answer to these questions is that the violinist's survival which you will stop is something he is yet to get, not something already given. It depends on the continued use of your body. But he has no right to this use simply because he needs it and/or because you voluntarily began aid. Nonetheless, does he obtain a right to the continued use of your body because we may not kill and harm him or because without such use he would be deprived of opportunities he would have had independently of you? No, because, if he is killed and harmed relative to his being alive in your body, he will lose only those benefits that would arise from the continued use of your body. You have not yet voluntarily given these benefits to him, and he cannot retain them on his own independently of the use of your body. So, even if you are morally responsible for having caused him to survive up to now, the prospects he would have if support continued is not the correct baseline with which to compare his being killed.

Figure 2.

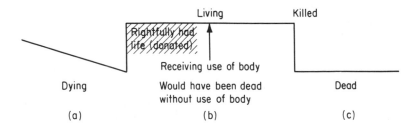

In a sense, his life as an entity has not been fully returned until the process of continued use of your body for the purpose of retaining the life is completed.

Baseline

One suggestion, therefore, is that in the case of voluntary attachment, the baseline with which we should compare the death that results from killing the violinist is b'. This is the state in which the violinist would be if he did not receive the continued support of your body. We compare death from killing with the state he would be in without continued use of your body (dead) to see if you have an obligation to provide continued use of your body on the grounds that he should not be killed. We decide it is permissible to kill and harm him, in part, because this is only taking away a benefit (continued life) of attachment, a benefit he would not have otherwise, to end an attachment which you are not required to give on other grounds. We have, of course, checked that that baseline b' is not a state in which he is harmed relative to the condition he would have been in without attachment at all (i.e., death).

Below we shall consider a revision of this suggestion for the proper baseline.

4. Your efforts to continue supporting the violinist are great enough that in conjunction with the truth of the other conditions, they justify our killing him in order to stop your making them.

5. In these circumstances, there are no other means of removing the violinist that do not require a greater burden for you than you would have to bear in order to avoid having him killed.

Therefore, the violinist does not have a right to continue to use your body, nor do you have an obligation to let him use it in virtue of his having a right not to be killed or a right not to be harmed relative to prospects he had independently of you. If killing and harming him causes only the loss of the benefit of otherwise unrequired support, not harming and not killing him cannot be used to morally require continuing this support.

Notice that we have decided this case independently of giving you moral credit for good intentions in volunteering aid. Nor have we made use of step 6, in that we have not considered that you should have some morally sufficient reason for putting yourself in a position where you might make use of the output cutoff argument. Suppose we did think that not only were higher efforts required to justify killing someone than were required to justify letting him die, but that you should do something to avoid being in a situation where we kill someone, even in accord with Conditions 1 to 5. Then we might point out that you are offering the violinist some chance of living when he would otherwise certainly die, and this may provide sufficient reason for putting yourself in the situation.

Now, however, suppose that someone else would have helped the violinist and would have continued this support to completion. But you drag away the violinist from this offer. If you then do not continue your support or you kill him in order to stop it, you will have harmed him relative to his preattachment prospects. Indeed, you will have made him worse off than he otherwise would have been. In this case, I believe, killing the violinist to stop supporting him is impermissible.

Some have suggested (in the literature on self-defense) that even someone morally responsible for causing another person to be a threat to him may defend himself, although this makes the threatening person worse off than he otherwise would have been. The perpetrator is liable for punishment for making the other into a threat, but he does not forfeit his right of self-defense. I suggest that the perpetrator loses his right to self-defense, when he is responsible for the size of the threat the other presents, i.e., it is not through escalation by the other that the other presents a large threat. This means that the self- and assisted-defense argument is even weaker compared with the output cutoff argument in cases of voluntary attachment than it is in the case of forced attachment.

There are types of intentional attachment cases in which making someone worse off than he would have been without attachment will not prevent a permissible termination of aid. Suppose, for example, that the violinist needed to be attached and that only you are willing to do it, but the unnatural removal procedure before nine months will make the violinist worse off than if he had never been attached. Still, if there is a good chance that you will go through with the saving operation and natural removal, it may be in his interest to risk being made worse off in order to gain the only possibility of survival. Here it is permissible to detach him, in part because it is permissible to impose the risk of being made worse off and the violinist still stands to gain something from being attached to you. Here we may impose a risk of harm relative to preattachment prospects on someone for the sake of a probable benefit to him.

Voluntary Act with Foreseen But Unintended Attachment

A voluntary act with a foreseen, but unintended, attachment refers to a situation in which you know that a voluntary act of yours will result in the violinist's attachment, even though you do not intend his attachment. For example, you know that walking down one street rather than another will trigger a magnetic reaction that will attach the violinist to you. The conditions in this case are the same:

1. The violinist's need by itself does not give him a right to start or to continue using your body, nor does it give you a duty to start or continue aid.

2. You have no special obligation to aid him. This is because your voluntarily performing an act for a purpose other than attaching the violinist to you does not by itself constitute a commitment to him or in some other way constitute giving him the right to use your body, even though you know what the consequences of your act will be.

Though his need and your acts, alone or together, give no right or obligation for him to stay, could the fact that the violinist will be killed if he is removed, and/or will be harmed relative to preattachment opportunities, give him the right to stay? In answer to this, we note the following:

3. By being killed and harmed, the violinist loses only the benefit he gets from the continued use of your body, a use not yet shown to be required; he is not harmed relative to his preattachment opportunities, and he loses nothing that you are causally responsible for his having that he could retain independently of you.

If we assume that you are morally responsible for his initial attachment, because you acted voluntarily and knew the possible consequences, then the discussion of Condition 3 and the proper baseline in the case of voluntary attachment applies here.

4. Your efforts to continue supporting the violinist are great enough that in conjunction with the truth of the other conditions, they would justify our killing him in order to stop them.

5. In these circumstances, there are no other means of removing him that do not require you to bear a greater burden than you would have to bear in order to avoid having him killed.

In discussing this case we have not used Condition 6. If we wanted to use it, what we might think about in connection with this case in particular is whether it would have been costly to avoid the voluntary act that led to this attachment. It might be thought that if it was easy to avoid, it would have been best to avoid getting into a situation in the first place in which we end up having to kill someone. On the other hand, the fact that Condition 3 is true could be a reason for not making significant efforts to avoid the act leading to attachment. For example, suppose that walking down another street—where there would be no magnetic pull between you and the violinist—meant entering a dangerous neighborhood. Why bother to take this risk when the possibility of the violinist's being attached and detached will not harm him in comparison with his preattachment opportunities?

The cost of avoiding a voluntary act, the probability of an attachment ensuing, and the permissibility of imposing risk are more likely to be important if the violinist would be harmed in regard to his preattachment opportunities and/or worse off than if he were never attached to your body, and stood no chance of receiving the benefit of being saved if attached to you. For example, not performing the voluntary act may be extremely costly, either immediately or in opportunity costs to you or to society, and the probability of attachment may be low. Then it might be permissible to kill the violinist in order to detach him even if he would be harmed relative to preattachment opportunities and had received no opportunity to benefit. The analogy here might be to driving a car when the costs of not doing so are significant. For example, suppose you must drive to get to work. Suppose that even though you took reasonable precautions, you had an accident and that you knew that there was some probability of this happening. If the accident resulted in your victim's being attached to your body when he had no need to be, could you have him killed to avoid his nine-month imposition? Is it unreasonable to think that this is permissible, because it is permissible to impose a risk on someone, even though this is not done for the sake of a possible benefit to him?

Should the Numbers Count?

All along we have been considering single cases, but perhaps the numbers should count. That is, suppose many individuals had to drive cars, with each person having a low probability of either killing a pedestrian or being attached to him and having to kill him in order to be detached. The numbers of deaths might be quite large if we permitted driving and also detachment, not to speak of the psychological burden of having to kill many people. If the pedestrian will be worse off than if never attached, there may be a certain number of deaths or killings to detach that was great enough to lead us to prohibit driving.

The alternative to prohibiting driving would be to require nine months of support to continue if attachment took place. Given that it is understandable for someone to interpret this to be a large imposition on him and to wish to avoid it, it would be reasonable if he instead chose not to drive. That is, it is not unreasonable for him to see the sacrifice of giving support as greater than the sacrifice of not driving. Of course, there may be conflicts of interest. For example, it may be in his employer's interest to have him drive, because for him the cost of the employee's not driving may be greater than the cost to him of the employee's having to provide support if detachment is not permitted.

If driving is not banned, those who refuse to drive for fear of risking uninterrupted attachment may be subject to additional pressures: There may be others who are willing to take the risk and drive. Then the nondrivers will lose job opportunities and may wind up with lower economic and social positions. Furthermore, if some drivers are not subject to the risk of attachment, this inequality may result in different social positions between this group and others. In this context the cost of not permitting driving with detachment rises for those who do not drive. The numbers may not matter, however, if those who are pedestrians on some occasions and who would not benefit from attachment on those occasions would want to be drivers on other occasions. For then they may be willing to risk detachment for the sake of also being drivers who may detach pedestrians.

What if there were many violinist cases in which there was foreseen attachment as a result of a voluntary act? Because the violinist would not be harmed relative to preattachment prospects, I do not believe there would be a significant effect on the moral permissibility of detachment. However, the psychological burden of frequent killings, even if the output cutoff argument were correct, might affect our policy. What if there were many violinist cases of forced and also of intentional attachment? Again, the fact that the violinist would not be harmed relative to his preattachment prospects would make the numbers less significant.

Notes

1. It might be argued that the baseline should be part (a) of Figure 1, because we use part (a) as a baseline when we disconnect someone from life support and then allow him to die, thus making him what he was—both alive and dying—before being connected. (I owe this observation to Joseph Rizzo.) Because it is not generally permissible to kill someone who will die soon anyway, it may be argued that it should not be permissible to kill someone who would have died soon if he had not been attached to you. In answer I point out that: (1) To produce a sufficient good, it may be permissible to kill someone who will die soon anyway; and (2) Suppose that we would not kill someone at $t1$ if he will soon die at $t2$. We might still think it is permissible to kill at $t3$ in the violinist's case because $t2$—when the violinist would have died—is in the past by $t3$, and the person would have been dead at $t2$.

2. A third type of case is that of a person who is not even causally involved in producing the threat but is on it. A villain may have put him there, or else a natural event (e.g., a gust of wind) blew him onto the threat, which has an adhesive surface. Such persons are referred to as *innocent shields*.

3. Nancy Davis, "Abortion and Self-Defense," *Philosophy and Public Affairs* 13(1984):175–207.

4. What if it were her duty to sit on an object before it became a threat? The object should still not become a threat to someone, and she should not be on it when it is a threat.

5. Likewise, someone who is afflicted with a disease that makes him a threat should be responsible for not harming others, even though he is not morally responsible for his illness.

6. I first made this point in "Problems in the Morality of Killing and Letting Die" (Ph.D. diss., Massachusetts Institute of Technology, 1980).

7. I first used this example in a discussion of what innocent threats owe their victims, in my article "The Insanity Defense, Innocent Threats and Limited Alternatives," *Criminal Justice Ethics,* Summer 1987, pp. 61–76. I tried to prove that the innocent threat has a duty not to cause harm, and I derived from this his duty to undo such harm if he were unable to prevent himself from causing it, as well as his duty to compensate anyone he does harm if he cannot undo the harm. I now suspect these conclusions go too far, but it is interesting, I think, to figure out why. Our discussion in this book summarizes part of this earlier piece.

8. Further discussion of what efforts we are justified in avoiding by killing, which completes the analysis of this topic, occurs in Chapter 3, and is summarized on p. 70.

9. Larry Crocker and Julian Lamont kindly commented on this chapter.

3

Variations and Alternatives

In this chapter we will consider how significant variations on the violinist case affect the output cutoff argument and also consider other arguments.

If Aid Is No Longer Causally Necessary

Suppose that the violinist needed to be attached to you for only a moment in order to be cured of some fatal disease. However, it is impossible to separate him from you for another nine months, even though the further attachment in itself does him no good. Or assume that the one moment necessary for the violinist's life-saving attachment had the remarkable effect of making you dependent on his body for nine months if there were no forcible detachment.

If the violinist's attachment is forced on you (by a person or by natural force), and if killing him is the only way to separate the two of you, it seems to me that such a killing would be permissible. The violinist still will lose a benefit he would not have had if he had not been attached to you, although he will not gain anything from being attached to you after the first minute. He is not harmed relative to his preattachment prospects, and the losses that you seek to avoid are as great as they are in other cases.

Your continued connection to him or his to you—a loss to you in both cases—is best seen, I believe, as an unavoidable extension of the process which occurred in the first minute that provided him with his benefit. Indeed, it is a part of the same process whose helpful component is already over. If you had wondered at the beginning, "What do I have to do to save this person's life?" you would have concluded, "Keep him in my body until he is detached after nine months." (Or, alternatively, "remain attached to him, with me in him, until I am detached.")

If you voluntarily attach the violinist, what he gains in the first minute is rightfully his. But you knew that he would need to remain attached as part of the only process that can give him the benefit. Seen in this way, if he is killed, we will be taking from him the benefit that requires the entire nine-month attachment in order to be effective. We thus will be killing him in order to stop that process; we will not be taking from him something that he now can retain on his own.

This analysis suggests, contrary to Figure 2 in Chapter 2, that if this aid is voluntarily begun, the baseline with which we should compare the violinist's state if he is killed is the state in which he would be if he had not been attached (that is, he would be dead.) We should not as Figure 2 suggests, compare it with the state in which he would have been—in this case, alive—if he did not continue to be attached after the moment in which the attachment actually, causally, cured him. Why is this? Because it is, in fact, impossible for him to leave your body, he still needs to be in you. The important question is in what state he would be if he did not get what he needs from you. We, therefore, compare his condition if killed with what he would have if he did not get all he needs from you. And that is the condition he would have been in (dead) if he had not been attached to you in the first place.

Those cases in which attachment is not causally required after a point have obvious relevance to the issue of viability in abortion. A viable fetus is one that no longer needs to be in a woman's womb, although as long as it is there it does receive sustenance from her body. In this violinist case we assume that after a time the violinist receives nothing from his attachment, even while he is attached, and also that it is impossible to remove him. We shall refer to this as a *superviability* case.

We stated that receipt of the benefit, in a sense, requires the entire period of attachment, not just the one minute. The output cutoff principle, however, dictates a close causal connection (such as exists in the first minute) at some point between the benefit and the use of the body. By contrast, suppose that a mugger murdered you and so satisfied his appetite for killing before he encountered someone else. In a sense, this second person owes his life to your having been unjustly killed. But this does not mean that it is permissible to kill the second person, even if that could somehow bring you back to life. (That is, we may not take away the "benefit" of your loss in order to prevent a further loss to you; the causal connection between your being used and the second person's being alive is not tight enough.)

Innocent Beneficiaries of Impositions

We can alter the violinist case in another way. Assume that the violinist is never attached to you but that his friends hook you up to a machine that will remove some of your blood from you over the next nine months. They will then transfuse your blood into the unconscious violinist. The only way to stop them from doing this is to kill the violinist, so that his friends no longer have a reason for their operation. In previous scenarios, because the violinist physically imposed on you, he could be regarded as a morally innocent threat. In this scenario, however, because he does not impose on you, I do not believe that we can regard him as an innocent threat (even though your life is in jeopardy as long as he is alive). Rather, he is what I shall term a *morally innocent beneficiary* of an unjust imposition on you.

Is it permissible for a third party to kill the violinist in order to stop the imposition on you? The output cutoff argument, leaves open the possibility that it is permissible, as it does not explicitly require that the person to be killed must be an innocent threat to the person who is being imposed on. We could say of the violinist, who is an innocent beneficiary, that he will lose only a benefit (continued life) of the continuing imposition on you, he is not harmed relative to the prospects he had prior to receiving benefits, and he is killed to stop a significant imposition which your initial behavior does not commit you to continue and which you would not have had to suffer to save his life.

If we permit killing in this case, should we also permit it if you are the victim of a natural event (rather than an act of injustice) whose consequence is that its damage to you saves another person's life? After all, we did argue that if a gust of wind, rather than a villain, made someone into an innocent threat to you, a third party might be permitted to kill him. But it may be wrong to extend the permission to kill innocent beneficiaries to cases in which nature causes an imposition by something other than the beneficiary; the element of injustice may be crucial to the killing of innocent beneficiaries. We do need, however, further justification for drawing such a distinction between cases, a justification I shall not provide here.

Efforts for the Sake of, Versus on Account Of

Suppose that the violinist is detached from you almost immediately after he is attached, but that you will continue to suffer losses over the next nine months that are equivalent to the losses that would have been imposed on you had he continued to be attached. That is, the losses are equivalent to having the violinist attached to you and then removed; they are the direct effect of the imposition that saved the violinist's life.[1] I suggest that in this case, it would not be permissible to kill the violinist after he has been detached in order to stop that further loss to you. (This variation in the case is relevant to Condition 4.)

The reason is that once something that is thought of as belonging to someone (in this case, this something is the life of the violinist) is completely and successfully retained by its "owner," without his now imposing on you for its retention, it seems impermissible to have it taken away from him, however illegitimately it was returned or retained, so long as he was morally innocent in the original imposition. (Simple stolen property can, however, be taken away. If the owner was not morally innocent of causing the imposition on you, it is, I believe, morally permissible to take what is his that he now retains independently of you in order to prevent the aftereffects of imposition. For example, if a guilty aggressor has used your body and as a consequence your kidneys fail, it seems morally permissible to remove his kidney to help you, even if he is now detached.) What is the difference between this case and the variation in which the violinist's bodily attachment continues after the minute for which it is needed (the superviability case)? I believe that in the latter case the onerous side effect of the causal means that saved the violinist is considered part (even if not a causally useful part) of the process of saving him. In the former case it is only an aftereffect of a completed process.

Nevertheless, the aftereffects of a process (rather than a part of it) often can help justify the permission to kill. For example, suppose that I want to tap someone lightly on the shoulder—an intrinsically small intrusion, permissible in itself for a good cause—but I know that he is a hemophiliac and also that the aftereffect of my tapping will be his bleeding to death. If I attempt to tap him, he or a third party may permissibly kill me if this were necessary to stop me. They could not kill me to stop the tap itself, only to prevent the aftereffects caused by the tap. It is one problem of the doctrine of double effect, as traditionally understood, that it does not rule out intending a small intrusion, even though we foresee great harmful consequences.

But now suppose that someone's life could be saved from a prior threat to it if he lightly tapped the hemophiliac. This person, however, does not know the consequences of his act; he is thus a morally innocent threat. Yet he too could be killed in order to stop the aftereffects of his tap.

What otherwise would be a permissible intrusion is turned into an impermissible one because of its aftereffects. We can kill to prevent such aftereffects of imposition when the imposition is yet to occur or when the imposition is ongoing. In short, we can kill to stop the minor imposition because of the losses that will ensue. But, it has been suggested, we may not kill in order to prevent the aftereffects when the imposition itself by the innocent threat has stopped.[2]

Assume that we are not permitted to kill the violinist after he has been detached in order to stop the aftereffects of the now-completed process that saved his life. Then we certainly should not be permitted to kill him in order to prevent the loss that you would suffer simply as a result of the violinist's survival. Suppose, for example, that during a famine you would have had the last bit of food available if the violinist had not lived to eat it instead. It would be wrong to kill the violinist so that you could get the food.

The point of these cases is that often we may kill someone in order to stop losses suffered for the sake of saving someone else, and such losses go beyond what is strictly causally productive of that benefit to someone else (this is the point of the superviability case). But we may not kill someone who is now independent of us in order to stop the losses we suffer on account of saving that person or because that person is still alive. We may, however, kill him in order to stop an imposition because that will prevent losses we would suffer on account of saving the person. We shall thus divide the cases we have considered into five classes, all involving morally innocent threats:

  1. Killing someone whose life is being saved, in order to end an

imposition on you, an imposition that is a continuing means of saving this person's life.

2. Killing someone whose life has been saved from a threat in order to end an imposition that is a necessary element of the life-saving process.

3. Killing someone whose life is being or has been saved, when this ends an imposition that is a causal means of saving him or is a part of the process that saves him, in order to stop losses that will be the aftereffects of this process.

4. Killing someone now detached whose life has been saved, in order to stop losses to you that are the aftereffects of the process that saved him but that are not considered as part of the process.

5. Killing someone whose life has been saved, in order to stop losses to you that are the side effects of the success of the process that saved his life, that is, the side effects of his merely being alive.

It has been suggested that killing is permissible in the first three situations, but not in the last two.[3]

Ending Attachment to Prevent Efforts on Account Of

One of the reasons that we might give for ending an ongoing attachment to us is that we wish to avoid the efforts that will follow on account of the attachment. One justification for doing this might be as follows: We are still providing support that we have no obligation to provide even if killing someone is necessary to end it (according to the output cutoff argument). But, the reason that we wish to end it is not that we object to the efforts themselves. Rather, we object to making efforts that we are not obliged to make when they will have further bad effects on us; for example, we will die during a famine. Therefore, you would have no right to kill the violinist after he has been detached from you, in order to prevent this same effect, but you may refuse to help create a situation that will be difficult for you, by continuing to make efforts that you need not make. It is because you have the right to kill to end your bodily support that you may end it for reasons other than an objection to the support itself. A second justification for ending the violinist's continued attachment because of what will follow that attachment might be as follows: Even though the imposition itself is something you would have an obligation to permit rather than kill someone in order to end, the imposition plus the losses that will follow if the imposition is not ended can justify ending it. Still, some imposition is necessary if we are to be justified in acting to avoid the aftereffects.

This argument can be used to criticize the view that it is not a right to bodily autonomy but simply a right not to be a parent that underlies the right to have an abortion. For if a fetus that is a person is growing in a lab, you would not have a right to kill it in order to avoid becoming its parent. But if it is growing in your body, you could refuse to provide bodily support that will have an ultimate bad effect on you.

Let us summarize the points we have made in this and the previous chapter pertaining to Condition 4:
It is permissible to kill someone in order to end significant efforts

1. That are causally necessary to provide life and also those efforts that are not causally necessary yet are part of the process necessary to provide life.

2. Even as a means of avoiding the effects on account of such efforts (and perhaps their success).

3. Because of their quality or quantity.

4. Perhaps even when they are not caused by the imposition of the person to be killed (recall the case of the innocent beneficiary).

5. If these efforts or their effects are to some degree beyond the maximum owed as aid to save a life.

6. Securely beyond the minimum that would be necessary in order for third parties to kill someone if the efforts or their effects were deliberately imposed.

7. Thereby accounting for the effort that should be made because of the moral innocence of the person to be killed and also for the fact of his not being harmed relative to preattachment opportunities.

Efforts That May Justifiably Be Avoided, Using the Self- and Assisted-Defense and Output Cutoff Arguments

We have already suggested, using the case in which someone took your $100,000, that it is not always permissible to kill someone in order to prevent a loss that you would not have had to suffer in order to save someone's life. This is true whether or not by being killed, the person would be harmed relative to the prospects he had before having the use of your $100,000. If the loss to you is low, the fact that saving someone's life helps him retain what is legitimately his will make killing in order to terminate this life support indistinguishable from killing him in order to stop an imposition on you that is not beneficial to him. That is, if you cannot use a self- or assisted-defense justification in such a case, you also cannot use the output cutoff argument. When the efforts are very large, an argument based on self- or assisted defense for ending the imposition that does not benefit the threat may be as strong as the output cutoff argument, at least in cases in which you are not responsible for the threat that the other person presents to you. It is with respect to middle-range efforts that the difference between the self- and assisted-defense argument and the output cutoff argument should show up most clearly (as well as in cases in which you are responsible for the person's being a threat). It should sometimes be easier to justify killing someone when the lost life was a benefit rather than when circumstances are such that the person ends up being harmed relative to prospects he had before his attachment to you. This statement holds even when the residual difference between killing someone and letting him die means that we must make greater efforts so as not to kill him than we must make so as not to let him die (see Table 1). Keep in mind, however, that sometimes a self- and assisted-defense justifies killing when the output cutoff argument would not, for example, when we would have to harm the person rela-

Table 1. Third-Party Killing

	Assisted-Defense Argument	Output Cutoff Argument
Low amount of effort		
Forced attachment	No	No
Voluntary attachment	No	No
Voluntary act	No	No
Medium amount of effort		
Forced Attachment	Maybe	Yes
Voluntary attachment	No	Yes
Voluntary act	No	Yes
High amount of effort		
Forced attachment	Yes	Yes
Voluntary attachment	No	Yes
Voluntary act	Maybe, depending on cost to avoid act and probability foreseen of attachment	Yes

tive to preattachment prospects we cannot rely simply on an output cutoff argument.[4] However, as the number of cases in which someone would be harmed relative to preattachment prospects increases, the self- and assisted-defense argument would be weaker. A comparable increase in numbers when the person killed would not be harmed relative to preattachment prospects would seem to have less of an effect on the strength of the output cutoff argument.

Comparing the Output Cutoff Argument with Thomson's Argument

We have already considered one alternative to the output cutoff argument, namely, the self- and assisted-defense argument, as well as these arguments supplemented by the idea of imposing risks. Now we shall see how the output cutoff argument for nonabortion cases compares with Thomson's discussion of nonabortion cases. First we shall summarize her discussion.

Baby in a House

Thomson begins by considering a case in which a baby and a woman are in a house together. The baby is expanding so that it will crush the woman unless she or some third party kills it. Thomson believes that the woman may kill the baby in self-defense, presumably even intentionally seeking its death if only that will stop its expansion. But it is not clear, she adds, that a third party may intervene. I have already argued that it is sometimes permissible for third parties to favor the person being threatened, and although there may well be limits on what can be done to stop innocent threats, third parties may well be able to impose greater losses on these threats than the threats must impose on themselves.

Baby in a Woman's House

Thomson then modifies her first case so that the baby and the woman are in a house owned by the woman (owned-house case). Thomson now believes that a third party is permitted to side with the woman and to kill the baby that threatens her life. What is her reasoning? Is it meant to be *additive?* That is, if the threat to the woman's life is not a sufficient loss to make the third party side with her, does the *addition* of the infringement on her property right make the loss to her great enough to kill the baby? But this does not sound right: It is as if we said that we may not kill someone who threatens another's life unless he is also stealing the silverware. Surely it is the loss of life that is significant, not the infringement on property.

I suggest that Thomson's reasoning in this case must be *multiplicative* rather than additive.[5] What she must think is important is that the threat to the woman's life occurs because of the infringement on her property right, that the baby threatens her life by infringing on her property. Something that is hers, and that should serve her interests, is being used against her. (However, is it worse to be shot by one's own gun than by someone else's?) Again, some people may worry whether if the baby does this as an innocent threat, there should not be severe limits on what a third party may do to stop it.

Coat Case

Thomson introduces a third case in order to defend her claim regarding the owned-house case. In this case, Smith, who would otherwise freeze to death, innocently finds Jones's coat, puts it on, and thereby saves his own life. However, Jones also needs his coat to survive (coat case). In this case, Smith does not impose directly on Jones, but he imposes on something that Jones needs to stay alive. (Should Smith's imposing on Jones's coat be treated any differently from his imposing on Jones's heart?) May a third party take away the coat from Smith and give it to Jones, even though Smith will then die? (This would be a foreseen rather than an intended death and would be the consequence of Smith's not having the coat.) Thomson believes that a third party may take away the coat from Smith.

Besides whether or not she is right, there is the prior question of whether it is appropriate to introduce this case as support for her conclusion in the owned-house case. I believe that Thomson failed to appreciate a crucial difference between the two cases: In the coat case, Smith—who will die if the coat is removed—loses the life-saving benefit of using someone else's property, a benefit relative to the position he would have been in if he had never had use of the property.[6] These factors are not present in the owned-house case: The baby faces no prior threat to its life from which it was rescued by being in the woman's house, and if it is killed, it will be worse off than it would have been had it not been in the woman's house to start with. In addition, there is a direct attack on the baby itself, not just the removal of someone else's property from it.

The argument that can be constructed to permit killing the baby, who will lose the life it would have had quite independently of using the woman's property, is the self- or assisted-defense of someone against a deadly threat. By contrast, the justification for taking the coat away from Smith might be the claim that when two people are in equal need of the use of property that belongs to one of them, a third person may take away this property from the nonowner in order to return it to the owner, even if the nonowner is already using it, if (1) the owner is not obligated to let the nonowner use the property and if the nonowner would have had no right to take it for his own use had he known of the owner's need, (2) if the nonowner will thereby lose only the benefit that he would receive from the use of the property, especially (3) if the nonowner will not then be harmed relative to the opportunities he had before using the coat. (In our case, neither Jones nor his third-party assistant would be harming Smith in regard to his earlier prospects, as they did not originally interfere with Smith's other opportunities. Smith also would not be harmed by anyone else or "by circumstances," as there was no other lifesaving option available. (This contrasts with some cases we have discussed.[7])

Violinist Case

The justification for taking away the coat from Smith may be compared with the justification for killing the violinist. In the violinist case, unlike the coat case, your life will not be at stake if someone uses your body. Indeed, you stand to lose much less—an imposition on your body but not permanent damage—if the violinist uses your body than he will lose if you do not let him use it. Nevertheless, Thomson's claim is that it is permissible to kill the violinist if this is required in order to remove him.

Even if Thomson's conclusion is correct, are her arguments in defense of it correct? She states that the violinist's right to life does not include the right to use your body merely because he needs it to survive. So it is permissible to allow the violinist to die, and it is wrong to force you to begin letting him use your body, even if all that were at stake for you was nine months' use of your body. Furthermore, she observes, his right to life is not a simple right not to be killed; it is, rather, a right not to be killed unjustly (some killings are not unjust). Why, then, is this killing not unjust? Thomson argues that it is not unjust because if it were not permissible to kill the violinist, he would have the right to use your body. But it has been agreed, she says, that he does not have a right to use your body, even to save his life.

We could understand this argument as providing a general way of deciding what efforts or losses we may kill in order to avoid: Whatever efforts or losses we need not suffer in order to save someone's life are efforts or losses we may avoid by killing innocents who are threats to us. Third parties may also defend us against enduring these losses.

Now consider the following objection to this argument: Someone may agree with Thomson that the violinist does not have a right to use your body to save his life but claim that he does have a right to use your body rather than be killed in order to be removed. Thus there is no conflict between not having to do something to save a life and having to do that same thing rather than kill someone.[8] Thomson responds to this conclusion by trying to defend the view that killing someone is not necessarily worse than letting someone die.[9] She does this by considering cases in which killing someone seems not to be morally worse than letting a person die. So if certain losses need not be suffered in order to save a life, she believes, at least sometimes they need not be suffered in order to avoid killing someone.

But this conclusion is problematic. The general claim that killing someone is not morally worse than letting a person die may not be true, even if killing someone in a particular case were no worse than letting someone die in a comparable case.[10] Therefore the general claim that we need not make greater efforts to avoid killing someone than we need make to avoid letting that person die may not be true. If so, we need more than a few cases where a killing is no worse than letting someone die to show that in regard to the violinist, not having to save his life by sharing your body with him proves that you do not have to share your body with him in order to avoid killing him. Further, the general claim that efforts that we need not make to save someone's life are also efforts that we need not make to avoid killing someone does not distinguish between our making efforts instead of threatening someone with death before he threatens us in any way, and our making efforts instead of killing someone who threatens us first. (The latter is what happens in the violinist case.)

In addition, I have already argued that those cases in which we kill someone in order to stop aiding him share a definitional property with letting someone die, and this helps account for these cases' being almost as permissible as letting someone die is. But then Thomson's argument should be supplemented by something like Condition 3, which emphasizes the definitional property of letting someone die: that someone loses life that would be the result of being aided.

If Thomson's argument is not supplemented in this way, her reason for permitting the violinist to be killed will not differentiate between killing him when he uses your body and receives life support, and killing him when he uses your body but does not receive life support. In the latter case we might want to kill the violinist in order to stop making efforts that we need not make in order to save his life, even though our efforts are not now saving his life. Yet it may be that (as I have argued) for efforts of a certain magnitude, it is more difficult to justify causing someone to lose his life that he would have had independently of those efforts than to cause him to lose what he has because of those efforts and would not have had without them.

Notes

1. Here the direct effect of the imposition is considered to be the effect of the imposition itself, independent of its success. That is, it is independent of whether the violinist lives or dies. In other variations, one might assume that it is the effect of the imposition plus the achieved aim (the violinist's surviving) that causes further problems for you.

2. It was a conflicting view, that we could harm an innocent to stop aftereffects, that I defended in "The Insanity Defense."

3. David Wasserman helped separate my cases into classes.

4. As I was reminded by Seana Shiffrin.

5. Indeed, I believe that this reasoning anticipates Thomson's analyses of the trolley problem, in "The Trolley Problem," *Yale Law Journal* 94(1985):1395–1415.

6. However, in connection with the second difference, suppose that someone else would have offered a coat had Smith not already had Jones's on. I do not believe that the fact that if we take away Jones's coat from Smith, Smith would then be worse off than he would have been if he had never had Jones's coat affects whether we may take it away. The reason is that in this case, it is not Jones who offered or is otherwise causally responsible for the use of his coat, and so Jones is not responsible for interfering with other offers that Smith might

have had. Furthermore, we are not even attacking what is Smith's (either his body or his property) but are taking away Jones's coat from him.

7. Smith has indeed actively taken the coat, but I am ignoring the fact that he is not a nonactive morally innocent threat.

8. Baruch Brody makes such a counterargument in "Thomson on Abortion," *Philosophy and Public Affairs,* 1(1972):335–40.

9. In Judith Thomson's "Rights and Deaths."

10. A comparable case of letting someone die is one in which all elements in the case of killing someone are present, except killing him. On this general issue, see my "Killing and Letting Die: Methodology and Substance," *Pacific Philosophical Quarterly* (Winter 1983):297–312.

4

May We Kill
in Abortion Cases?

Assuming that the fetus is a person (infant) and accepting the output cutoff argument with its five conditions for the violinist cases, we shall now consider an analogous argument for the permissibility of abortion. We will consider objections to it in Chapter 5.

A Basic Abortion Argument

1a. *Need alone does not confer a right to have aid begin, nor a duty to give it.*

The efforts required in even a normal pregnancy, labor, and delivery are strenuous and risky, not merely inconvenient, and so they extend beyond what a woman is obligated to provide merely because it will save a fetus's life. To give meaning to this observation, imagine a case in which a fetus is growing in a lab but will die unless it is transferred to a woman's body. Is she morally obligated to have it transferred, solely because of its need, even if it is a stranger to her?

We must be convinced that Condition 1a is true even if we consider the fetus to be an infant, if there are morally significant reasons why we are more protective of infants than of adults.

1b. *Need alone does not confer a right to have continuing support, nor a duty to give it.*

If it is morally permissible to let the fetus die, then its need for survival alone cannot morally require continuing support that has already begun as a result of a pregnancy started in a woman's body.

2. *There is no special obligation to aid.*

In the case of pregnancy, unlike the violinist case, we must deal with this condition before we can decide whether we may even allow a fetus in a lab to die. The reason is that the woman may have created the fetus and so had a part in its needing her body, whereas you did not create the violinist's original need for your body. Therefore, we should be concerned with the following conditions:

2a. *There is no special obligation to begin support.*

This includes (a) no obligation to create a fetus, (b) no responsibility in virtue of a woman's actions to begin support if the fetus is growing in a lab, and (c) no responsibility to begin support because of the fetus's genetic connection to the woman, a factor also absent in the violinist case.

2b. *There is no special obligation to continue support when a pregnancy (assumed to begin in the woman's body) has begun.*

This means no obligation in virtue of a duty to have created the fetus, or because of the woman's actions or the genetic connection. It might be claimed that intentionally and voluntarily beginning a fetus—let alone unintentionally becoming pregnant as a result of a voluntary act—does not by itself commit a woman to begin or continue her support of the fetus. We may sometimes begin projects, intending to complete them, but stop if they become too strenuous, for example, if the person we support is not harmed relative to preattachment prospects as a result of our starting and stopping than if we had never started. If this is true, then if the fetus fell out, the woman would not be obligated to reattach it, even though it needed her body to survive. Support requires her continued efforts, so she might refuse to give further installments. It is perhaps relevant here to point out that the fetus is not conscious and that beginning existence and support arouses no expectations in it.

Given that need or types of actions (or other grounds for special obligations), either alone or together, do not confer a right to be in a woman's body, one possible ground for a woman's obligation to keep the fetus in her body is that its removal would harm it relative to the opportunities it had before its attachment to the woman's body. This possibility might also be a ground for not allowing a lab fetus to die and for obligating a woman to begin supporting it. Another possible ground for a fetus's right to remain in a woman's body is the impermissibility of killing and harming it relative to the life it would have if it remained attached.

But it could be counterargued when pregnancy begins in the body:

3. *By being killed and harmed in order to end a pregnancy, the fetus loses only the life that is provided by the woman's support, support which is not required by its need and any special obligation; it is not harmed relative to prospects it had before its attachment to the woman's body (and it is not worse off than it would have been if it had never been in the woman's body); and killing the fetus does not cause it to lose anything that the woman is causally responsible for its having that it would retain independently of her.*

That is, the fetus had no opportunities before being attached to the woman's body (i.e., before its conception) of which it would be deprived, and it would have had no opportunities other than being attached to the woman's body. It is also no worse off being dead because it was killed than if it had never existed. It may lose the life (considered as an entity) that the woman is (in certain types of cases) morally responsible for having given to it. But this is not a life that the fetus could retain independently of the woman or could have received without this leading to its continued residence in the woman's body.

We may summarize this as follows: We need not deny that we harm the fetus in killing it relative to the condition it would have been in if the woman continued support. But it may not be wrong to harm it in this way, because we may be obliged only not to harm it relative to the condition it would have been in if it had not been attached. If the woman has no duty to aid it because of its need or other grounds of special obligation, any condition it is in as a result of her support is not something it has a claim to keep, at least as long as it continues to need her support to maintain it. Therefore, its condition when attached cannot be the baseline relative to which we must not harm it.

Things might be different if it did retain what it had gotten from the woman's support independently of her, even if not independently of the aid of others. (This is the point of the last clause of (3).) Analogously, suppose we find someone who is dying. We give him a medicine, and he is much improved and no longer needs our help. We may not kill him simply because he will not be harmed relative to the condition he would have been in if he had never gotten aid.

The fact that if left to die (versus being killed), the fetus begun in the lab will not be harmed in regard to precreation opportunities is sufficient, in combination with Conditions 1a and 2a, to also conclude that we may let the fetus die (so the argument claims).

4. *Efforts involved in supporting the fetus and also removing it are significant enough that in conjunction with the truth of the other conditions, they could justify killing the fetus in order to stop them.*

5. *Killing the fetus is the only way to end its support that is not excessively costly to the woman, given the aim of not killing a person and the fulfillment of the other conditions.*

If procedures can be used that are not excessively costly, given the aim of not killing a person, and the fetus could retain its life independently of the woman, then these procedures should be used. We must determine how to evaluate the costs of such procedures.

The killing justified here includes not only abortions in which the fetus's death is foreseen but also abortions in which its death is intended as a means of removing it. (This is different from feticide, in which we would intend the death of the fetus even though this is not necessary for removal.) It sometimes is permissible to intend that someone lose the benefit (continued life) of certain forms of support in order to stop that support. Put another way, suppose that the fetus has no right to support and the woman has no duty to support it simply so that it can obtain or retain its life, and that beginning to support a needy person does obligate continuing. Then, the argument claims, the fetus cannot obtain the right to remain in the woman's body, and she cannot be obligated not to kill it, simply because ending its support would require that we take away the life that it has only because it received the support. This holds even if we think of support as helping the fetus retain the life (considered as an entity) that belongs to it. It is sometimes wrong for us to retain an entity that belongs to us if we retain it by improper means.

The basic strategy of this argument, which I shall call the *cutoff abortion argument,* is similar to the strategy of the output cutoff argument in the violinist cases. Very generally, it has two components: to show that it is permissible to let the fetus die and, if letting it die is permissible, then to show that sometimes killing it is permissible as well.

We have not relied on Condition 6 in this argument. It says you have no special obligation not to kill someone in accord with Conditions 1 to 5, because there is sufficient reason to be in the situation where you would kill the person. If we thought it beneficial to add Condition 6, we would have to consider the cost of avoiding a voluntary act that was foreseen to have the possibility of producing a fetus, and be sure it was not morally necessary to pay the cost in order to avoid being in a situation where we would kill the fetus in accord with Conditions 1 to 5. This cost could be sexual abstinence or use of birth control. We would also have to consider the possible gain from a voluntary pregnancy or the cost of not deliberately beginning a pregnancy, and be sure it was not morally necessary to pay these costs in order to avoid being in a situation where one would kill in accord with Conditions 1 to 5. If Conditions 1 to 5 hold, and have the dominant role in justifying abortion, then, I believe, the costs that are morally necessary to avoid these voluntary acts resulting in a new fetus would not be great.

Since Condition 6 may not be necessary if 1 to 5 are correct, and because we will eventually criticize the cutoff abortion argument and develop a new argument making use of the costs of avoiding acts leading to pregnancy, I shall not mention Condition 6 again.

Like the argument in the violinist case that concludes that killing the violinist is permissible even if after his original attachment, *you* become dependent on *him,* the cutoff abortion argument would, if it were correct, show that abortion is permissible even if the fetus grows around the woman, not in her, and she becomes dependent on it after it is conceived.[1] The fetus's growing around her is an imposition on her bodily integrity, too. Therefore the fact that the fetus is inside the woman's body is not crucial.

The abortion procedures that such an argument tries to justify fall into the four categories discussed in the violinist case: death as a consequence of loss of support, death in the process of removal, death as a result of an intentional attack, and intended death as a means of removal. This is an argument for the permissibility of abortion not only in cases in which the woman will die or suffer a severe impairment of health, or in which she faces economic hardship or responsibilities to other family members, or is very young. It also aims to justify abortion in cases in which a woman does not want to continue a normal pregnancy simply because of the effort it requires and the loss of autonomy that the bodily imposition of pregnancy involves (including labor). It is nonconsequentialist in that it does not require that her life be more valuable because of her talents and work than the life that the person she bears might eventually be, nor that she stand to lose more than the fetus will.

We have pointed to the following differences between the violinist and abortion cases: (1) fetus considered as an infant; (2) genetic connection; (3) the possibility that one's acts are responsible for causing the fetus's need to be in one's body, but not that of the violinist's; (4) the fact that letting the fetus die requires more conditions (1, 2, and 3) than it takes to justify letting the violinist die. There are other differences which we shall discuss below.

Let us now consider the steps in the argument in more detail, considering three different kinds of cases.

Rape

It is natural to think that rape is analogous to the case of forced attachment of the violinist. In the violinist case, however, a person intends to put someone in your body. In rape, usually no one intends to force a fetus on the woman. Rather, someone intends to force himself on her, and a natural consequence of this act may be a fetus within her. (So a more closely analogous violinist case would involve someone forcing himself on you with the violinist attached as a side effect.) I do not believe this difference should make a difference in the argument for the moral permissibility of killing the fetus.

In the case of rape, the following conditions apply:

1a. A fetus that you are not responsible for creating needs to begin to use your body in the manner of pregnancy for nine months. You need not allow it to do this.

1b. A fetus that you are not responsible for creating is in your body. The fact that it needs your body to survive does not, alone, justify your having to continue aiding it. For example, if the fetus drops out, you need not return it to your body.

2a. Assume that someone deliberately intrudes on your body and as a side effect acquires your genetic material. The material happens to fall into a test tube and develops into a fetus growing in a laboratory. He (this someone) then calls you up and tells you that the fetus will die unless you put it in your body for nine months, all the while enduring the burdens, changes, and risks of pregnancy and labor. In this case you have no obligation to support this fetus that someone else created. You are not causally responsible for creating this fetus or for its needing your aid. In addition, I believe, its genetic connection to you would not make it impermissible for you to let the fetus die. Even a genetically related fetus does not have an inherent right to your bodily support simply because it needs it, nor do you have a duty to provide it.

2b. In the case of rape, where a forced sex act begins the fetus in your

body, you have made no commitment to continue support already begun, and no special obligations exist (e.g., because of genetic connection) which require you to continue your support of the fetus.

Assume that need or other factors (genetic connection, or the actions
and duties to create that are absent in this case) alone or together do not
require you to continue your support. You still might have a duty to let
the fetus use your body because otherwise you would have to kill and
harm it in order to remove it, or you might have a duty to continue your
support because not doing so would harm the fetus relative to prospects
it had before becoming attached to your womb. In answer to these
possibilities, we note the following, when pregnancy begins in the body:

3. By being killed and harmed, the fetus loses only what it gains from
your support (its life, arguably a benefit); it is not harmed relative to
opportunities it had before its attachment to you; and it loses nothing you
are causally responsible for its having that it could retain independently
of you.

Comments on Condition 3

Rape involves somewhat different issues in reference to Condition 3
than the violinist case does. Unlike the violinist, the fetus did not exist in
need of being attached to you before being in your body, as it did not
exist at all. Does this fact mean that the fetus will be worse off if it is
killed than if it had never been in your body or will be harmed relative to
the opportunities it had before being attached to your body? A suggested
claim, adequate or not, is that it is no worse to live a short time and then
be permissibly and painlessly killed than never to have lived at all.[2] One
is not harmed by living such a life rather than never living at all. One
reason is that the principal misfortune of death is not receiving any more
of the goods of life, but not receiving more goods is not worse than not
receiving any in the first place. One is not harmed by receiving something rather than nothing. Further, if the killing were permissible no
injustice would enter into the life.

Let us expand on the first claim, defending it as best we can without,
however, committing ourself to its truth. Death is bad for a person
primarily because it deprives him of more life.[3] If this is true, then why
should it be better for him, from the point of view of his best interests, to
have had no life at all than to have had a short life? It is true that we are
susceptible to the harm of being deprived of more life only because we

do have some life. Yet, the suggestion is, avoiding this harm of deprivation does not seem to be a reason to avoid creating some life. That is, in this case one is not harmed overall by coming to exist and then having the harm of being deprived of life happen. If death is bad for a person primarily because it prevents more goods of life, it may make sense to create a greater loss, such as the loss of eternal life, in order to produce a small amount of good, such as sixty years of life, or even two years. In short, death, including its deprivation of more life, may be the sort of bad thing that it makes no sense to avoid for the sake of the person (the fetus) created, by not creating it at all.

There are obvious problems with the claim that someone is or is not worse off than if he never had existed. How can he be no worse off than he would have been if he had not existed, if he then would not have been? Asking whether he will be no worse off if he dies (when he will not be) than if he were never created seems to compound the problem. But many of these same problems arise in discussing whether someone will be worse off if he dies (i.e., goes out of existence) than if he goes on living. Yet in some sense we can understand this claim. That is, we can compare the type of life a person would have if he continued living (good or bad) with no life at all (assuming that death is nonexistence), and then we can try to decide whether this is a plus or a minus. In this sense we can also understand that a fetus who is living a life of uninterrupted pain will be worse off than if it never existed.

Likewise, to say the fetus is harmed or not harmed in regard to prospects it had before being created seems odd, as it had no prospects before its creation, given that it did not exist. But, I believe nonetheless that we can understand that if the fetus is living a life of uninterrupted pain, it will be harmed by having been created, relative to the prospect before its creation of never being created.

Further Evidence: Miscarriages

We might further buttress the claim that the fetus is not harmed relative to the prospect of never being created and is no worse for living a short time and then dying than never having lived at all, by considering the following: (1) a woman who deliberately becomes pregnant, even though she knows that she has a very high risk of miscarriage; (2) a woman who knows that she will lose her first conceived child but becomes pregnant anyway because she is told that this is the only way to have a child eventually; (3) a woman who knows that her pregnancy will end in a miscarriage but would have to make a significant effort to avoid getting pregnant (taking a dangerous birth-control drug or avoiding heterosexual intercourse altogether). Must these women avoid getting pregnant only for the sake of preventing a fetus that will die?

If some life and an early death were worse for the fetus than never living at all, if creating that short life were comparable to making an existing innocent bystander worse off by exposing him to a cause of death that he otherwise would not have faced, then these women should be required to do a great deal to avoid becoming pregnant. This is true even though they would not kill the fetuses but rather put them into a situation where nature will kill them. However, the women who know that they will lose their fetuses are encouraged to become pregnant if they want a child, or at least are not discouraged for the fetus's sake. But if the fetus is a person, if it is worse off for living and dying, if it is harmed by living a short while and then dying, perhaps such women should not become pregnant.[4]

But suppose that living a short while and then dying a natural death is not worse for the fetus than never living at all and does not harm it relative to precreation prospects. Then the permissibility of producing this short life by creating and later killing it cannot be disputed on the ground that death harms the fetus relative to its options before being in the woman's womb. (We are not here arguing that simply because putting a fetus in the way of foreseen death is permitted, killing it is too.)

Assume that it is no worse for the fetus to live for only a short time than never to have lived at all, that it is not harmed relative to preattachment prospects (i.e., nonexistence). It may still be true that a world in which a creature that had the chance to live a long life never fulfills its potential is a worse world than one in which such a creature never lived. The first world contains a waste; the second does not. If this is so, the next question is how much effort should someone make in order not to produce such a worse state of the world (even if it is still not worse relative to pre-attachment prospects—the appropriate baseline—for the fetus)? The answer may be that we are not obligated to make a large sacrifice to prevent waste that is not worse for anyone. Perhaps we should also balance the waste of destruction of the fetus against the possible waste of opportunities in the life of the person who might have to carry it. In any case, focusing on waste seems not to be quite the right reason for opposing abortion. Suppose the cells on your hand, which you now destroy by scratching, could have been cloned and turned into many persons. Would we bemoan the waste? It is, rather, the fear of interfering with (or perhaps not assisting) a life form that on its own is developing that worries many about abortion.

Does the Fetus Lose a Benefit?

The fetus loses its life, the result of its support, but is the life it loses a benefit? We can agree that once it is alive, it is a benefit to it to continue to live. But the benefit that results from support need not be contemporaneous with residence in the womb. Rather, it may be the life that the developed person would have later if given the bodily support now. (On the other hand, some theories hold that the time spent in the womb is the best time of our lives and that we are constantly trying to return there.) All this, however, does not commit us to the view that coming to life from nonexistence is a benefit to the person so conceived. For the cutoff abortion argument we do not need to argue for this further view. (We will discuss it somewhat later.)

If these points were correct, we could conclude that Condition 3 is true. That is, the fetus loses the output of its attachment but is not harmed relative to its prospects before its attachment. If we assume, for the moment, that it continues to require support, we also do not take from it anything that the woman has caused it to have and that it could retain independently of its attachment to her. (We will consider later the case in which the fetus can retain its life independently of such an attachment).

Let us continue with the conditions applying in the case of rape:

4. We kill to stop efforts significant enough to merit killing, given the other conditions in the argument.

Here, I shall assume that the efforts in question are bodily support and the changes and risks of pregnancy and labor. If the output cutoff argument is correct in the violinist case, these efforts are significant enough to kill in order to avoid making them. Perhaps the cutoff abortion argument should be phrased so that it permits abortion only at certain times during pregnancy, for a very late abortion might be undertaken to avoid only a few days' efforts, and a few days' residence in someone's body may be something that it would be morally wrong not to give. But what is a small effort in itself may be more burdensome if it follows large efforts already made. In addition, there is the effort and risk of labor.

5. There are no procedures for removing a fetus to another life-sustaining environment that cost a woman no more than she would have to pay in order to avoid having the fetus killed. For the time being let us assume that this is true.

Comments on Condition 5

Note that use of procedures that do not kill a fetus is reasonable only if the fetus could retain its life outside the womb independently of the woman's significant efforts. So condition 5 and the last clause of 3 are related. The two conditions are also related in that, if the fetus needs a woman's excessive efforts to be removed, it thereby cannot retain its life independently of her, even if it can live without her once it has been removed.

Even if Condition 5 is true, it presents complications. Suppose that the procedure for removal that kills the fetus late in pregnancy is itself slightly more costly to the woman than is a procedure that does not kill the fetus who will then survive. Each procedure considered in itself, however, is excessive in regard to the aim of not killing the fetus. Given that if we kill the fetus, we will be using the more costly procedure, is there an obligation to use the less costly procedure even if, considered by itself, it is excessive in regard to not killing the fetus? It may seem that we should use the less costly procedure. Yet it is possible that if the efforts required are beyond the call of duty (supererogatory), one may always retain the option of choosing what to do. For one may be willing to make a supererogatory sacrifice for one goal but not for another. (We shall return later to the problem of alternative procedures.) Figure 3 represents this case of rape.

Figure 3.

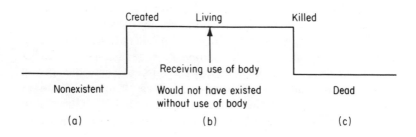

This argument has sidestepped a defense based simply on self- and assisted-defense. But we should keep in mind that rape is taken to be analogous to forced use of your body in the violinist case. We argued in the violinist case that it would sometimes be permissible for third parties to kill the violinist even if he were thereby made worse off than if he had never been attached to your body in the first place. This same should be true in rape cases. It should be even more clearly permissible for the woman to let die a lab fetus, created from her stolen genetic material, even if it would be worse off than if it had never existed.

Voluntary Pregnancy[5]

In the case of voluntary pregnancy, we assume that the pregnant woman recognized the need for her continued support. We shall review the conditions of the abortion argument:

1a. Again we imagine a fetus in a lab who needs to be attached to your body in the manner of pregnancy (including labor) in order to maintain its life. Its need alone, however, does not obligate you to begin supporting it. (Abstract from voluntary creation here.)

1b. Likewise, need alone does not obligate you to continue supporting the fetus begun in your body.

Now imagine that you voluntarily began the fetus in a lab, knowing that it would need to be transferred to your body or else would die. Are you permitted to let it die? When you volunteered to attach the dying violinist to your body, you were not responsible for his needing to be attached. You did not give him his mortal illness. But if you voluntarily create a fetus, you are, in a sense, responsible for its need to be in your body. Of course, you have not specifically given it that need, that is, instead of making it a fetus that can continue to grow independently. We assume that the latter is not an option. (Cases in which this is an option will be dealt with later.) But you did voluntarily create the fetus knowing it would have such a need, and intending its existence.

2a. The simplest ground suggesting that your voluntary act alone or combined with its need does not commit you to start support, and that you are permitted to let the fetus die, is the claim that the fetus will still be no worse off than if it had not been created at all and will not have been harmed relative to the prospects of nonexistence.

Some philosophers have erred in their attempt to distinguish between voluntary and involuntary pregnancies. That is, they have distinguished between cases in which someone is called upon to save an innocent person that he did push into the water and those in which someone is called upon to save a person that he did not push into the water. In the former case the agent voluntarily caused the need of the person that he must aid, and it is this case that, some claim, is analogous to voluntary pregnancy. So, the philosophers conclude, abortion cannot always be justified by an argument based on not having an obligation to aid. But if someone pushes an innocent person into the water, that person will presumably be harmed—if he is not saved—relative to his prospects if he had not been pushed in at all. This obligates the culprit to save this person. If the fetus that is deliberately created is not harmed by living with the need for support and dying without having that need met— relative to never living, then this case is not analogous.

2b. Voluntarily beginning support by conceiving a fetus in one's body does not, by itself, constitute a commitment to continue supporting the fetus. One could try to create a new life in this way, and if it fell out not have to put it back—the claim might be—if the fetus would not be harmed relative to the prospects of nonexistence, and the support was burdensome.

If need and voluntary acts, or other special factors either separately or together, do not commit you to supporting the fetus, then the fact that it would be killed and harmed might give the fetus a right to remain in your body. Alternatively, if not continuing support of it or killing it made the fetus worse off than it would have been had it never been attached to you or harmed it relative to its prospects before its attachment, this also might constitute a ground for a right for it to remain or a duty for you to aid. However:

3. By being killed in order to end your support, the fetus loses only the result of your support, is not harmed relative to preattachment prospects, and does not lose anything you are causally responsible for its having that it could retain independently of you.

Comments on Condition 3

Why has Condition 3 been satisfied? The following might be argued: In this case of voluntary pregnancy, you are responsible for the original donation of life and the life now belongs to the fetus. But, suppose that the fetus causally requires your continued support in order to remain alive. By killing it, therefore, you are taking away no more than the benefit—the continued retention of its life—of your bodily support. Therefore, if it is killed—a harm to it because it loses the future goods of its life—it still is not harmed relative to the condition it would have been in without your continuing bodily support. It is no worse off than it would have been (dead) without your continued bodily support which has not yet been shown to be required; it would have no better prospects than death if it were independent of the support of which killing it deprives it. In other words, although you are causally responsible for having given life to the fetus, you are not yet causally responsible for allowing it to continue that life and are indeed refusing to provide the support necessary for that. Because without your support the fetus cannot retain the life you gave to it and so would be dead, it loses nothing you are responsible for causing it to have that it could retain independently of you (see Figure 4). According to this view, how the fetus would have been without your continuing support is the appropriate baseline for comparison with its fate if it were killed. (As with the case in which the violinist was voluntarily attached, we may find, as a result of later discussion, reason to revise this analysis of the appropriate baseline.)

4. We kill the fetus to stop efforts significant enough to make killing it permissible, given the other conditions of the argument (e.g., Condition 3).

5. There are no other ways to remove the fetus to another life-sustaining environment that would not require more from you than you are required to give instead of having the fetus killed.

As with our discussion of the voluntary attachment of the violinist,

Figure 4.

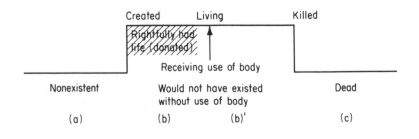

we have not focused on the motives of those who voluntarily begin pregnancies to see whether this would affect the argument or on the benefits to be gotten from the pregnancy or the costs needed to avoid it.

Voluntary Act with a Foreseen but Unintended Pregnancy

In the case of voluntary intercourse engaged in though knowing—but not intending—that it might lead to pregnancy, the conditions are as follows:[6]

1a. Its need alone does not give a duty to aid a fetus incubating in a lab.

1b. Need alone does not give a duty to continue support resulting from a pregnancy begun in your body.

2a. There is no special obligation to begin supporting a fetus arising simply from the fact that a voluntary act created it, for, it is claimed, if the fetus were no worse off for living and dying than if it had never lived, and not harmed relative to preattachment prospects, its existence as a result of a voluntary act would not be the deciding point.

2b. There is no special obligation to continue supporting a fetus begun in your body arising from the voluntary act that caused the pregnancy, it is claimed, because if the fetus were no worse for living and dying than if it had never lived, and not harmed relative to preattachment prospects, it would be permissible not to return it to your body if it fell out.

There is even less reason in this case to think you have committed yourself to allowing the continued use of your body than there is in the case of a voluntary pregnancy. However, the aim of creating a child present in voluntary pregnancy is absent. If this aim is motivated by the desire to produce a nice new life, one type of good motive for the sexual conduct is absent. However, other good motives for sexual relations may be present instead and/or the cost of avoiding such relations may be high. In any case, the motive for creating the fetus is not relevant to the abortion argument being presented here, nor are we now focusing on the costs necessary to avoid a sex act.

3. By being killed, the fetus loses only the output of support, is not harmed relative to its preattachment prospects, and loses nothing that you are causally responsible for its having that it could retain independently of you. This argument here is the same as for Condition 3 for voluntary pregnancy, assuming a case in which the fetus needs to remain

in your womb and also that you are morally responsible for creating the fetus.

4. The fetus is killed in order to end efforts that are significant enough to make killing it permissible, given the other conditions.

5. There are no alternative ways of ending the pregnancy that do not kill the fetus and do not require more of you than you would be required to do to avoid having the fetus killed.[7]

Superviability

Suppose that at a certain point the fetus were what I shall call *superviable*. This is the (unrealistic) state of not needing and also not deriving any sustenance from residence in the woman's body but not being removable from the woman. We might then use the reasoning in the comparable violinist case in which a cure is effected in the first minute of attachment. The conclusion there was that even in voluntary attachments, the baseline with which we should compare the person's fate if he is killed is the state in which the person would have been if he had not been attached at one time. This represents an alternative position from that reflected in Figure 4, that in voluntary attachments we must compare the prospect that results from killing the attached person with the prospect that he would have had if his attachment had automatically ended after the period of voluntarily donated support. In the case of superviability, the fetus would have lived if its attachment had automatically ended. According to this alternative position, if the fetus is still inside the woman and cannot be removed, but her body no longer enables its survival, we can still conceive of the fetus's residence as part of the process that was necessary to give it life.

Therefore, we are taking away the fetus's benefit (life) resulting from its residence as a whole in order to end its continued residence. This continued residence has not been donated and, therefore, neither has what it is necessary for (the fetus's life). One reason that a woman might be obligated to grant continued residence to the fetus is that by killing it she would be taking away something that she was responsible for its having and that it could retain independently of her. But if the entire residence is what gives it life, then she will not be taking away anything it has already been given and that it could retain independently of her. In addition, if we know that Condition 5 is true, then we know that the entire period of residence is morally necessary for the fetus to survive, since it could not retain life without her at a cost that is not excessive to her.

So, if the woman is not obligated to provide the use of her body— except possibly on the ground that she may not kill the fetus in order to terminate this use—she may in fact kill it to end this use. In a voluntary pregnancy, it is permissible to kill the fetus, even though it would then lose something voluntarily given to it that it could have retained without further use of the woman's body had it been physically possible to be free of her at reasonable cost.

Viability

The point made by using superviability bears on the relevance of ordinary viability to the permissibility of abortion. This is the time in a pregnancy when the fetus can live outside the womb (albeit with mechanical support), though in fact it is still in the womb and deriving sustenance from the woman. If we assume that it can live outside if removed, but removal before a nine-month attachment is not in fact physically possible, then killing the fetus ends a process that as a whole is necessary for giving life to it, and the fetus loses what, in fact, it cannot have without the woman. If removal is possible, but at a cost beyond what the woman would have to make in order to avoid killing the fetus, it will be no worse off by being killed than it has any right to be, given that it has no right to the means necessary to get it outside her and no right to all the body support it needs otherwise. That is, the fetus will not retain its life independently of her if it needs her help to be free of her, and if these efforts are excessive, it has no right to them. We must compare how the fetus would be if it were not getting what it needs from the woman (rather than how it would be if miraculously independent of the woman) with its fate if killed. If exit from her body is possible only at excessive cost to her, one thing it needs is that excessive cost. How would it be if it did not receive that excessive cost of exit? It would be alive and in her body. But then it would need the period in her body that she has not donated and that extends beyond the point of viability. Therefore, the baseline we must use when considering whether we may kill is how it would be without either of the things it needs from her, that is, the cost of exit or the entire period of residence in her body for nine months. It would be nonexistent.

This leaves the case in which it is not too costly to the woman to transfer the fetus to an external womb. Briefly, in this case, a woman who prevented a fetus's being removed and then had it killed to remove it would make the fetus worse off than it had a right to be. She would have harmed it relative to prospects to which it had a right. Abortion should not then be permissible. Therefore, one reason that viability may be morally significant is that it is the point at which it is possible for a woman to make the fetus worse off than it would be in an alternative state in which it had a right to be. Notice that in this last case the fetus still could not retain its life independently of her efforts, but either it has a right to those efforts or she has a duty to give them.

Alternative Arguments: Equality, Self- and Assisted-Defense, and the Permissibility of Imposing Risks

No version of this cutoff abortion argument is based solely on one's right to one's own body or on the right to engage in private, protected acts, such as sex, or solely on the inequalities between the sexes that would result if females were required, against their wishes, to bear persons in their bodies. For suppose that everyone knew that whenever a woman had sex, her body—but not a man's—had a peculiar magnetic effect: It drew an innocent healthy bystander off the street and into her body, where he would have to stay for nine months or otherwise be killed in order to be removed. Both the output cutoff argument and the cutoff abortion argument are consistent with the impermissibility of killing the bystander in this case. If he is killed, he will be made much worse off than he would have been if the woman's actions had not caused him to be attached to her.

Other arguments may support the permissibility of killing such an attached bystander in order to remove him, even when the attachment was a result of committing a voluntary act with foresight to its possible effect. Comparable arguments can be used to justify killing a fetus if it would be worse off living and dying than never living at all. For example, the self- and assisted-defense argument works best when attachment is not the result of a voluntary act by the woman. But supplemented by the consideration of the cost of not acting, the probability of harm, and the permissibility of imposing risk, the argument may be used when the act of attaching someone is voluntary but the attachment is unintended. For example, we voluntarily drive a car knowing the risks of killing someone. Suppose that we nonnegligently hit someone while on a voluntary drive. He will die unless we attach him to our body for nine months. Suppose that we are not required to attach him, given that we drove non-negligently, the costs of not driving are significant, and the probability of hitting someone is not too high.

Based on these conditions, we can construct an argument for the permissibility of killing the car accident victim in order to detach him if it were a consequence of the crash that he became attached to our body and would otherwise remain there receiving life support for nine months. Although he would be worse off than if he were never attached to us, did not stand to gain from attachment, and we were voluntarily driving our car, we need not use our body merely to save his life. Further, his imposition on us would be sufficiently serious to justify a third party's killing him, given the other conditions. If nothing we have done obligates us to let him use our body as aid, why should what we have done significantly raise the cost we need to pay in order to avoid having him killed from what it would be if this person's attachment were independent of our act?

If this argument can be applied to driving, cannot it apply to killing the innocent bystander or the fetus placed in the woman's womb as the consequence of a voluntary sex act, even if he would then be worse off than if never attached? It should apply if sex is an intrinsically important activity and/or one whose avoidance is costly and is nonnegligently engaged in. This may mean, for example, using reasonable—but not every possible form of—birth control. (Notice also that the fetus, unlike the pedestrian or bystander, may stand to gain from attachment. We shall consider this further in Chapter 5.)

This argument still is problematic when applied to abortion in cases of voluntary pregnancy, however. In regard to such an abortion, if the fetus were harmed relative to its prior prospects and had not stood to gain anything from attachment, the case would be comparable to one in which a driver deliberately endangers a pedestrian and then refuses support to save him. Furthermore, if the number of merely foreseen attachments becomes large, we may rather curtail the acts leading to them than permit detachment, when there is the possibility of harm relative to preattachment prospects.

Another Alternative: The Equality Argument

As noted, another argument for abortion is based on grounds of equality.[8] If applied to our other hypothetical cases, a simple concern for equality would imply that a woman should be allowed to have an innocent bystander killed if she unintentionally attracts him to her body as a consequence of having voluntary sex. That is, those whose principal concern is equality of the sexes may wish to allow women the same freedom of action as men have—even though men cannot attract others to their bodies in the same way—even if these freedoms lead to different morally relevant consequences because of the biological differences between the sexes. Such people may argue that preserving equality (with respect to freedom of action and social position) between the sexes overrides what—suppose for the sake of argument—would otherwise be reasons for different responsibilities in life. This would, of course, create another sort of inequality in the treatment of the sexes, in that a woman would be treated differently from any man who had a sex-divergent magnetic effect; she would be exempted in one respect from the ordinary code of responsibility. Such an equality argument could apply, even though the innocent bystander would be much worse off if killed than he would be if the woman had not caused him to be attached.

This argument, unlike all those we have looked at so far in connection with variations on the violinist case, emphasizes that those who may end up supporting others in their bodies are female rather than male and that women have a distinctive, and (at least seemingly) a socially subordinate, relation to men. The equality argument suggests that the conclusion regarding the permissibility of terminating support in a case in which attachment is the result of a voluntary act might be different if men as well as women could have people attached to their bodies.

If the equality argument does imply this, it would straightforwardly permit killing such attached people in order to avoid losses (in social equality) that would occur on account of one group's members carrying people in their bodies. That is, social inequality is not a loss for the sake of support but a loss on account of support, and the equality argument suggests that efforts for the sake of support (pointed to by the cutoff abortion argument) are not sufficient to justify killing (i.e., because if both men and women could get pregnant, we might not have an argument for the permissibility of abortion in either sex).

This interpretation of the equality argument is consistent with its claiming either that social equality alone is sufficient to justify killing or with the view that social equality is a necessary supplement to bodily efforts and that having to make bodily efforts is necessary, though not sufficient, to justify killing. On the other hand, the equality argument may simply be considered as just another independent argument for killing that does not deny the sufficiency of other arguments.

In any case, I am not relying on such an equality argument in constructing the cutoff abortion argument. Indeed, I believe that we may want to question the equality argument on three points: (1) It may be wrong if it suggests that abortion would be morally impermissible if its permissibility were not necessary to achieve social equality (that is, if women were socially dominant to men, or both men and women could get pregnant would abortion be impermissible?). (2) It may be wrong if it claims that one may kill someone simply because this is necessary for social equality. For example, in the attached bystander case. Also, one cannot kill infants, detached from anyone's body, if their existence led to social inequality for women because women but not men could not resist taking care of them. (3) It would be wrong if it suggested that abortion would not be permissible if a right to decide whether to abort actually reduced women's power relative to men's overall, because women's power stems from having many children.

This does not mean, however, that we should not consider a role for equality in the cutoff abortion argument. For instance, equality might be a relevant consideration in justifying one's exercising a right to decide whether to have an abortion, a right that is justified on grounds other than a concern for equality. Or it might combine with the fact that one's body is being used so as to provide someone with life and yield a right to abort on the grounds that even a small imposition may be stopped if its after-effects will be inequality. We shall consider these possibilities below.

More Differences Between the Violinist and Abortion Cases

Having constructed an abortion argument on the basis of the output cutoff argument, we shall now consider additional differences between the violinist and abortion cases to supplement differences we have already considered. Even if we eventually reject the cutoff abortion argument, these differences will be important to any other argument.

The Naturalness of Pregnancy

Pregnancy is the "normal" use by (what we are assuming to be) one person of another person's body, but the attachment of the violinist to someone's body is not such a normal use. Does this make a difference? Another way of putting this is that the fetus is made for the womb; it is a womb-resident by nature. But the same cannot be said of the violinist in relation to your body. Still another way of stating this is that the function of some female organs is to house a fetus. (Some might even say it is a woman's function to do this. But a woman may have no function, even though her organs do. Even if a woman considered as part of nature has a function, it may be bad for her as a person to perform this function, and she may not want to do so. The natural is not always the best, e.g., we give drugs to cure natural disease. And even if she wants to perform this function, she may have second-order desires or values that give her reasons not to have, or to act on, these first-order desires, etc. This is structurally similar to a person who has a compulsion but wishes he did not have it. This is consistent with the Kantian idea that rational beings are not mere means, that they are not simply tools to produce certain states of human welfare; rather, they are ends in themselves, capable of reflecting on and assenting to or denying the practical force of certain desires.)

There are genuine problems in this area, I believe, centering on whether and when a person can claim that his body belongs to him and to no one else. In the violinist case, the person whose aid is needed can claim that it is his body—the body that belongs to him—that would be used. Can a pregnant woman claim that her body, in the sense of the one she lives through as a person, belongs to her alone rather than to the fetus as well? Is it a body that the fetus has as much right to as she has?[9]

The answer to this question is relevant to the entire cutoff abortion argument since this argument depends on the view that her body belongs to the woman alone.

In this connection, consider the following scenarios:

1. Suppose that new people come into existence simply by budding, as persons, inside the bodies of already existing young people and that these young people have no control over whether or when this happens. Furthermore, the new people (Buds) come into existence simply by taking over the bodies of already existing people, who die in the process, losing out on further good life. This is the "normal" course of nature. If the already existing person refused to die, would it be permissible for him to claim that the body was his, because he was its first "occupant" and then, using this as one premise, argue that he should be allowed to abort the bud?

2. Alternatively, suppose that newly created people always come into the world in sets. The body of (only) one of every two physically separate people eventually wears out in mid-life, and the body of the second member of the set is specifically constructed to provide life support for this first member. (Assume that our best scientific understanding of life makes it clear that this is the natural order.) We may further imagine that in mid-life there is a natural magnetic pull of the first to the second member of the set.

Even more in Case 2 than in Case 1, we can get a sense that someone's body is jointly owned by him and another person (i.e., the second member of the set), even though he is its sole occupant at the outset. We have a greater sense of this in Case 2, I believe, because there exists a person from the beginning who may claim the body used by the other person, though he has not used it yet. In Case 1, the second person comes into existence later.

The difference between Cases 1 and 2, on the one hand, and pregnancy, on the other, lies in the fact that in pregnancy as we know it, the other person does not exist unless a woman does something (or has something done to her). Usually this is sex, which is considered by many to be a normal and, for most people, even a physically or psychologically important part of life. (If it is possible to abstain from sex, however, it is significant that pregnancy occurs as a result of it rather than from, for example, eating or moving one's bowels. These latter activities, at least seemingly, unlike sex, are currently unavoidable if one wants to remain alive.) If one wants to make certain that a new person will not unexpectedly show up, one should not use or let one's body be used in this way. In addition, Case 2 differs from pregnancy as we know it in that the person who will share one's body exists all along.

One question to ask about both Cases 1 and 2 is whether we would consider it permissible for the person who must die (in Case 1) or share his body (in Case 2) to resist nature and to have the second person killed or left to die. The second person is not only a morally innocent threat which comes about without any unjust human acts, by a natural force (a gust of wind). He is also a "natural threat," a threat expressive of the natural order. The more basic question, however, with which I am currently concerned, is whether a person who resists nature can at least defend the claim that the body is his and not jointly owned and then use this as a premise in an argument for killing the coresident. (An alternative argument would be that the body does belong to both people in Case

2 or eventually to Bud in Case 1, but when someone is a threat to one's life, one is permitted to do what one can to defend oneself.) One reason to think it is his body is that he acts and feels through it.[10] But suppose one sign of Bud's presence is that the first occupant notices his arms and legs moving in response to Bud's expressed desires and Bud suffers when the first occupant is physically attacked. Still, my sense is, it is not Bud's body, because someone else is its first occupant. (By contrast, Siamese twins are simultaneous occupants.)

Suppose that we think it reasonable for him to make this claim and thus oppose nature's "plan" on grounds that he is defending his body in the sense that it belongs to him and is not merely used by him. Compare this with the claim of the pregnant woman that her body is hers and not held jointly with the fetus simply because of the naturalness of its position. (Again, this is different from the additional claim that she may remove the fetus.) Her claim would surely be stronger (i.e., more powerful than the claims of those in Cases 1 and 2) as in her case a fetus is not created independently of what she does, nor does it come into existence at the same time as she does. Although some people may believe that a woman's responsibility for allowing a fetus to use the body that belongs to her is greater when the fetus's existence is a consequence of her actions, this does not conflict with the fetus's claim to her body as also its body being weaker when its existence is due to her act.

Of course, whether a case for resisting imposition is successful cannot be settled by answering the question, Whose body is it? In particular, the fact that the fetus is created because of what the woman does may make her resistance less appropriate morally.

I do not intend to pursue the issue of ownership here. I shall simply assume, for the sake of argument, that the facts of nature as we know them do not by themselves defeat a woman's claim that the body that she and the fetus share belongs to her alone. I also believe that the fact that a person is a natural threat will not, by itself, rule out resistance.

Another point should be made about the normal and natural aspect of pregnancy in contrast with the imposition of the violinist. Suppose that we are not permitted to terminate a natural and normal process, as opposed to an artificial one such as attaching a violinist. Then the person who is subject to the natural imposition—but not the person who is subject to the artificial imposition—may come to be considered, and to think of himself, as merely part of nature. This contrast between a woman as a part of nature and a man as a person with dominion over nature has been said to be characteristic of the female–male distinction and the female–male relationship. (A somewhat different view sees men as themselves part of nature, though its controlling part.) If this is so, then the fact that pregnancy is natural and normal, but the violinist's imposition is not, might make disallowing abortion even more burdensome than disallowing the detachment of the violinist. Understanding abortion as a matter of morally permissible choice helps save people who become pregnant from being treated as mere parts of the "natural world," even if they do not choose to have an abortion. This is one significance of the term *prochoice* rather than *proabortion*. (In general, the reasons for supporting any prochoice position need not be the same as the reasons, if there are any, for justifying the selection of one of the options, for example, to have an abortion. Indeed, one might hold that it was morally permissible to have a choice to do what was morally wrong, and hence a prochoice position need not even be committed to the moral permissibility of abortion.[11])

There is a concomitant psychological difference between a person who unwillingly has a violinist attached to him and a woman in an unwanted pregnancy. We can imagine the first person as resistant, frustrated, and perhaps angry about his state. This is part of the cost to him of the state. But pregnancy, because it is "natural and normal," is more likely to result not only in an immense physical transformation of the woman—as evidence of the fact that her body is serving the needs of someone other than herself—but also in an immense psychological transformation: Her biology may pull her toward psychological identification with the fetus, and the boundaries of her ego dissolve with respect to it. Further, because pregnancy is a natural process, a form of pleasure is likely to accompany this quasi-dissolution of the individual into an instrument for the ends of nature.[12] This may seem to lessen the cost of pregnancy, as it helps break down both the resistance to it and the desire to separate. But it is just this ending of resistance that the woman who does not yet want to be pregnant may oppose.[13] This resistance need not necessarily represent a value judgment on the undesirability of ever being fused in this way; it may only represent the value judgment that it is undesirable for her now, perhaps because she identifies psychologically with some other person or activity. Such a woman might find the cost of pregnancy to be lower if she were sure that she would remain someone to whom the attachment was indeed a source of frustration, because she then would retain a strong sense of her separateness as an individual. A woman who resists pregnancy does not now want to become a person who will value things (e.g., the fetus) other than what she values now, and she believes that she has a right to act on her current values, not the ones she might have if she became pregnant.[14] (In general, resistance to sharing one's body in "natural ways" may have more to do with mental than with physical effects of sharing.)

If pregnancy is natural, it may be further argued by some, it always must involve real benefits to the woman. But what is natural is not always best for an individual. Still, suppose there were such benefits. It would be necessary to show that the benefits outweighed the burdens, but still paternalistic to assume the woman should accept even such outweighing benefits when she does not want them.

The naturalness of pregnancy therefore does not alter to whom a woman's body belongs, and indeed it may increase the cost to her of an unwilling pregnancy. The latter point means that the efforts the woman makes for the sake of the fetus are in some ways greater than those the person who supports the violinist makes for the sake of the violinist. This affects Condition 4. Why are these efforts thought to be made for the sake of the fetus rather than on account of the fetus when it is not necessary that the support be natural in order for the fetus to benefit from it? The reason is that the added burden is a characteristic of the very bodily efforts that are made for the sake of the fetus. Psychological fusion may also directly benefit the fetus and so is for its sake.

Some may believe that although naturalness and normalness do not directly create a greater obligation to a fetus, they do create an obligation to nature itself, with the fetus as the beneficiary of this obligation. Indeed, some think of nature as sacred and as punishing those who act against it. (This may be projection of the human unconscious, but in some views the unconscious reflects the real order of nature.) But human beings on so many occasions think it morally proper to resist nature—it is sometimes said that it is human nature and the basis of civilization to do this—that unless one believes that only women must not resist nature, there is not much to be said for this argument.

Perhaps the fact that pregnancy, at this time in history, is necessary for the continuation of the species makes abortion significantly different from detaching the violinist. After all, killing the violinist is not terminating an instance of a type of support that is necessary for the species' survival.

If most women refused to bear children, then some women might have to be drafted or induced by payment to do so, for then saving a species, not just one life, would be at stake. But it seems unreasonable to object to ending an instance of a type of activity necessary for the species' survival, when the instance itself is not necessary for its survival. After all, the fact that killing all people would eliminate the species does not mean that particular killings for reasons of self-defense that do not threaten the species' survival are impermissible.

The Postnatal Burdens

In the violinist case, our argument focused on the imposition on and the losses suffered by the person who objected to his body's being used. But after the violinist is detached, he and the person who supported him would lead independent lives. We did consider that there may be costs after detachment and that someone might offer them as reasons for terminating support. In the case of abortion, this problem looms even larger. A pregnant woman may not object to the use of her body by the fetus; rather, she may object to her interdependence with the child after its birth, having to raise it once it is out of her womb. This is a cost on account of pregnancy and its success, rather than one for the sake of pregnancy, though it also is a cost for the sake of the child. (In this way it differs from some other costs on account of pregnancy.) Even the child's adoption by another family is sometimes considered to be an emotional burden to the biological mother. For some people the existence of their biological offspring, even when they are raised by others, creates a new inescapable orientation, from independence to relatedness to another person.

It is sometimes said that avoiding these postnatal burdens might justify abortion. But if a fetus who was a person grew in a lab, presumably one could not kill it to avoid the postnatal burdens associated with having it adopted. If it is permissible to use as a justification for abortion these postnatal burdens, which are really losses suffered on account of pregnancy and its success in producing a child, it may be because they can justify (i.e., provide reasons for) exercising a right to have an abortion already granted on grounds of avoiding bodily imposition. But it may also be permissible to kill someone to stop an otherwise minor intrusion that on its own would not justify killing, if we knew that it would lead to very bad aftereffects. A person may sometimes prevent what is his (e.g., his body) from being used against his best interests. This means that "efforts on account of" could supplement the reason of bodily intrusion so as to make the total losses sufficiently significant that we may grant a right to kill someone in order to avoid them. If this is so, then we should add such costs, efforts, or losses to Condition 4.

Suppose a woman had a right to an abortion based on a claim to the exclusive use of her own body (i.e., use of her body is, by itself a sufficient effort to justify killing). Then it might be argued that she may permissibly exercise a prerogative not to let her body be used by others, even though its being used was not disturbing to her in itself, because she did not want to contribute her bodily efforts (which she is not obligated to make) to bring about an end (e.g., the existence of a child to be raised by someone else) that she opposes for serious reasons.

This type of argument finds its analogue in other contexts. Even if we do not look favorably upon a certain state of affairs (e.g., a particular candidate will win an election), there are some things that we are not permitted to do in order to see that it fails to occur (e.g., we may not interfere with the candidate's legal political efforts). But there are certain things that we may do, such as refuse to contribute our money to the campaign, even if we do not object to contributing on grounds of the money in itself. Similarly, even if a woman does not want to raise a handicapped child, she may not have it killed if it is born alive (assuming that it has the rights of a person). Perhaps, however, she may permissibly refuse to make significant efforts, which she would not have to make if she objected to making them per se, if such efforts would help promote a state of affairs that she does not desire, i.e., the existence of the handicapped child.

If this argument is correct, a woman can permissibly refuse to give bodily support to a fetus for reasons other than that she objects to the efforts themselves. To be more precise, there are four types of situations in which the desire to do this might occur: (1) A woman might want to refuse to make significant efforts that she need not make because of what they are in themselves, in order to avoid the consequences of the pregnancy itself rather than the consequences of producing a child. (2) A woman may want to refuse to make an insignificant effort that she would be required to make, considered in itself, in order to avoid the significant consequences of the pregnancy itself rather than the consequences of producing the child. (Justification for this is similar to that given for not tapping the hemophiliac, a small imposition can be refused because of its big effect.) (3) A woman may want to refuse to make significant efforts that she need not make because of what they are in themselves, in order to avoid the consequences of producing a child. (4) A woman may want to refuse to make an insignificant effort that she would be required to make, considered in itself, in order to avoid the significant consequences of producing a child.

The suggestion is that refusal is permissible in Situations 1, 2, and 3 but is not permissible in Situation 4. That is, although the consequences of the pregnancy itself could combine with what we hypothetically imagine is an intrinsically small effort during pregnancy to make a cost that we may kill to avoid, it is not true that the costs imposed by a new person's existence can combine in this way with such a small cost to make a cost that we may permissibly kill to avoid. This is analogous to the impermissibility of our refusing to make a minor effort in order to save someone's life just because he then will quite fairly consume a crucial resource that we would otherwise have consumed ourselves. On the other hand, to make a big effort that will result in someone's survival when the survival itself poses a threat to us (even by fair means) seems too much to require of us. (The big effort may be the result of a small bodily use followed by large consequences of that use itself, independent of its causing someone's survival.)

Do all these reasons for terminating support require intending the nonexistence of a person as a means of avoiding future psychological burdens due to his existence? Not necessarily. A woman may wish to avoid postnatal stresses; she may therefore refuse bodily efforts, despite foreseeing death of the fetus but intending only not to participate in helping it survive. The stresses, produced by the existence of the person once outside the womb, presumably are not by themselves sufficient grounds for killing the new person once he is out of the womb. Yet according to our current analysis, it sometimes is permissible for a pregnant woman to have an abortion because by means of an abortion she stops herself from helping bring about the state that she finds stressful. If she were not helping to bring about the state of affairs in the particular way that she is, she could not interfere with its coming about.

Even though such an argument may be strictly correct, it does not mean that reliance on it is to be commended when the stresses result from the existence of the new person per se. It might be suggested to a woman who does not find the pregnancy itself burdensome, even when it is in itself a significant effort, that it is morally better to learn to detach herself emotionally from the child that someone else will then raise than it is to destroy it. However, if she frequently becomes pregnant, non-negligently let us assume, both the psychological burden of such delib-erate emotional detachment and the physical burden of multiple preg-nancies will become stronger reasons for terminating the pregnancies rather than continuing and arranging for adoption.

There is another way of understanding a woman who resists continu-ing a pregnancy and putting up her child for adoption, a way that provides a different argument for the costs of not having an abortion. Putting up her child for adoption is not understood as merely a cost to the woman. Rather, she sees it as conflicting with the psychological pres-sure to continue an involvement that has already exacted a large cost.

If she is not obligated to continue her pregnancy merely because she has begun it, this psychological pressure to continue it will not be equivalent to a sense of moral responsibility. Still, the more sensitive the woman is and the longer she bears the fetus, the more likely it is that she will become committed to it. This non-obligatory commitment, in turn, will ground her belief that she must make further sacrifices for it. Rather than reducing the amount she feels she should still do, the fact that she has made some sacrifice for the fetus already will cause her belief that she should do more. Indeed, the greater the effort the woman makes for the fetus, the larger the sunk cost will be—and continuing the pregnancy is indeed a big effort—the stronger her sense of involvement will be-come, and the more appropriate additional big efforts will seem. (Al-though a woman can predict what she will feel psychologically com-pelled to do, her will and choice are in part responsible for this "compulsion." Her postnatal efforts need not follow as a matter of physical necessity.)

Therefore, a woman who is considering whether to have an abortion may well consider that the costs of not having one encompass not only the sacrifices required in pregnancy and giving birth but also the cost of raising the child (or alternatively the cost of breaking the non-obligatory commitment). The reason is that she can predict that the tendency of involvements to be self-sustaining in the manner described will make it impossible for her to give up the child at birth. If this is true, then the more sensitive the woman is to the pressure of involvement, the greater the cost will be to her of not having an abortion (it will be the cost of raising the child). Furthermore, she is more likely to fail to respond to the following argument: If you could ignore your sense of involvement after giving birth, then the cost to you of not having an abortion will be lower. This in turn will make having the abortion a less pressing need. And this will save more fetuses, which is a better result. This is a consequentialist, and indeed a pareto optimal, argument, as everyone may well be better off if we do as it suggests. I believe, however, that not only a deontologist but also someone sensitive to the pressures of involvement and high sunk cost, will find what it requires unacceptable: One cannot behave improperly at a certain time in regard to one's duties or the values of involvement simply to maximize the overall best consequences. That is, one cannot abandon the child post-natatly, having sunk cost and built ties to it during the pregnancy.

Two situations which raise the same issue with respect to duties rather than mere pressures of involvement are useful to consider: First, suppose that voluntarily beginning aid to the violinist did lead to an obligation to continue this aid. Then people would be less likely to start aiding, as they would know that they should not stop. Overall, fewer lives would be saved if this were true. That is, more lives would be saved if we allowed people to start aid and then to ignore an obligation to continue it, for then they would be more willing to start and might well complete the task. Still, we might refuse to allow such a scheme on the ground that we cannot manipulate the requirements to which circumstances give rise for the sake of overall good consequences. Second, consider the case of the disturbed visitor: I know that someone will come to town who will need a lot of help from me during his emotional crisis. I want to avoid being in this situation, and so I plan to leave town. If I stay in town, this person could receive useful travel instructions from me at a minimal cost to myself. It would improve the outcomes for both of us if I did not leave and he got instructions, on the condition that when he had his nervous breakdown I would not be bothered. Yet, I believe that such an agreement could not release me morally from any duties that I have to help someone who, in my presence, undergoes a severe crisis. Because, I believe, it is still permissible to leave town, I may do this, even though it is not pareto optimal, and ignoring my duties is.

The Burden of Uncertainty

If it were not permissible to interrupt pregnancy, a woman may not be able to do certain activities that require her to be sure that she will be free of interfering commitments. Thus the possibility (and hence the uncertainty) that one may have an uninterruptible pregnancy—even if one never has one—may itself impose significant losses. Women who will never become pregnant may be seen—for example, when being hired for a job—in light of the possibility of an uninterruptible pregnancy.[15] The fact that many women may possibly have uninterruptible pregnancies if abortion is not permitted—rather than just one person actually having just one violinist attached to him—results in the entire class of females being perceived differently. Rather than a cost that one woman takes into account when deciding on one abortion, so that she will suffer the cost if she does not have the abortion, this is a cost to all women even if not pregnant of all women's not being permitted to have an abortion. Such costs can be referred to as the *externalities* of any given pregnancy.

This issue raises the problem of other people's acts; that is, the burden of uncertainty may be an effect of others' refusing to hire women if they cannot interrupt their pregnancies. If others refuse to share the burden (e.g., in the form of a less efficient business) of not permitting abortion, then if a woman refuses to bear the career costs of not having an abortion, and not having the permission to abort, she can rightly believe that those others are, in part, responsible for the need to make abortion permissible or for her choosing to have an abortion. The reason is that they have made the costs of her not having permission to abort or not having an abortion very high. This, of course, does not mean that she is absolved from responsibility for her decision: The bad behavior of others is often a test of our resolve not to be pressured into behaving badly ourselves. In addition, this sort of differential burden would not be present to so great a degree if men had to leave work—at least as often as women did—to care for the children they helped create. For then, from an employer's point of view, men would present the same problems as women, and also raise the issue of uncertainty.

The Social Inequality

Pregnancy (unlike the attached violinist) produces broad social costs, notably a differential status for members of a group that is characterized not only as "all (possibly) pregnant persons" but also as "female" rather than "male." (The violinist case focuses on a single burdened person rather than a class of persons.) For example, as discussed above, since it seems rational to take into account the greater likelihood of a woman's having to interrupt her work than of a man's having to do so, if one pregnant woman cannot have an abortion, the burdens involved may extend to nonpregnant women as well, but not to men. The women will not be hired for fear they too will have an uninterruptible pregnancy. Notice also that it is not merely that social inequalities along sex lines may result from uninterruptible pregnancies. These social inequalities may benefit those (men) who have had a role (via sexual relations) in causing the pregnancy itself. That those who have had this causal role benefit from it is likely to be an additional negative.

One implication of this is that those who want women to carry all pregnancies to term should—with an eye to not creating social differences along sex lines—reduce the burdens of pregnancies. Because men cannot literally carry and deliver a fetus, other means for spreading the consequences of pregnancy across the sexes would have to be developed. For example, one might allot to men who have children the predominant responsibility for postnatal child care for at least several months. A consequence of such measures taken in order to prevent abortions might be less efficiency in society overall. But, of course, the benefit might be worth the loss if the fetus were a person.

Note that such programs that try to prevent abortion by compensating women for disadvantages that would otherwise flow from pregnancy may in some sense also alter their status negatively: Women may become more dependent on the aid of either men or governmental programs than other citizens are, that is, they lose their independence.

So far we have considered social costs of not permitting abortions. But even if abortion is legally and morally permitted, an adverse effect on women as a group can occur, as a result of individual women's decisions not to have an abortion. That is, what seems like a personal decision—if enough women make it—may result in very different, unequally advantageous positions for women and men. The creation of such differences along sex lines may be a harm that individual women should consider when deciding what the costs of not having their abortion will be. To prefer that no other women act as one acts—that is, to prefer that no other women refuse to have abortions, even though one is oneself refusing to have one—is problematic. But in thinking that it would be wrong for anyone in her position to have an abortion, a woman is approving of a standard that would result in unequal social positions along sex lines if everyone lived up to it—unless the costs of pregnancy were distributed across the sexes. (To decide how to act by considering what the consequences would be if everyone acted in the same way, is a consequentialist universalization procedure.)

It is interesting to try to figure out why or whether the fact that pregnancy is associated with another characteristic such as femaleness makes for greater concern with its effects than it would if both men and women could become pregnant. If both men and women could get pregnant, should the woes of the class of "all possibly pregnant people" matter less than if this property is uniquely female (or male) and results in social differences between the sexes? The association of one characteristic with another characteristic does seem to make some difference. For example, if most and only blacks (not whites) could become pregnant or provide assistance to ill people, the question of whether people who are able should be required to give aid might be answered differently than it would if the same number of people, but distributed over all racial groups, had these capacities.

One suggestion is that it is important if a unique capacity for pregnancy or for aiding ill persons is associated with some other characteristic that marks an already downtrodden group, like blacks, whom we are loath to burden further. But suppose that we are loath to burden women with unwanted pregnancy because they are an already downtrodden group. We may find that unlike blacks, women are downtrodden simply because of their capacity to become pregnant.[16] Likewise any group, otherwise diverse, that could become pregnant would be downtrodden. Should we care less for their fate than for the fate of any group distinguished by some other characteristic if pregnancy would itself make them downtrodden? That is, suppose that all and only blondes, not previously a downtrodden group, had the capacity to become pregnant. Would one treat the cost of pregnancy differently than if pregnancy were not restricted to this group, simply because now blondes will become a downtrodden group, distinguishable by blondness as well as by pregnancy?

The association of one group characteristic with another characteristic raises a special problem, I think, because it makes the first characteristic susceptible to being liked or disliked just because of the other characteristic. Suppose that someone's stupidity was a result of her genetic inheritance and was not related to any other characteristic she had. Then she can dislike her stupidity as a genetic inheritance, but need not dislike anything else about herself. But if she discovers that she is stupid because she is a female (or blonde), she will come to dislike being a female (or blonde) as well as being stupid, at least if intelligence is more important to her than any virtues associated with being female or blonde. If one's identification with a group characteristic is psychologically significant—as it may be for femaleness but not, perhaps, for hair color—a negative association to it will become even more significant. Further, there being a connection between a group characteristic and burdens (such as a pregnancy when unwanted) makes one feel even more trapped in those burdens. Perhaps the reason is that when we consider the counter-factual—what would have to be true in order for one to be rid of the burden—one focuses not only on being rid of the burden itself but also on being rid of some other characteristic which is, however, irrevocable.

The flip side of this is the attitude of people who do not possess the group characteristic associated with pregnancy: They do not think of the pregnant person as just another person who became pregnant. Rather, they can safely distance themselves from the pregnant person because they lack the characteristic (femaleness or, hypothetically, blondness) with which it is associated. This makes them feel freer to treat the pregnant person in a way very unlike the way that they would treat themselves (and any other man, or nonblonde person) if they became pregnant.

Suppose that this analysis of the significance of conjoined characteristics is correct. Then we have an answer to why an equal concern for each person, regardless of group membership, is compatible with a special concern if all those carrying a burden share some other characteristic, especially one with which they (understandably) identify significantly. That is, we may have a special concern when one group carries the burden, because each of the members of the group pays the additional costs just described, as well as the cost that would be paid if a more diversified population carried the burden. Because equal concern is appropriate when equal burdens are at stake, a greater concern for a greater burden does not violate it. In sum, it seems we could prefer a burden to be distributed across sexes rather than among one sex, compatibly with an equal concern for each individual man and woman.

If not permitting abortion placed an added burden on one sex as a group, this effect "on account of pregnancy" would have an impact on each individual; for example, each person would identify femaleness as associated with a negative. But it is not the sort of bad effect that an individual would likely give as an explanation for having an abortion. The cost from the idea of women as alone subject to uninterruptible pregnancies results mostly from the prohibition of abortion rather than from an individual woman's choosing not to have an abortion. (If such costs did occur because of an individual's choice not to abort, they are not costs to her. We have noted the difference between a straightforward *consequentialist* argument—that is, if I do not have an abortion, it will have a bad effect on my sex group—which is unlikely to be a strong argument, and the *consequentialist universalization* argument—that is, if I think that it is wrong for me to have an abortion, then I should will that no one else have one. If I cannot will the consequences of this universalization, I am using the idea of the counterfactual world in which no one has an abortion as a consequence of my not having one as a ground for having an abortion. But I do not have to expect that there are such real consequences.)

Therefore, it may be appropriate in regard to Condition 4 to consider not only those costs that it is permissible to avoid by having one person killed on one occasion but also those costs (e.g., the burden of uncertainty) that it is permissible to avoid by permitting abortions on many occasions. Nothing I have said about the additional costs of group inequality should be thought to imply that bodily imposition of pregnancy is not sufficient to justify abortions.

Inequality and the Worst Off

Suppose that a cost of the impermissibility of abortion would be greater inequality between the sexes. If we are concerned about this cost because we are concerned about inequality in general, ought we not consider that more severe inequality of a different type will occur if abortions are permitted? That is, if we assume that the fetus is a person and it will be killed at a young age, then surely it will be the worst off person. Ought we correct for inequality between those who are already better off, at the expense of the person who will then be worst off?[17] A related point is to note that every woman who may suffer inequality if abortions are not permitted, would herself have been in danger of being killed as a fetus (arguably a worse fate than adult sex inequality) if abortions had been permitted.

It does indeed seem possible to be concerned about one type of inequality, because it is inequality, that will be generated if we were to relieve an even worse form of inequality. Suppose, for example, that only blacks were capable of helping the poorest class of whites, by performing certain menial tasks. Helping the poorest whites would then be possible only at the expense of racial equality, which, however, would not leave blacks as badly off as the poorest whites would be without their help (by hypothesis). We still might rule out helping the poorest whites because it introduced inequality on the basis of race. In this case, of course, the blacks had no chance of being among the poorest class themselves. By contrast, adult women had a chance of being among fetuses threatened with abortion. But consider that everyone who is now an adult was once a child. Suppose that only adult blacks turned out to have the capacity to save children (both black and white) by donating certain of their organs. Could we object, out of concern for racial equality, to a policy which required adult blacks to donate their organs to save the lives of young children, even though dying at ten is worse than being required to donate on the basis of race at forty. (That we might favor the young in distributing organs which have already been voluntarily donated is different from taking organs from the old of any race—or permitting a comparable imposition on their bodies to continue—in order to help the young.)

In sum, the additional differences we have considered between the violinist and abortion cases are the genetic relation, the infant-like status of the fetus (if morally relevant), various aspects of the naturalness of pregnancy, post-natal burdens, the uncertainties engendered by uninterruptible pregnancies, and the difference in status between the sexes as social groups. As relevant, these factors should be considered when determining the costs which restrictions on abortion involve, and whose avoidance may help ground the permissibility of killing. A person may refuse to provide support that results in such further costs as inequality.

Liberalism, Equality, and the Theory of Value

We have considered the different factors that might count as costs of either not having an abortion or not having the permission to have an abortion, because arguing for the permissibility of abortion requires, I believe, the conviction that there are such costs. In a public discussion of the abortion issue, those factors that some people see as costs must be understandable by others to be costs. If we cannot see how uncertainty or not being able to pursue certain types of work or not being able to support one's other children or being intermittently dependent on the assistance of others is a cost to a person, then we may not see how there is an argument for the permissibility of abortion. I have, however, emphasized that if these costs are to help justify killing, they should result from and be reasons for ending bodily support that provides life for the fetus. One could not kill fetuses in incubators, assuming they were persons, because only women could not resist the need to take care of them, and this resulted in inequality. And, as noted, it may also be crucial that it is bodily imposition of the degree involved in pregnancy, not other forms of support (e.g., working for the fetus) that one would seek to terminate. I noted that this was in keeping with the great respect which is prevalent for bodily privacy. (However, I do not pretend to have justified our greater resistance to bodily intrusions than to other forms of imposition on persons, though I have pointed to humiliation and sexualization.)

How can others be made to see that these are costs? They may share one's own values and immediately recognize that these are costs. Then one can essentially say, "I want to have and avoid the same things in life that you want to have and avoid." But in a pluralistic society it is common for people's values not to coincide. Liberal political theory has attempted to describe the ways in which individuals with different conceptions of the good life can communicate. One might try to describe one's concerns in a higher-order language that another party can understand. For example, suppose that being required to work on Sunday conflicted with one's religious beliefs. Others who do not share one's specific beliefs may have a hard time understanding why working on *Sunday* is a burden. But put in more general terms, others may understand that working on a day—perhaps for others it is Saturday—that interferes with deeply held religious convictions is a burden.

One important implication of the possibility of such higher-order descriptions is that in order to convince others that one will suffer a burden, it is not necessary to convince them that one's particular values, one's conception of the good life, are correct and demanded of everyone in the society. For example, one need not prove that having sexual intercourse but not a child at a certain point in one's life is the best way to live, in order to get someone to understand that it is not unreasonable to think that avoiding intercourse or having a child at a certain time could be burdensome. Using a model of contractualist reasoning,[18] we could say that the proposition that "*x* is not a burden" is something that it would not be unreasonable to reject. One need not prove, as a defense of a particular theory of the good life implies, that it would be unreasonable to reject the proposition that "*x* is a burden." (That is, it is not unreasonable for some to find *x* not a burden and not unreasonable for others to find it is a burden. It is enough to show that it is not unreasonable to find it a burden in arguing for the permissibility of stopping the burden.)

Reference has been made to a certain form of social equality between men and women as a good whose absence was considered a cost. Is the sort of equality that might be used in the abortion argument the sort that we need only show it is not unreasonable to consider a good, or is it the sort of equality we can rationally require that everyone support? What is usually referred to as the political equality of men and women, for example, equal civil liberties and the right to political involvement, and perhaps equal provision of some baseline economic support, is thought to be a component of the theory of the right, that is, the theory of justice.[19] As such it is often thought to be rationally demandable that everyone accept it; that is, one's proof should show that it is unreasonable to reject it. But can such a thin conception of equality support the claim that a cost of the impermissibility of abortion is loss of equality; that is, would society's satisfying the thin conception of equality be put in jeopardy by the impermissibility of abortion? Probably not. Indeed, the ideal of moral equality of the sexes may actually require us to tolerate different outcomes in their life-style. The reason is that taking seriously the full moral status of women and men and their responsibility for dealing with their given biology may result in their each having different responsibilities. One can be treated as an equal, even if one is not treated equally (i.e., identically). (Similarly, we treat someone as an equal when we give him his due, even if he deserves something different from someone else because of his health condition.)

Therefore, if one wants to use an equality component in the cutoff abortion argument, a stronger conception of equality would have to be used, for example, equality of income and personal and social power. Such equality may be part of a theory of the good life, or at least part of a theory of extrapolitical justice. Its supporters need only show, I believe, that it is not an unreasonable view of the good life, whose absence is a cost, in order to be justified in using it in an argument for the permissibility of abortion. (This is not to say that they could not also show that it is a view rationally demanded of everyone.)

An alternative may be to distinguish, as Rawls typically does, between formal political equality and its worth or fair value. It might be argued that if economic, personal, and social equality are not present this will affect the worth of formal equality. So if abortion were necessary for strong equality and strong equality were necessary for the fair value of political equality, abortion would be necessary for the fair value of political equality. Analogously, if we all formally have the right to free speech, but only the rich are able to buy television time to make their views known, it may be claimed that everyone's formal right is not worth the same. Therefore, some equal economic power is necessary for equal free speech.

I must admit to thinking that, given the comprehensive nature of the strong conception of sex equality, if one did not think it worth supporting for its own sake, it would be reasonable to reject the equal worth of political equality as a goal rather than support strong equality only as a necessary means to its achievement. Analogously, the right to free speech is probably worth less to those who are not intellectually gifted than to those who are, but presumably, we should not require equality of intellectual talent in order to produce equality in the worth of that right.

In sum, the suggestion is that the formal conception of political equality is not strong enough to support the permissibility of abortion and the strong conception of equality may not be something everyone is rationally required to agree upon for its own sake or just to produce the equal value of formal political equality. But if it is not imperative that everyone agree on the strong conception, only imperative that everyone agree that the strong conception is not an unreasonable view to hold, then it can still be used to support the permissibility of abortion, for everyone could understand how failure to achieve strong equality is seen to be a cost by some. (If this suggestion is wrong, then it is still possible that one could prove that the stronger conception of equality is rationally demandable and its absence a cost.[20])

Alternative Means of Ending a Pregnancy

Suppose that there were ways of removing a fetus from a woman's body without killing it. This would affect Condition 5.[21] Some of these procedures, which will result in a live birth, are, let us assume, less burdensome (including less risky), just as burdensome, or more burdensome to a woman than having an abortion is. Those that are less burdensome still may or may not, when considered alone, demand more from the woman than she would morally have to endure in order to avoid having the fetus killed (see Table 2). They all involve some bodily imposition, as does the abortion procedure. Let us consider ways of reasoning about these alternatives.

Table 2. Removal Procedures Compared with Killing the Fetus

Less Costly Burdens or Effects	More Costly Burdens or Effects	Equally Costly Burdens or Effects
(a) More than morally required to avoid killing	(a)	(a)
(b) No more than morally required to avoid killing	(b)	(b)

One fundamental issue in considering obligations to avoid the abortion procedure is whether the costs of the different procedures include not only the burden of the procedure itself but also the costs resulting from the procedure itself and also from the consequences of a live birth. Our previous analysis suggests that it is often permissible to consider all the postnatal costs (although those stemming from the existence of a new person itself is morally problematic if the procedure and its other effects are not very costly), when evaluating how weighty the different procedures are. For example, suppose that a removal procedure by itself involves a sacrifice that a woman should be required to make in order to avoid having the fetus killed; but it entails a bad consequence for her after the birth. If the aftereffect independent of the new person is great enough, it could make the procedure costly enough that it would fall into the class of those demanding too much of her.

A second fundamental issue is whether we can decide what procedure can be required (1) by determining whether the difference in cost between abortion and other alternatives is too large to require a woman to pay it in order not to have the fetus killed or (2) by examining each procedure and its effects individually to determine whether its cost is too great to require. The first proposal seems more reasonable, for if a woman will suffer cost x anyway if a Procedure A is used, which kills the fetus, and Procedure B, which does not kill the fetus, costs $x + n$, where n itself is small, why should we not require her to use Procedure B? Furthermore, if Procedure C, which does not kill the fetus, also costs x, and Procedure D, which does not kill the fetus, costs $x - n$, is there not even more reason for limiting her choice, on the grounds that by means of a small reduction we can avoid killing the fetus?

But now, suppose that the less or the only slightly more costly procedures involve costs that are, considered separately, more than a woman would be required to pay in order to avoid having the fetus killed. Perhaps, if all the procedures involve such costs, the woman may choose whichever one she wishes, for whichever one she chooses, she will end up bearing costs she need not bear for the specific end of not having the fetus killed.

Consider a somewhat different problem in another context: If someone chooses to suffer great costs that he need not suffer, in order to achieve a certain end, he cannot be required to achieve another end at only a slightly higher cost. Nor would he be required to do for another end a less costly but still supererogatory act. The claim in the abortion case is that even if something else that we want the woman to do is what she could be required to do at cost n alone, she cannot be required to do it at cost $x + n$ (which itself is supererogatory) rather than to do something else at cost x. This is all separate from the objection that even if n is small, there is always a straw that breaks the camel's back. That is, if she has given so much she cannot be required to do any more.

Now consider the procedures that may be used to remove the fetus by themselves rather than with their effects. The procedures that would spare the fetus's life are slightly more burdensome, less burdensome, and as burdensome as is the procedure that produces a dead fetus. If the procedure that produces a live fetus is less burdensome, it may still be more costly overall for a woman to use the less burdensome procedure because of the postnatal effects of the procedure itself. Further, by going through the slightly more burdensome, less burdensome, or equally burdensome procedures, the woman knows that she is making large efforts (even if not much larger efforts than otherwise) to produce a sort of world that will be more costly to her.

I suggest, therefore, that given the spirit—right or wrong—of the cut off abortion argument, the wording of Condition 5 should stay as it is. We should consider whether the overall cost of each procedure (including its postnatal effects) is more than one would have to pay in order to avoid having the fetus killed. (But the effect of the new person is counted only when the cost of the procedure itself and/or its other effects is large.) We should not make this judgment only about the difference between it and another procedure. In some cases, even the differential cost will seem too large. If this is true, then we must ask whether, for example, a caesarian section (which is a considerable imposition) plus the effect of live birth are costs that a woman would have to pay rather than to use a procedure that is almost costless to her but kills the fetus. The fact that part of the burden here is considered to be in the simple existence, undetached, of another person makes this a morally problematic calculation. However, if the differential cost of the life preserving procedure over the cost of abortion is in itself great enough so as not to be required, then a woman might refuse to make this large effort to bring about a state she does not want to exist. When the differential cost of the procedure itself and/or its other effects is small the existence of the new person is not added.

Finally notice that the issue in this discussion is somewhat different from those that arise in court cases in which the question is whether women are required to undergo surgery to save a fetus from a natural death (rather than to avoid an abortion-induced death). In the court cases we consider what costs it is permissible to impose in order to save a life rather than to avoid killing it. Even if certain efforts were morally required rather than have the abortion, they might not be required to save the fetus from a naturally arising problem. (Similarly, the *Roe v. Wade* Court held that normal costs of pregnancy were not necessarily reason enough to justify an abortion after viability, but this still does not mean that such costs could be morally or legally required to save a post-viable fetus still in the womb from dying of a disease.)

Notes

1. A suggestion by Judith Thomson.
2. We are here assuming that abortion is permissible only to see if a life which ends with no injustice would still be worse than never living. Some may think that the reason for concern with abortion is the possible pain to the fetus. A

life with pain and no goods is worse than nonexistence, but this cannot be the problem with abortion. If it were, the moral problem of abortion would disappear if we gave the fetus an anesthetic.

3. This view is well expressed in Thomas Nagel's "Death," reprinted in his *Mortal Questions* (Cambridge, England: Cambridge University Press, 1979).

4. I first used the case of women who miscarry in my "The Problem of Abortion," in Raziel Abelson and Marie Friquenon, eds., *Ethics for Modern Life*, 2nd ed. (New York: St Martin's Press, 1981). Dr. Robert Morris, of the New York University Medical Center, confirmed my suspicions about actual attitudes toward such women. Of course, actual attitudes may be based on the supposition that the fetus is not a person. Suppose we think it permissible to allow someone to try to have a child, even though there is a very high probability of miscarriage. Would we think it equally permissible to allow someone to try to have a child, even though there is a very high probability that the child, who will definitely survive, will be retarded? (We shall assume it has limited capacities, but its life is not so bad for it that death would be preferable.) I suspect we would be more reluctant to begin a pregnancy that would end with a retarded person than one that would end with the death of a fetus.

This may indicate that we do not believe the fetus is a person and so prefer the death of a nonperson to a not very good life for a person. Alternatively, it may indicate that although we do believe the fetus is a person, we think it less serious that a person may die before "beginning life in earnest" (a phrase used by Ronald Dworkin) than that a person lead a life of normal length but with abnormally limited capacities.

The latter analysis, however, faces the following problem: Suppose a fetal person is about to die and we can save it, but only by a means that causes some retardation. I suspect that we think it would be in the interest of the fetal person itself to be saved. If we consider its interests, we will save it. This means that we should save it from death for a retarded life, though we would do more to avoid beginning a pregnancy that would end in a retarded life than in death. How can these be consistent attitudes? It seems as though in the first response we think that retardation is better than death, and in the second response we think that death is less bad than retardation. I suggest the following answer to this puzzle: Before a created person exists, there is both no one to be harmed by his own nonexistence and no one who literally needs to be conceived. Therefore, there is no good reason, from the point of view of the person that we would create, to create him as a retarded person rather than to create nothing. However, from that same perspective, the prospect of living a short time and dying could seem no worse than total nonexistence; there is at least no retarded life that one has to endure. But from the perspective of someone already in existence, staying alive even in a limited condition may be preferable to death. Consider an analogous case: It is possible that when one is still mentally normal, it is in one's interest to die rather than live on in a demented state. Yet if one survives to that demented state, we evaluate the prospect of one's future relative to that of one's new identity as a demented person. It may then be in one's interest to survive in this diminished state. (This analysis was prompted by consideration of an alternative view held by Ronald Dworkin.)

In such cases, if one dies before the shift in one's values and concerns, then death was in one's interest, but if one survives the shift in one's values and concerns, going on living is in one's interest. In the case of creation, if we consider outcomes before the existence of the person, death may be acceptable when living in a diminished state is not. From that perspective, being saved for a diminished life is not the preferred course of events. But if the created person will not necessarily die and can be saved, from his perspective it is preferable that he be saved.

5. It might be argued that no pregnancy is fully voluntary if there is a biological pressure to reproduce, but this can be disputed.

6. It might be suggested that heterosexual sexual intercourse is never, or only rarely, truly voluntary for women or men. I shall simply assume for the sake of argument this is not true but discuss the issue a bit later.

7. We are leaving out consideration of the possibility that if the abortion procedure itself is very dangerous to the woman, one might be obligated to use a procedure less dangerous though intrinsically requiring more than a person would be obligated to sacrifice rather than to kill. We shall discuss this issue below.

8. The equality argument seems to be favored by, for example, Catherine MacKinnon, Sylvia Law, and Cass Sunstein.

9. Different but somewhat similar issues arise when considering whether the body of a married person belongs equally to his or her spouse.

10. Ronald Dworkin's suggestion.

11. I owe this point to Seana Shiffrin.

12. Arguably, this is what goes on in sexual intercourse as well, and at the time of death also when a person's blood chemistry is said to alter so as to diminish fear of—and resistance to—the end. These are illusions and dissolutions. Indeed, there are interesting parallels between positions on abortion and on the right to die: Some in the right-to-die movement are interested in giving people control over their death, so as to make it less a matter of nature. Others are not so much interested in giving a person control over when he or she will die as in not interfering with nature by artificially prolonging life, which, it is said, does death so much better (pleasanter) than doctors do. If control is lost over nature in abortion, there will be fewer abortions; if control is lost over nature at the end of life, there may be more deaths, in part because a pleasant death is confused with a death that is in the interest of the person who dies. (Only the latter is truly euthanasia.)

13. This is structurally analogous to the person who resists brainwashing, even though he knows he will not object to his state if the brainwashing is successful and will even feel happier as a brainwashed person than as one who has not been brainwashed. He resists the brainwashing because it conflicts with things that are valuable besides feeling happy. But, it may be said, those are only his current values; after brainwashing he will value happiness above everything else. Why should he give more weight to his current values, than those he would have? He does in fact have a right to do this. Julia Driver reminded me that we must assume the priority of present values in describing this position.

14. For discussion of some issues concerning psychological separateness and the loss of separateness, see Robin West, "Jurisprudence and Gender," *University of Chicago Law Review* 55 (Winter 1988):1–72.

15. I credit Laura Shulkind for consideration of this social cost of the impermissibility of abortion.

16. This claim would be challenged by, among others, those who believe that it is femininity itself that is the source of women's lower status, independent of capacity for pregnancy.

17. Ronald Dworkin's point. But perhaps the fetus is not worst off.

18. Provided by Thomas Scanlon in "Contractualism and Utilitarianism," in A. Sen and B. Williams, eds., *Utilitarianism and Beyond* (Cambridge, England: Cambridge University Press, 1982).

19. Here I am using the distinction between the good and the right that has been commonplace in political philosophy at least since John Rawls's *A Theory of Justice* (Cambridge, Mass.: Harvard University Press, 1971).

20. My discussion of strong equality, formal equality and its fair value was prompted by discussions of Rawls'.

21. And hence the last clause of Condition 3.

5

Creating Responsibly

In this chapter we shall consider problems with the cutoff abortion argument and then examine two alternative arguments for the permissibility of abortion.

Problems with the Cutoff Abortion Argument

The cutoff abortion argument has many problems. The one that I want to focus on now is that when creating new people, just making sure that they will be no worse off than if they had never existed and will not be harmed relative to prospects they had before being conceived are not sufficient conditions.[1]

For example, on the continuing assumption that the fetus is a person would it be permissible for a woman to begin a pregnancy knowing that she will intentionally abort it? One such case could arise if a woman's chance of developing breast cancer would be reduced by becoming pregnant and then having an abortion. In another case, perhaps a woman wants to get pregnant as a summer project—just to see what it is like—and also intends to abort. Avoiding cancer is a weighty reason for pregnancy; a summer project is a frivolous one. Yet both cases seem to carry with them an inappropriate attitude toward creating a new person. In these cases, pregnancies are begun as a means to some end other than having a child and with the intention that they will end with an abortion.

Suppose that abortion involved intending the death of the fetus as a means to—not merely foreseeing its death as a consequence of—freeing a woman's body. Then in these two cases someone would intend to intend the death of the fetus, as well as to intend to become pregnant for a reason other than having a child. The second, rather than first, factor seems to be the crucial mark against these pregnancies. For consider another case in which one intends to intend the death of the fetus: you are dying of a disease, and the only thing that can save you is taking a drug that, in addition, will make you pregnant. Suppose you take the drug knowing that you will end the resulting pregnancy, and you must intend the death of the fetus in order to do this. In this case, the pregnancy is only a foreseen side effect of the cure rather than the intended means to the cure. It therefore seems permissible for you to take the drug, even though you intend to intend the death of the fetus.

Even if we do not begin a pregnancy with the intention, or for the sake, of ending it, we can begin it foreseeing that the new person will get very little out of life. This also may be morally incorrect to do. It seems that we sometimes should avoid bringing people into existence, even if we expect that their existence will not be worse for them than if they had never existed and will not be a harm to them. Which sorts of lives it is wrong to create may change over time. That is, if we had always imposed a high standard, cave people might have lacked a moral right to reproduce, except possibly to keep the species from becoming extinct, and even that might not have been a sufficient overriding reason.[2]

Alternatively, suppose that the analysis in Chapter 4 is incorrect. That is, assume that creating a life that will soon end, either naturally or by means of human intervention, will harm the person who lives it, relative to the prospect of never living. The discussion of abortion must then take into account this wrong.

Examples

To reinforce these points, we shall use an example suggested by Derek Parfit.[3] He considers a woman who is told that if she has a child now it will be mildly retarded but still will have a life worth living. If she waits a few months, however, she will have a normal child. But if she has the first child, he will be no worse off than he otherwise would have been, as he otherwise would not have been, given that the child she would have later would be a different child (because a different egg and sperm would be joined).

Understood literally, this would apply even to someone who had only a short life of pure suffering, that he is no worse off than he otherwise would have been, as he otherwise would not have been at all. Yet, I believe that understood nonliterally, a life of suffering does make someone worse off than if he had never lived, and does harm him relative to the prospect of never living. But it might be said of the life of a retarded person that even in this nonliteral sense it is not worse than nothing, considered from the point of view of the child himself. Yet we still think that the woman in Parfit's example will be doing something morally wrong if she does not wait until she can have the better-off child.

Will she have done something wrong in creating the retarded child because she harmed it relative to prospects of life it otherwise would have had if it had not been created? No, because it would not have lived at all. Will she have nonliterally harmed it relative to its nonexistence? It is plausible to say no. Yet we nevertheless think she will have done something wrong. Now consider a different case.

Suppose that a woman is told that she will have a child with a 120 (normal) IQ if she conceives it now or will have a child with a 140 (superior) IQ if she waits two weeks. In this case we might also think she will be doing something wrong if she does not wait. Yet she does not do wrong because she literally harms the infant she creates, relative to the prospects it otherwise would have had; it had no other prospects. And it is correct to think that she will not have harmed it relative to its nonexistence even nonliterally. Furthermore, it seems that she will have done wrong in a different way from the woman in Parfit's case.

When judging the woman in the first example, we seem to use an objective standard of defectiveness—the child is below normal. It is for this reason that we think that the woman will have done something wrong in producing it rather than a normal child. Indeed, even if she could produce no child except a mildly retarded one, it might be better for her not to produce any. Why is this? Because there is no one to lose out in not being conceived, and the child would avoid the difficulties of abnormality. This implies that given that there is no one who loses out in not being conceived, it can be wrong to create a life that is still worth living and not worse than nothing. (Some might even want to say, on the basis of this analysis, that the child is harmed in being assigned to such a life, though I shall not say it.) So the first woman would do wrong to produce a defective child when she could have easily avoided it.

The second woman will not have produced a superior child. The wrong she will have done is not apparent in any objective defect she produces. Rather, she will have done wrong in not choosing a better state of affairs when she could easily have done so.

In both cases, the less gifted child would lose nothing if he were never conceived. Yet we treat his creation as though it were a matter of creating one particular person who will lose out on something, and wind up in a worse rather than a better state he might have occupied.

The Fetus Versus the Violinist

We will harm the violinist if we kill him, for we will deprive him of the life he could have had. But we do not thereby necessarily harm him relative to prospects he had before his attachment. It has been argued that this helps make killing him permissible. But the satisfaction of the same factors in the case of the fetus may not make killing it permissible. Let us assume that even if it is sometimes wrong to create a life that is not worse than nothing, we will not have harmed someone (even non-literally) relative to the prospect of nonexistence in doing so. Still, there seem to be requirements other than not harming a fetus relative to prospects it had before its conception and avoiding giving it a life that is not worth living. This is what the cases of the pregnant women seem to indicate.

One reason for this is suggested by a contrast between the violinist and the creation cases. When we kill the violinist, we bring about a bad state of affairs that would have existed anyway—the violinist's death—in order to stop the aid that prevented his death in the first place. In the case of the fetus, the state of affairs that is bad for it—its being dead or defective—would never have existed if we had never created the fetus. We are not merely trying to end efforts that stopped a bad state of affairs from coming about in the first place. This is the first time that these bad states of affairs will exist. Because there is no one in existence before his or her creation who needs to be created or who is harmed by not being created, we want to know why we bring about for the first time the possibilities of defective existence and someone's losing further life after only a short time alive.

Why Death Is Bad

Is it also possible that what makes death bad—contrary to the analysis in Chapter 4—makes living a short while and then dying worse for the person than not living at all? It was suggested that death is bad primarily because it deprives a person of more of life's goods. Why then should the prospect of death stand in the way of producing any goods at all? Prenatal nonexistence also deprives one of (having had) more goods of life: That is, if you had been created earlier (without dying sooner), you would have had more goods of life. Yet much as we recognize this as a true loss, we do not have as great concern with the prenatal loss as we do with the loss to come because of death. Does this suggest that death is bad for some reason other than that it deprives us of goods?[4]

One suggestion is that death may not be intrinsically different from prenatal nonexistence, but it is of greater concern to us because it lies in the future. That is, we care more about bad things to come than we do about equally bad things that are over and done with. Derek Parfit describes a case that demonstrates this in relation to pain.[5] Suppose that you awaken in a hospital not knowing whether it is the day after you have suffered greatly or, its alternative, the day before you will suffer moderately. If you were concerned about having a life with the least amount of pain in it, you would prefer it to be the day before the moderate pain. In fact, however, most people would prefer it to be the day after the worse pain (so long as there are no aftereffects), as the pain then would be in the past. If we apply this analogy to the case of death, we can say that the loss of goods caused by prenatal nonexistence is no less bad than the loss caused by death, that it is just behind us and so we care less about it. If this were true, it reduces the significance of death as a distinctive harm, I believe. It should stand in the way of creating a person no more (or no less) than the fact that when he is conceived he will be someone who has not always lived. (In addition, the fetus does not even care more about its future than its past, as it does not yet care about anything.)

Before considering whether this is the complete truth about the distinctiveness of death, it is important to emphasize that what seems to be true of pain is not necessarily true of other goods and bads of life; that is, if we prefer that pain be in the past rather than in the future, do we prefer that goods be in the future rather than in the past? It is not true that we would prefer fewer overall goods of life if this meant that we would still have a few goods of life in our future rather than many goods over and done with in our past. Nor would we prefer it to be true that we have overall many more bad things in our life if this meant that we would have fewer bad things in the future than otherwise. The reason is that some goods of life are achievements; they represent what we amount to as persons. They are what we see when we evaluate our life from the "outside," so to speak, rather than evaluate it from a point now, within our ongoing life. Thus we should prefer to have written great works or have had important relationships in the past and have little to look forward to now, rather than to have had none of these past goods and be about to experience some small pleasures in the future.

We do not express such a temporally neutral preference in Parfit's pain example because we do not consider a life with overall less pain in it to be an important achievement. This is consistent with our being concerned with pain to come from the point of view of now in the living of life. The "outside" view that tells us what an achievement is, is courageous in a way that we may not be able to live up to from the "inside" view.

I shall refer to the goods and bads that are important to us when we consider our lives from the outside as the *formal* (or structural) goods and bads and those that are important to us only as we live our lives (leading us to avoid as much pain as possible in the future, but not overall or in the past) as the *experienced* (or experiential) goods and bads.[6]

Let us now consider what else may make death bad besides being deprived of more goods of life. If additional factors distinguish between death and prenatal nonexistence, they might also explain why death can serve as a reason for not creating a new life even if the prenatal nonexistence of anyone we will create cannot.

Death, but not prenatal nonexistence, takes from someone what he has already had, what he already is; it happens to someone and demonstrates his vulnerability. (Prenatal nonexistence does not happen to someone who already exists, it does not take what one already has, and no one is shown to be vulnerable because he did not exist sooner.) Death is a decline (from the good of life if life is good), whereas going from nonexistence to life can be considered an incline. All these factors make death a sort of insult to the person that prenatal nonexistence is not, whether or not he is aware of the insult.

Death, of course, also represents the impossibility of any future for the dead person. This can be distinguished from simply not obtaining quantitatively more goods of life in the following way: someone might enter a limbo state containing no goods of life, and return to complete his conscious time alive thus extending his time alive without increasing the goods in his life. This would be done merely to delay his end and the end of the possibility of obtaining more goods, since so long as he stays in limbo there is the possibility of return. If someone, call him the Limbo Man, is understandably not indifferent between, on the one hand, going into limbo and, on the other hand having the same amount of goods and length of consciously experienced life only continuously, then we will have located yet another reason besides the reduction of total goods of life why death is bad: the end of the possibility of life.

Prenatal nonexistence, of course, does not eliminate the possibility of obtaining more goods of life in the future. But it does eliminate the possibility of having obtained more goods of life in the past. Why do we care more about the loss of possibility in the future than in the past, other than that it is in the future? That is, this additional reason why death is bad may again distinguish prenatal from postnatal nonexistence on the basis of our concern for the future, even if the insult factors discussed previously do more. If so, it may then provide no more reason for not creating someone than that someone will come to be who was not always in existence. Of course, such a person will, in losing the possibility of future goods, be losing something that he cares about having. By contrast, once he exists, he will not care as much about not having the possibility of past goods. But this is compatible with his losing something just as intrinsically valuable through prenatal nonexistence as through future nonexistence. (The fetus, of course, even if it is a person, is not yet capable of caring about the loss of its future.)

Is Mere Fetal Life a Harm?

Where are we in the end? If the fetus is a person it will lose many goods of life it might have had and, at the least, suffer an (unfelt) insult in having life taken from it. We already said (in Chapter 4) that independently of concern for it, it is worse from the point of view of the world that there will be waste if a creature dies young. For all that has been said, is it still possible that someone is not harmed overall by having a bit of life and then being a person who is to be pitied for having lost so much and been insulted in having lost so much? That is, it is not for this person's sake that we should not create him. If the formal characteristics of his life are not good (i.e., his having lost out on practically everything and been insulted), should this weigh more with us than the fact that his experiences are not negative and perhaps even positive? I am sympathetic to the view that respect for persons should lead us to emphasize the poor formal characteristics, and hence to avoid creating out of respect for the person herself, but that a love for life itself (a prolife view in a sense) might lead us to see no harm in creating such a short life.

There is, furthermore, a comparative question: Is it worse, on the one hand, to create someone who will soon die or, on the other hand, to make or allow to become worse off someone who is already in existence? For example, suppose that we have only a few dollars and must decide how to spend them. We could prevent traffic accidents and provide funding for the sick. However, imagine that the world is also such that without any human intervention, new persons are spontaneously conceived who will die shortly thereafter, having lived experientially adequate lives. We could spend our scarce money on preventing this spontaneous conception (though we could not develop a procedure to save the people once they came alive.) How should we spend our money?

I suggest that we might permissibly choose the first use of our money. The reason might be that certain bad experiences count more than do certain formal properties of a life, but the reason might also be that preventing conception and death does not save someone's life, even if it prevents the formal property of a short life. (Furthermore, choosing how to spend our money is different from causing damage to someone in order to prevent the spontaneous conceptions and different from requiring people to make sizable sacrifices to prevent them. These moves would be even more morally problematic.) In abortion we kill a creature who could be saved; it does not unavoidably die a natural death after spontaneous conception. But here we are concerned only with whether simply losing its life harms the fetus relative to its noncreation, as part of seeing how significant killing is and what costs we should impose on the person who is responsible for creating the fetus. Therefore considering how comparatively bad spontaneous generation and early death are is relevant.

In sum, I shall assume that the fetus is no worse for living and dying than if it had never lived, nor harmed relative to prospects it (nonliterally) had prior to conception in the *experiential sense*. By this I shall mean that it does not have bad experiences, and also that it is not deprived of any goods of experience and activity that it might have had if it had not been conceived. I shall leave it open that there is some other, *formal,* sense in which the fetus is harmed in being created to a short life. To indicate this, I shall say the fetus is not *worse(e)* off and not *harmed(e)*. But I shall not assume that if it is harmed in the formal(f) sense, much sacrifice is morally required to avoid the harm(f) per se. Nevertheless, independent of whether it is harmed (e) or (f) it is owed more than not being harmed (e) or (f).

The Minima

Therefore, let us suppose that we should not create persons at will unless we have good reason to believe that they can have some—just how many is deliberately left open—number of years of life with some degree of health and welfare, and let us call these things that they should have the *minima*. I do not pretend to have given an argument that proves this conclusively; nevertheless I shall assume it henceforth. (From the claim that one should not at will create life without the minima, can one separate out the claim that persons should not exist without the minima? Not if the latter claim implies that noncreators as well as creators are obligated to provide the minima.)

The violinist and abortion cases differ in that the same reasons are not available for owing the violinist such minima; that is, we may attach him at will without having good reason to believe that he will receive such minima. Although the greater significance of killing (interfering with life) than of letting someone die might increase not only the efforts we must suffer rather than have him killed but also make us prefer letting the person die straightaway than beginning a saving operation that may result in killing him. That is, because killing adds an additional negative, we may avoid beginning aid without some confidence that we will carry it through. (Hence the possibility that Step 6 is needed.) But this still leaves the following difference between the violinist and abortion cases: Assume that you knew the violinist would fall out of your body and need to be reattached. Then you would not face the problem of killing at all, just the problem again of letting him die. It would then be impossible to construct an argument for beginning aid, since any argument for minima in the violinist case would be based on the need to avoid killing. But in the abortion case, the argument for not creating at will without a reasonable possibility of offering minima would hold strongly even if we had to deal only with letting the fetus die.

A crucial question for our purposes then in the abortion case is how much or what kind of effort persons are entitled to, and from whom, if they are either to have minima or not to exist at all if they cannot obtain minima. In particular, do they have a right to the minima at such costs as (1) being carried in someone's body (I shall assume that this also includes labor, delivery, and the risks and changes of pregnancy), (2) someone's forgoing a heterosexual sex life, or (3) surgery on someone's body (e.g., a caesarian section or to do fetal therapy). (I shall refer to these efforts as *carriage, abstinence,* and *surgery,* respectively.) As we pointed out in Chapter 4, there may be additional psychological costs of an unwanted pregnancy (e.g., the woman may be thought of as part of nature, she may lose her sense of separateness as a person, economic, career, or familial troubles may come) as well as social costs if abortion is not available (e.g., more social inequality between the sexes). Even if we reject the adequacy of the cutoff abortion argument, we should keep these other costs in mind in constructing another argument, and ask whether someone has a right to bodily aid for the minima when these costs follow as well. Though I will not refer to these other costs repeatedly, we can label them costs of *status.*

Veil of Ignorance

One way of determining acceptable costs for achieving minima or avoiding lives without minima might be reasoning behind a veil of ignorance.[7] (The veil deprives us of knowledge about the particulars of our circumstances in society, so that we are unable to allow a bias in our own favor to influence our decision as to what social policies should be established.) But it might seem that this would yield the impermissibility of abortion, for the following reasons: From behind a veil of ignorance, one would not know whether one was a pregnant woman or a fetus. Given that the woman has lived longer than the fetus has and will not die if the pregnancy continues, should one not choose, by banning abortions, to improve the prospects of the worse-off fetus who has had no life so far and will die? (All this, of course, assumes that the fetus is a person.) Although this might seem the way to reason from behind the veil, there are grounds to suspect it, for the type of reasoning it exemplifies would have radical implications if applied elsewhere. For example, if one cared only about length of life and maximizing the number of lives saved, one would also decide behind the veil to kill one older person to save one younger person or to kill one person to save five people. Yet we do not institute such a policy. It may well be that other factors besides equal lengths of life or maximizing individuals' chances to live should direct our reasoning behind the veil.[8] For example, preserving the status of people as to some degree inviolable, where this includes not enduring an imposition on oneself already underway rather than just not being interfered with to begin such an imposition.

We can discover what additional types of factors should weigh behind a veil by engaging in the actual process of moral argument in an unbiased manner.

Factors That Determine Efforts

I suggest that the following factors should be part of our reasoning in regard to how much must be done to provide the minima or to avoid creating lives without them. Much would need to be said to defend the truth of these factors, but I shall not attempt proofs here. Instead, I am concerned with setting out certain factors which at least have some plausibility in order to see what they might imply if they were true. (I shall not even claim that these are necessary implications.)

a. It is important that the new person will be no worse(e) off having lived without minima than never having lived at all and that he will not be harmed(e) relative to prospects he had before being conceived. (I shall continue to interpret these phrases nonliterally and shall not rely merely on the fact that this person literally had no prior prospects and would not have existed.) This factor has already been discussed in the context of the cutoff abortion argument. If these conditions hold even if the minima are not provided, they should help set an upper limit on the sacrifices that are required in order to prevent the occurrence of a life without minima. That is, if the consequences of not providing the minima do not reach a certain negative upper limit, less must be done to achieve the minima. If the new creature would be in large amounts of uncompensated-for pain, and so worse(e) off than if it had never existed, greater efforts might be required of its creator to avoid creating it. (I emphasize that among the ways to avoid such a life is to make efforts to avoid creating the fetus as well as to make efforts once it is alive to give it the minima.)

b. When determining the efforts required of you, we do not necessarily compare the condition in which the new person will be with the condition in which he would have been had other people cared for him. For example, the fact that a millionaire offered my child a better life does not mean that I must meet that standard in order to avoid losing my rights to my child. So the standard "he will be worse off than he might have been" is generally not operative, even if it does have a role with respect to nonexistence in the manner described in Factor a, that is, even if being worse(e) off than not existing at all is a serious matter.

c. There is an "internal logic" associated with creating a new person that may include some idea of human normality. It would be wrong, therefore, to create a human being who was in a happy psychological state when living a life functionally equivalent to that of a normal rabbit. This internal logic may also include the idea that some efforts are required to make the next generation at least as well off as the present one is and that creatures not be created solely as tools for others. These ideas set minimum standards below which we must not fall, but they also help set standards that we need not make great efforts to exceed.

Could we fail to abide by Factor c, even while creating a good life with the minima, if we create for the wrong reason? Consider a family who conceives for the sake of having a child whose marrow might be able to save their other child. They are quite willing to give this child a happy life and love it even if its marrow does not match their first child's. Does this mean there is no problem? Rather than having the child for its own sake, they created it for the sake of another. This may be a problem. (This is a separate issue from taking the child's marrow without its consent. The latter act could be committed on a child who already existed. In this latter case, it might bbe said that the child would later regret not having helped its sibling. This cannot, of course, be said of a child who would not have existed if it had not been created to help its sibling.)

In such cases, it is creating one person for another's sake that is problematic, not creating without the consent of the created, a fact true of all creation.[9] To understand this, suppose that a mother's giving marrow to save her leukemic child was known to make the mother pregnant. This foreseen pregnancy (resulting in a child that the woman would treat well) would not be morally objectionable. Indeed, this shows that it is creating for the sake of saving the child that is morally problematic.

It is often pointed out that the Kantian injunction is to treat people always as ends and never merely as means. It does not require us to treat people only as ends, and so we may treat them as means as long as we also treat them as ends. One way of doing this is to intentionally use them as long as this does not conflict with their interests and in fact promotes their interests. (In the case of already existing people one may need their consent as well.) Then creating a child who will be loved, when one creates it for the sake of its sibling, does not, perhaps, violate the Kantian injunction. But consider the following points, inconclusive as they may be: (1) The child did not need to be created, and so strictly speaking its interests are not served by being created. (2) It may be that in some contexts, our acts can be justified only if at least one of the aims of our acting is that a good come to that person. It is not enough that this benefit is a foreseen side effect, or even intended, but not an aim of the act of creation. (3) This is consistent with the permissibility of aiming at the benefit as a means and not only as an end in itself. (Although sometimes it may also be important that we treat the person solely as an end and not as a means at all.) Suppose that a couple decides to have a child in order to prevent their marriage from crumbling, because they think that loving the child will be the means of saving their marriage. Then they still have the child in order to love it. This is different from having a child to save someone else's life and then loving it. In this case one does not create the child in order to love it as a means of saving someone else's life, for loving the new child is not necessary in order for it to be the means of saving the sick child. (4) Will the child be treated as an equal? Suppose not only that its marrow did not match its sibling's but that it fell ill of a disease that its sibling's marrow could cure. Would we now be willing to impose the same risk on the older child that we would have imposed on the newborn, for the sake of saving the newborn?

To make clearer the internal logic of creating, let us compare it with the ideals and requirements of being a host. They apply independently of whether abiding by the requirements makes the guest better or worse off than he would have been if he had spent the weekend somewhere else. However, suppose that the host is morally responsible for having brought the guest to his house. Then, in addition to any obligations internal to the role, he should see to it that his guest is no worse off than he would have been elsewhere. This is one difference between the logic of being a host and that of being a creator, as emphasized by Factor b.

d. What can be done to a new creature by its creators is constrained, minimally, by the requirements that a stranger would have to meet in dealing with the new creature. For example, its rights as an individual person must be respected. That is, creators do not own their creations and may not treat them less well than strangers are permitted to, simply because they have given them life.

e. No one exists before conception. Therefore one cannot literally be benefited by coming to life. And as we emphasized earlier, no one is literally harmed by not being created. Yet we do and, I believe, we should, consider creating a good life as similar to bestowing a benefit on someone. We can, in good conscience, think of ourselves as creating for the sake of the created person.[10] (If there is no overpopulation, some births can also be benefits to the society at large.) I consider this a prolife assumption.[11]

f. Assume this prolife view of creating, according to which the new person may permissibly be treated, to some degree, as though he is benefiting from receiving life. Then might it not be fair to require him to bear some risks to obtain this benefit? Might this not even include some risk of being worse off than if he had never existed (i.e., the risk of living a life of pain?) Is not the (hypothetical) willingness to accept such risks part of a (prolife) view that life is like a great gift?

An objection to this view is based on the claim that because a person is not waiting to be created, no one will literally be benefited by being created. Because of this, an agent for all future fetuses might easily hold out for better terms, that is, no risks at all for them. Suppose such a model, involving an agent bargaining in this way, were the appropriate basis for determining what is due any given fetus. In this case, an aborted fetus would indeed have been harmed relative to better prospects it had a right to have.

I do not believe that this view of creating—which gives the fetus essentially a veto right—is morally required or is even morally acceptable. We must give weight to the fact that there is no real moral alternative to procreation. We say this on the basis of two imperatives. The first is reproduction of the species or, more appropriately, "the continuation of humanity," insofar as this phrase expresses more than its mere biological continuation. The second imperative is the need of many individual humans to reproduce (as a biological urge) as well as to pass on their individual humanity (in the nonbiological sense). In the face of such strong reasons to reproduce, demanding complete security for the fetus seems unreasonable. Indeed, even in the absence of a strong personal desire to reproduce, many people consider there to be strong reasons to

create just because of the worth of the enterprises of continuing humanity and involving oneself personally in creating a new generation.

Given this, we might almost say that in a non-literal sense, fetuses-to-
be are sometimes under a duty to allow themselves to be created. They
must play their part in the human enterprise. It does seem true, however,
that we allow ourselves to take advantage of their nonexistence before
being in someone's body, in thus requiring their participation. If we
needed the involvement in our project of someone who was already in
existence, had no great personal need to participate in our project, and
might be made worse off by it, it is unlikely that we could justify
involving him without his consent, even if he had a good chance of
receiving a large benefit. But if we required the consent of those who are
created, no creation would be morally permissible.[12]

Suppose that fetuses have been permissibly "called upon" (or
drafted) to participate in the human enterprise, and the reasons that
creators have for creating are (in part at least) as just described. Then
there must be some sort of balancing of interests and rights in deciding
what freedoms the creators have and what the fetuses are owed.

When deciding this, we must consider that all people, including each
generation of creators, once were fetuses and also that every fetus is a
potential creator. To hold the creators to the standard of no risks at all is
also to hold fetuses to that standard when they become creators.

g. Intentionally providing a benefit to someone is a good thing to do
(assuming creating a good life is in some ways like giving a benefit).

h. Intentionally creating usually means creating with the knowledge
that fetal needs will then exist that would not exist otherwise.

i. As things are now, the newly created person requires extraordinary
efforts from others to meet its needs, efforts that we do not usually
require on behalf of just anyone.

j. Although the need for these efforts is usually foreseen as inevitable,
given the creation of the new person, the creators of the new person do
not specifically make it the case that the need for these efforts exists
(rather than does not exist) in the new person. That is, they do not
choose to make the new person dependent when it could have been
independent.

k. There may even be weighty sacrifices necessary in order to avoid
creating the new person. These may include not having a heterosexual
sex life, using dangerous contraceptive drugs, or not trying to have
children when one strongly desires them. At this point it is relevant to

recall the imperatives of humanity as a whole, and of some individuals in particular, to reproduce. There are costs of not reproducing that correspond to these imperatives. (Not permitting abortion can interfere with a need to have children that is not all-consuming by dissuading people from trying a pregnancy for fear it cannot be ended.)

l. This last factor implies that voluntary creators themselves can obtain benefits from creating; that is, they do not create for totally altruistic reasons. Rather, they want children and, in some cases, need children.

I believe that Factors a, b, c in some respects, and e in some respects, and f, g, i, j, k, and l in some respects, help reduce the sacrifices that one is obliged to make either to support the fetus or to prevent its conception. Factors c, in some respects, e in some respects, and d, h, and l, in some respects, work to increase such sacrifices. Next I shall explain how these factors do this, referring to them as the *creation factors*.

Relation Between the Cutoff Abortion Argument and This Discussion

One component of the cutoff abortion argument is the claim that the fetus is losing only the benefit (continuing life) that results from the use of a woman's body and that this is a use which is not required merely to give that benefit. The following discussion can be taken as reexamining Condition 2(a) and (b) that a woman has no special obligation, given that the fetus's simple need is not sufficient, to let the fetus use her body and make the attendant sacrifices. The discussion should help decide how much a woman must do to provide the minima because a creator has a special obligation to provide the minima (at some as yet undetermined cost). So the discussion also bears on Condition 4. Focusing on whether there is such a special obligation reduces the role of Condition 3. Suppose that the fetus has a right to a certain effort to obtain the minima and a woman has a duty to provide it. Then if it were killed to stop that effort, the fetus would lose more than the benefit of efforts to which it had no right and that the woman had no duty to make. But assume that there are efforts to which the fetus has no right and that the woman has no duty to provide in order that the fetus obtain the minima. Then we can assert Conditions 2a and 2b, that there is no special obligation at certain costs, and proceed with the rest of the cutoff abortion argument, as described in Chapter 4, which is supposed to derive the permissibility of killing. Therefore though we criticized its adequacy, the cutoff abortion argument still provides the structure for this new approach.

Rather than begin with a detailed general proposal based on the creation factors, let us use them to construct proposals regarding abortion in different cases. These proposals should not be considered to be attempts at sound arguments for the permissibility or impermissibility of abortion in these cases. Instead, one way to construe them is as hypothetical arguments: If, and only if, it is appropriate to give certain factors a certain amount of weight, will abortions be permissible. (This makes the argument strict but not sound, that is, valid but not necessarily having true premises.) On this view, we hope to show what conditions would have to prevail if abortions were to be justified, without proving they do prevail or in fact have the necessary weight.

Another way to construe the proposals is as attempts to show that certain positions on abortion lie within the scope of the reasonable, since it is not unreasonable to believe that certain factors are true and not unreasonable to believe that they have the needed weight from which to derive a conclusion. (This makes the arguments for this position nonstrict.) We try to demonstrate at least the moral plausibility of certain positions, that they can be reasonably considered to be positions that a reasonably moral person could adopt regarding the moral permissibility of certain abortions and the adequate sensitivity of those who seek them. (All this is not to say that one could not also prove that these proposals are demanded by reason.)

I shall consider these cases as involving individual, one-time pregnancies. Any conclusions we reach about individual cases may have to be modified if there are multiple pregnancies. One reason is that we may sometimes not be able to demand as much of someone who has already made an effort in a previous pregnancy. Alternatively, we may think it appropriate to penalize someone for repeating past negligent behavior.

The frequency with which women get pregnant and require abortions is also an important issue for historical reasons. If risk-free contraception were available and forced sex were an infrequent event, unwanted pregnancies might be rare. But when thinking about whether abortion should be permissible, we must also think of ourselves as deciding whether women in past ages who sought abortions would have been doing something morally impermissible. For in the past, at least, contraception was not very effective; sex was frequently forced; and abortions might have been commonly sought if they had been permitted. We thus should think of ourselves as judging the moral behavior of all those past women (and the doctors and men who helped them obtain their abortions), as well as that of contemporary women and their associates.

Put most generally, we shall propose that maximally there is a duty to provide minima only at cost m, if one could not avoid being pregnant at a cost less than c, *or* there is a duty to provide minima at cost m + x if it was foreseen that much more than m would be required and the cost to avoid being pregnant was less than c.[13] The fact that the new person may be treated as one who benefits from creation, and so may appropriately be asked to take risks for that benefit, has a role in setting what m, x, and c are. If being created would always be worse(e) than never existing or there was a very small chance of "benefiting" from creation, c, m, and x would represent greater efforts. What this very abstract and rough formulation amounts to should become clearer by considering the particular cases.

Proposal 1 for Voluntary Creation Without Foreseeing a Need for Carriage

People who voluntarily, and not for "reasons of state,"[14] create a new person must attempt to obtain the minima for the new person[15] and provide these minima by undergoing up to cost m, where cost m is lower than carriage, abstinence, or surgery. (Alternatively, they may find someone else to provide the minima for cost m.) They need not provide the minima by means of carriage, abstinence, or surgery if before creating the person they could not reasonably predict the need for these to provide minima. (How could abstinence be a sacrifice required of a voluntary creator to get minima? Is it not instead a way of avoiding an unintended pregnancy? I am imagining, for purposes of argument, a hypothetical case in which a creator's abstinence for the rest of his reproductive years would be useful for providing minima to the created person. As we shall see, we can use the fact that someone need not do something for a fetus once it exists as evidence for what someone need not do to avoid creating the fetus in the first place. We must assume that such long-term abstinence is required of the voluntary creator—rather than abstinence merely during pregnancy—to maintain the analogy with avoiding pregnancy.) One implication of this position is that even if one does not foresee cost m as necessary, one may owe it nevertheless.

Let us clarify this proposal. First, being a voluntary creator can be understood as a weaker relation than that of being a parent to a child, because I shall assume that the parent–child relation means acceptance of a long-standing commitment to a dependent person. One point of Proposal 1 is that one need not be an accepting, committed parent in order to have obligations to the person that one has voluntarily caused to exist.

Proposal 1 would be consistent with court decisions refusing to require parents to give up their bodily organs or bodily products (such as bone marrow) for older children if in those cases the parents could not have reasonably predicted the need for those things when they created the child. It also implies that a voluntary creator has no duty to undergo surgery on his body for the sake of the fetus if the fetus develops a problem that could not have reasonably been predicted when it was created. Nor would the creator have a duty, according to Proposal 1, to endure an unexpected[16] serious threat to her health in order to continue a pregnancy.

The Difference Between Parents and Creators: Commitment

The difference between a fetus's rights vis-à-vis its voluntary creators and their duties to it and a child's rights vis-à-vis its parents and their duties to it must be kept in mind. The parents' willingness to undergo carriage, abstinence, and surgery for their children on all relevant occasions could be retained as an ideal without its being a moral requirement. But suppose that parents were morally required to do these things in order to provide the minima, because they are committed to an active, long-term relationship with their offspring. For the voluntary creator and bearer of a fetus who is not yet committed, these moral duties may not exist at all. That is, even if the internal logic of morally correct creating carried with it the obligation to become a parent, voluntary creating alone does not make one a parent.

There currently is much emphasis on encouraging the formation of a parent–child bond as soon as possible in pregnancy, to help ensure that the fetus will receive better care. But this may be a problem if those who are unsure about their willingness to go through with a pregnancy really do have a right to remain more detached. If the fetus is not a person, then the fiction that it is may be useful in getting it better care so that the person-to-be will not be damaged, but it may also lead to unwarranted negative attitudes toward these people who have abortions. It may also lead to inconsistencies, for example, wanting to abort a fetus that is shown to be defective when one would not abort a person if it had a comparable defect. We assume the fetus is a person, but not one with whom someone has been involved in a committed or long-term relationship, especially one where expectations have built up.

When considering the difference between parents and voluntary creators, it is important to define what we mean by commitment. Perhaps we mean only psychological commitment. Parents may well be more psychologically committed to their offspring than creators are to a fetus in the early stages of pregnancy. But it is difficult to see how we can generate duties from the parents' psychological state, because the psychological ease with which someone can make a large sacrifice if he is psychologically committed does not reduce the objective size of the sacrifice. And it seems correct to determine whether someone has a duty to sacrifice something on the basis of the objective size of the sacrifice, not its subjectively felt difficulty or ease. That is, if someone says it is easy for him to give up his life, this does not make it permissible for us to ignore that he is sacrificing something objectively large—his life.[17]

It has been suggested[18] that when one psychologically identifies one's interests with those of another, as a parent may do with a child, the parent's autonomy is not violated if there are duties of aid from him to the child. The reason is supposedly that one's separateness is not infringed upon if one is called upon to aid what one conceives of as an extension of oneself. According to this view, it is not that the subjective, rather than the objective, weight of sacrifices should count. Rather, it is that being required to make an objectively great sacrifice for oneself is different from being required to make it for someone else. (The psychology enters not as the ease with which one sacrifices but in the description of the person—oneself or someone else—for whom one sacrifices.)

There are problems with this view, however. First, there are few cases (if any) in which one has a duty to aid oneself. Therefore, the fact that it is another person with whom one identifies must still be crucial to generating duties to aid. Given this, it seems odd to try to generate duties to aid another person from one's psychological identification with him. This argument for duties may, therefore, still depend on the greater psychological ease associated with aiding a person with whom one identifies. But this does not mean that the objective burden is any less, and it is the objective burden that still seems relevant to whether we should generate duties.

On the other hand, a nonpsychological, normative notion of being committed just encompasses the idea of being responsible for the welfare of one's offspring. From this notion, duties can analytically be generated. Then should someone who has voluntarily created a person be held to have (normatively, nonpsychologically) committed himself or herself to it from the time of its creation? Can we make moral sense of the idea of a trial or grace period during which we are not as responsible for the welfare of the person as its full-fledged (psychologically committed) parents will be?

In order to generate duties for carriage, abstinence, or surgery in parents but not in all voluntary creators, the idea of a morally permissible grace period may have to be employed. Its moral permissibility would depend on the absence of duties being an appropriate risk to impose on a fetus in order to give even voluntary creators time to decide, once the person has been conceived, whether they want to be parents. The ground for this, in turn, has much to do with the fact that being created into a nice life is seen as a benefit that exacts rather unusual costs. Therefore, we might argue, it is appropriate to have the new person accept risks for the sake of a sufficiently high probability (but not a guarantee) of gaining the benefit of life with minima. Alternatively, it may be incorrect to generate such duties to share their bodies, even in parents who are both morally and psychologically committed to their child's welfare, if they could not foresee with reasonable probability that such a need would arise.

Qualitatively Different Sacrifices

We have described cost m as lower than that of carriage, abstinence, or surgery. But suppose that cost m comprised something comparable to the ordinary responsibilities of raising a child for several years. How can we then say that cost m is lower than nine months of bodily support? To repeat what was said above, an important issue here is how we should measure and compare types of impositions or deprivations. For example, someone may find it much more onerous to be without a new car than to be without a constitutional protection of free speech. Yet it is debatable whether a system that exchanges basic liberties for economic status (once a certain level of economic security has been achieved) can be morally justified. Likewise, working for forty hours a week may be more of a burden to someone than having his body examined. Yet we think we have a right to sentence a criminal to hard labor (or service to the community), but not to physical testing or involvement in (even nonrisky) research experiments that intrude on his body. (We may, however, allow the criminal to decide to exchange his hard labor for participation in such research.)

These analogies suggest that the distinction, if there is one, between the use of someone's body and other losses must be drawn qualitatively, in terms of privacy or integrity of the body. It cannot be drawn in terms of degree of strenuousness alone. In this sense, therefore, saying that cost m is lower than that of carriage or surgery is misleading.[19] But further, bodily invasions themselves can differ qualitatively. A forced bone marrow transplant may be strenuous, if not very damaging in the long run. But a nonvoluntary rectal exam, which causes less damage and is not strenuous, may be humiliating. Sexualized bodily impositions can be like this, and real pregnancy (if not the ersatz one in the violinist case) is a sexualized imposition, as well as a strenuous use of a body.

Now that I have (merely) gestured in the direction of a possible qualitative distinction among these efforts, I shall nevertheless continue using such quantitative notions as lower or less than to distinguish among losses and impositions. In addition, remember that abstinence does not involve invasion of the body. In the case of this sacrifice, then, is greater strenuousness the basis of comparison with cost m? Or can we also seek a qualitative distinction based on the importance of sexual expression to personality formation or "mental health" or based on its being less subject to personal control, and allow that a voluntary creator's (or parent's) abstaining from it for many years is not required to save his or her offspring, whereas raising and supporting a child can be required?

If y represents the foreseen probability that a new person will need a sacrifice like carriage if it is to obtain the minima, making Proposal 1 more liberal will mean raising the value of y at which voluntary creators will not be morally obliged to carry the new person if it turns out to need carriage.

What is the rationale behind not ensuring that a new person always obtains minima at the cost of carriage, abstinence, or surgery (let alone at a higher cost), given that we can always foresee that there may be some chance that the new person will need them? One proposed rationale is based on the fact that being created into a nice life is seen as a benefit that exacts a rather unusual cost for its provision. Therefore, it is appropriate to have the new person accept risks for the sake of a sufficiently high probability (but not a guarantee) of gaining the benefit of life with minima.

Proposal 1 and the Cutoff Abortion Argument

Suppose that Proposal 1 is correct for the case it describes and that such a creator is not obligated to provide his fetus with carriage, surgery, or lifetime abstinence in order for it to receive the minima. We then shall apply this conclusion to the general structure of our cutoff abortion argument. In particular, we plug into Conditions 2a and 2b, which are concerned with whether there are special obligations to aid, the claims that voluntary action with no reasonable foreknowledge of the need for carriage carries with it no special responsibility to provide this aid, in part because it is permissible to impose on the fetus the risk of not receiving a benefit and, in part because of the lack of reasonable foreknowledge. However, we noted that the efforts that should be made rather than kill someone (even to stop aiding) may be somewhat greater than the efforts required to aid someone. Therefore, showing that carriage, abstinence, and surgery are not necessary to aid a fetus does not show that they are not necessary rather than have it killed. The next question then, is whether carriage, surgery, and abstinence are great enough impositions to sanction killing the fetus, given the other crucial properties of the abortion case. If they are, then Condition 4 in the argument for abortion can be accepted. Suppose we take seriously the qualitative line between certain bodily invasions and other losses or the invasive surgery is major. It seems reasonable (keeping in mind our discussions of this issue in previous chapters) to regard the losses as significant enough that if they are not required as aid, killing the fetus in order to end them can be justified as well, if the other conditions in the cutoff abortion argument have been satisfied. What remains is Condition 5, that there are no other alternatives that are not excessively costly. As we shall see, taking seriously the need to provide minima may also alter Condition 5, so that the cost difference among alternative procedures, rather than the cost of any procedure judged separately, becomes relevant to deciding whether an abortion is permissible.

I shall refrain from laying out the total set of revised steps in the argument until we reach the end of our narrative discussion of several types of pregnancy. But we may assume for each subsequent proposal for a case that it will be fit into the structure of the cutoff abortion argument in a similar way.

Proposal 2 for Voluntary Creators Foreseeing a Need for Carriage

Now consider a second proposal for a second type of case: Suppose that the voluntary creators knew with certainty before creating a new person that it would need carriage to have any chance at all of receiving the minima. This is the case for most voluntary creators in ordinary pregnancies. It would also be true of a male creator who was told, before conceiving his child, that at the age of one day his child would need to be attached to the father's body for nine months in order to survive.

Proposal 2 states that voluntary creators are morally required to provide carriage for the fetus if they could easily have avoided creating it. For example, they would be required to provide carriage if all that was required was that they not deliberately create.

But is the decision not to deliberately create without cost? Or does it have a personal cost, such as when one is uncertain about whether one will complete the carriage? What is the cost of refraining from creating, when one is uncertain whether or not one will carry the fetus? It is the cost of not having a child that one might otherwise have had because one would in fact have completed the carriage. (Strictly speaking, this cost should be the value of the child to oneself, multiplied by the probability that one would have completed carriage. I consider the child to have value to someone even if he or she wants only to produce genetically related progeny but has no desire to raise the child.) Call this the *refraining cost*.[20]

This cost is presumably lower than the cost of being committed to provide carriage if someone is willing to accept the cost rather than commit herself to carriage. That is, this particular potential creator is more willing to pay the refraining cost than to pay the cost of required carriage, in order to ensure that she does not create a person without minima. (It is worth emphasizing that we do not use the refraining cost to argue for the permissibility of abortion by appealing to the cost of not having a child as a reason for the refusal to go through with the efforts of pregnancy! This would make no sense. Instead, we appeal to the cost of not having a child to explain why we want to be given the opportunity to start a pregnancy without giving up the option to end such efforts as carriage: If we could not retain this option, the cost of starting the pregnancy might seem great enough that we would never attempt it and thereby would suffer a lesser, but still a significant, refraining cost. Because we might have completed the pregnancy, enduring the refraining cost might have been a waste, except insofar as it provided absolute security from abortion by preventing conception.)

Proposal 3 for Voluntary Creators Foreseeing a Need for Carriage

The third proposal also applies to situations in which voluntary creators foresee with certainty the need for carriage. However, unlike Proposal 2, it takes into account the refraining cost. In this way, it reduces the efforts required of the creators, on the principle that if the cost of avoiding an act is great, the cost imposed for performing the act will be less. This takes into account the refraining cost, in part because our reason for "charging" carriage if a woman tries to have a child is not to discourage her from having a child per se but only to ensure minima for the child.

In many cases, however, it would not be correct to take into account—as a cost of not performing an act—the loss of the benefit that would be gained by the act. (This is what is involved in the refraining cost.) For example, it may be morally acceptable for me to harm someone because it would cost me $10,000 to buy the equipment to prevent the act which harms him. It is less acceptable, however, to harm someone because I am in a hurry to make a business deal from which I will make $10,000 in profit that I do not already have. It is even more clearly morally inappropriate to harm someone because if he is harmed I will inherit his $10,000. It is also inappropriate to harm someone because someone else will pay me $10,000 to harm him. In the latter two cases, unlike the first two, someone's harm is a means to secure the $10,000. In the last three cases, the loss of the $10,000 to me is not a cost of my not harming per se; it is an opportunity cost—that is, I lose an opportunity to make $10,000. This also makes it more difficult to use the loss to argue for the permissibility of harming.

A similar problem arises in the context of pregnancy, because theoretically a refraining cost could be conceived of in two ways. Each yields a different view of what efforts should be morally required of a voluntary creator in order to provide minima. Suppose that the refraining cost were something like a rigorous exercise necessary to stop conception. Then the fact that we would have had to pay the cost would help reduce the efforts that could be demanded of us after we had conceived if we decide to create rather than pay the cost. (In this case the refraining cost is like my having to pay $10,000 for equipment to prevent harm, or like the cost of abstaining.) On the other hand, suppose that the refraining cost is defined as the loss of the good produced by creating (which is, in fact, what it is). Then the emphasis is on the fact that the person who acts instead of refrains stands to gain a benefit from acting. (This is on the model of gaining $10,000 if someone is harmed and losing it if not.) Seen in this second way, our analogies suggest that the refraining cost should not reduce the efforts that one is morally required to make after conceiving a child in order to provide minima for it. The reason is that the cost of refraining does not excuse not refraining—not refraining from harming someone or from becoming pregnant, as the case may be—when the cost of refraining is the loss of the possible benefit that is the result of not refraining.

Need Versus Benefit

Perhaps we can resolve this problem by distinguishing between not fulfilling a need and merely not improving one's present state. That is, we must understand that for some people, not having a child leads to a worsening of their present condition, through their unhappiness and frustration. Having a child would prevent their expected prospects from being worse than their present condition. This is consistent with it also giving them prospects that are better than their present condition. Indeed, the presence of a need for x (in this case a child), rather than just a desire for it, may be shown by the fact that one will become worse off than one currently is if one does not have x. This is consistent with x's also making one better off than one currently is.

The proposal is that when the absence of the beneficial outcome of an act (or its omission) results in a situation worse than the status quo, it may be legitimate to let that absence enter our calculation as a cost of not performing the act (or its omission). We may count this cost just as we count the costs of taking the necessary precautions to avoid an act.

Notice, however, that this reasoning does not excuse my harming someone in order to inherit his $10,000, even though I need the money to save myself from a disease that will make me much worse off than I currently am. In this case, someone else's $10,000 is a means to my not becoming worse. The case suggests that it is impermissible to take what belongs to someone else, even if it will prevent me from becoming significantly worse.

We can also imagine a case in which unless I harm a person in the course of carrying out some business, I will lose $10,000 that is already mine. In this case that person's death is not a means to prevent my condition from worsening, but doing what harms him is a way to avoid becoming worse off. Suppose, however, that I am already very well off and that $10,000 does not mean much to me. The fact that I will be worse off if I do not harm does not mean that harming is permissible. This last case suggests that my being worse off than I am now without a particular item does not necessarily mean that I need this item. Rather, whether I need it depends on how badly off I will be if I do not get it, and this may be just as badly off as I am now.

The Need to Benefit

How do we distinguish pregnancy from those cases in which it is impermissible to include the loss of the benefit of a particular behavior as part of the cost of refraining from that behavior? First, we must argue that not having a child will result in a serious loss and so that having a child can be a need. Second, we must emphasize that pregnancy itself does not take away something from someone in order to satisfy another person's need. Rather, it creates someone and, in a nonliteral sense, "gives" him (life) and thereby (nonliterally) benefits him. Indeed, a creator does these things in order to satisfy his own need. So, it might be said, someone needs to (do something like) benefit someone (through creating, however, because she or he does not feel the need to benefit an already existing person). However, it is still true that the fetus will be killed if the pregnancy is discontinued. In nonpregnancy cases, would the fact that someone truly needs to "benefit" someone else play a role in relieving him of some responsibility for continuing to provide such aid? The claim is that it could when other factors hold, such as if the potential beneficiary will not be harmed(e) if aid is discontinued, relative to prospects he had beforehand.

The refraining cost in pregnancy may not always be large, however. (For example, people may think they need children, when they really do not. Of course, they may procreate not because the cost of not having children is so great per se, but because they think that they will lose out on other successes if they do not have children.) If the cost is not large, its role in reducing requirements in pregnancy will likewise be diminished, unless having children does have a real, objective value. Then what may be relevant is that people should sorely miss the children they could have, whether or not they actually miss them.[21] If trying to have children is something they should do, then this may also help reduce the requirements of pregnancy. This is so because if one had something like a duty to have children, it would not be held against one that one began a pregnancy, but it is not true that we have to discharge such a duty at such a large cost as carriage, abstinence, or surgery. That is, one could present the desire to avoid these costs as reasons for not getting pregnant without being accused of shirking one's duty. Therefore, if a woman does her duty, only a lesser cost should be required if other conditions permit (for example, the fetus is not harmed(e), it is permissible to impose risk, and so on).

Proposal 3 and the Chance of Being Born

Proposal 3 also considers it sufficient that there be some significant chance of the offspring's receiving minima, at the foreseen cost to the woman of carriage.[22] That is, it would allow the new person to bear the risk of being aborted in exchange for a significant chance of gaining the benefit of a life with minima, taking into account the costs both of refraining from becoming pregnant (discussed earlier) and of the significant imposition represented by carriage. More specifically, suppose it was foreseen (by everyone) with certainty that the fetus would need carriage in order to receive the minima. At what level would Proposal 3 for these situations set the acceptable risk of the fetus's not receiving the carriage that we know it would need? Perhaps at the same level as the risk of its developing a condition for which it would need carriage, when carriage was otherwise not foreseen as necessary, and yet permissibly being denied carriage by its creators (this level of risk was referred to earlier as y).

Consider an extension of Proposal 3. Suppose that a voluntary creator decides in the middle of her pregnancy that she no longer wants to raise a child. That is, she no longer is willing to do all of m, which is essentially eighteen years of child raising. Furthermore, assume that there is no one available to adopt this new person. A proponent of Proposal 3 might concede that the creator knew that m was necessary in order for the new person to receive the minima, and that m is, in fact, required of voluntary bearers at some point if adoption is impossible. Yet this proponent might also claim that because m is significant, voluntary bearers may at certain times stop carriage because they are not willing to do all of m. In support of this claim the proponent might also point to the high refraining cost. (The proponent of this view may still deny that it is permissible for creators to have abortions because they are not willing to do merely some parts of m.)

This further liberalized Proposal 3 is in fact a revision of Proposal 1. Proposal 1 suggested that all voluntary bearers, rather than just parents, must do all of m for a voluntarily created person if no one else can. Proposal 3 sees a moral requirement to do all of m even if need for it was foreseen only after a grace period for voluntary bearers. Again, the suggested grounds for this grace period—persuasive or not—might be the claim that given the size of m, it is permissible to make a fetus bear risks in order to receive benefits, especially given the refraining cost.

Brief Summary. Let us summarize the overall strategy we have used up to now in deciding how much aid the voluntarily created fetus has a right to and the creator has a duty to give. Voluntary creation of the fetus and foresight to its need for aid move us in the direction of greater responsibility to aid. On the other side, there are the (supposed) facts that the fetus is (in a nonliteral sense) benefited by a life with minima, there is a good intention to create a life that benefits the person born, and the costs involved both in not creating and in supporting a new person are great. These factors move us in the direction of less responsibility to aid and the permissibility of imposing risks on the fetus. It may seem paradoxical that deliberate creation has factors that move morally in two different directions, toward and away from greater responsibility. Yet, I believe, this is a plausible portrayal of its role in a theory of the morality of creating people. Finally, the fact that the fetus is (or is reasonably expected to be) no worse(e) off living and dying than it would be if it had never lived helps set an upper limit to efforts that might be demanded for the sake of preserving it, even in the presence of the goal of seeking more for it than its merely being no worse(e) off than if it had never lived.

Proposal 4 for Unintentional Creation and Voluntary Sex

Consider a third type of case: Suppose that a woman unintentionally becomes pregnant as the result of a voluntary sex act. She always intended to end any unwanted pregnancy; she has a legal right to end such a pregnancy; and she would have had to give up her sex life during her reproductive years in order to avoid the chance of becoming pregnant. Such a person consciously refused to abstain from heterosexual sex even though she knew that abstaining was necessary to ensure the nonexistence of a new person who would have no significant chance of receiving minima.

For this situation, consider Proposal 4: This woman would have needed to make the sacrifice of abstinence in order to avoid a pregnancy in which she must provide carriage if her fetus is to receive the minima. This relieves her of any responsibility for having to provide carriage (at least if she had no good reason to believe that a fetus who is not carried will be much worse(e) off than if it had never existed at all.)

Proposal 4, hence, states that it is not immoral for this woman to use her legal right to abort. The basis for this proposal is the claim that neither man nor woman need abstain totally from sex to avoid causing pregnancy. Nor need one carry someone in one's body if, hypothetically, this prevented pregnancy. If making these sacrifices is the only way to be certain of avoiding pregnancy, then if a woman becomes pregnant she will not be morally responsible (although she is causally responsible) for putting herself in the position in which carriage becomes necessary; and so she is not required to provide this carriage. She is required to do for the fetus what someone who had not caused its existence would be required to do for it.[23]

The Cost of Not Having Heterosexual Sex

Some people believe that for women, heterosexual sex is hardly ever truly voluntary. They believe that coercion, both blatant and subtle, is often responsible for making sexual relations compulsory. Suppose, for the sake of argument, that this were so. Then the cost of abstaining would not be only losing the good involved in sexual relations per se. It would also be whatever (supposed) penalty would be imposed on women for not having sexual relations that constituted the coercive pressure, for example, bad economic or social consequences, physical or mental abuse. Some analyses of coercion claim that there are not only coercive threats but also coercive offers. The former would make one worse off than one would otherwise have been. The latter offer one an improvement in one's prospects one finds it difficult to turn down and deny one an improvement in one's prospects, if one does not behave in a certain way. If there were indeed coercive offers, they would have to be taken into account as well. There are cases in which one could not achieve an improvement in one's condition unless one behaved in a certain way yet the behavior was not coerced. Suppose it were necessary for one to genuinely want to perform a certain act, in order to receive the improvement, and no benefit comes to those who merely pretend to an interest. Even if this does not result in a coerced act per se, men and women might still object to receipt of the improvement being contingent on an act that seems as if it should be irrelevant to a distribution of the benefit.

If there were such a cost for refusing to have sex, then it should be taken into account in discussions of abortion. (This leaves it open that it is still more honorable to pay the cost than to have sex.) If there were not such a cost, it could not be included in the cost of abstaining.

The voluntariness of sex might also be affected by pressures that do not involve costs, for example, social or environmental factors that encourage sexual relations. Even if these factors did not affect the voluntariness of sex, they might send a message encouraging rather than discouraging it. To encourage rather than discourage sex—if birth control is not perfect and if abortion is not permitted—has the effect of making both men and women become creators of persons. Penalizing women for refusing to have intercourse or encouraging them to have intercourse, and then refusing to permit them to have an abortion, would pressure women to risk becoming child bearers. Social encouragement of sexual relations transmits the message that it is right and good to have sexual relations even when no pregnancy is intended. If women follow this advice and then become pregnant, something like "moral coercion" will have put them in the position of being pregnant. On the other hand, one of the costs of not having sex then will be the sense that one has failed to do one's duty. But if the cost to them of doing the good act— which social encouragement says sex is—is carriage (at minimum), then they would not truly have been obliged to perform the good act. This is simply an instance of the view that we have a prerogative not to do the best if the cost to us is great. If women were convinced by society, nevertheless, that they should perform this act and if this made them faultless for being in a position in which duty did not require them to be, then this may be grounds for thinking that they do not have to assume responsibility for continuing carriage. If they had a duty to have sex, they do not have a duty to have it at the cost of carriage. If the cost does not relieve them of the duty, they may perform the duty without paying the cost.

Even if there are no coercive threats or offers on any given occasion, and no encouragement which suggests a duty, some may believe there is a sense in which having sex is still not voluntary. That is, suppose one chooses to have sex for pleasure and out of attraction. Suppose this meant that the occasion and person are chosen voluntarily. Furthermore, suppose that one could have abstained on this occasion and with this person. Still, if one had no choice to abstain altogether, from everyone on all occasions, and if one had counterfactually tried to, penalties would have been exacted, then sex would again not be completely voluntary and not engaging in it would be costly. (This model has some of the features of Locke's case of the man locked in a room, which Locke uses when discussing the problem of free will. The man chooses to stay in the room, but he could not have left if he had wanted to.) Of course, this picture may be an illusion; it may be quite possible always to refuse to have sex, without penalties or the deprivation of any benefits other than those involved in sex per se.

The cost of not having sex per se (i.e., the loss of the good it is in itself) is also a matter of dispute. Some think that sex is a great intrinsic good, an expression of love or an energizing force, crucial to creativity and sociability, with these goods accruing to both men and women. Abstaining then involves a great loss. Some believe that only one party may benefit in these ways, with the other party having sex in order to help the first. Finally, some people dispute the worth of sex for anybody; they may or may not deny its necessity. Therefore, to the extent that an argument concerning the morality of abortion depends on one's view of the value or necessity of heterosexual sexual relations (more frequently than necessary for intentional reproduction) and to whom it is valuable or necessary, the conclusion will be indeterminate.

Suppose that sex relations were important, although they were not thought to be—reflecting the pursuit of real value—in other words an activity we should invent if it did not already exist. Then its real value, and the real cost of abstaining despite beliefs about its value, might count in a prochoice argument as well. But if sex that cannot cause pregnancy is a good option, abstinence from other sex is not costly.

Should Sex Be Avoided?

Ordinarily, if an activity should be avoided because it is bad, engaging in it could not provide a justification if the activity resulted in harm to others. An interesting possibility is that this may not be true when the reason that one should have avoided the activity is also a reason that we give for harming someone in order to end the consequences of that activity. For example, some say that heterosexual sex encourages passivity and loss of independence in women, destroys their intellectual creativity, and is essentially a way to tame and control women.[24] Some say it is the cause of all corruption.

As much as one may reject such views (or their application to one sex rather than both), suppose, for the sake of argument, that such views were true. Suppose also, for the sake of argument, that pregnancy stimulated some of these same psychological states, for example, passivity and loss of independence, and that these were states worth avoiding. If it were true that a woman could not protect herself from becoming passive and dependent by avoiding sex, then, it might be further argued, she would just be trying to minimize the damage by at least avoiding the passivity and loss of independence that pregnancy imposed. If she should be avoiding these things, then she would be trying to do the right thing belatedly rather than never. Notice that this sort of argument will work only if one has a moral duty to avoid certain types of character traits, or to prevent certain states of the world (e.g., the control of women by men). It will not work if one merely has a prudent interest in avoiding certain burdens, because it may behoove one to endure burdens as a result of not doing what one should have done to avoid them in the first instance. But character defects or domination are (prima facie) always to be avoided. Of course if pregnancy even when unwanted, is morally beneficial for a woman this argument will not apply. (There may be other reasons to avoid sex that have this feature of being available as reasons to avoid pregnancy as well. For example, a person may be too young to engage in it: If one should avoid sex because one is too young, one presumably should also avoid childbearing for the same reason.)

A consequentialist counterargument might be made, however: If we permitted abortions on grounds of avoiding (the supposed) passivity induced by pregnancy, no one would be motivated to avoid passivity by avoiding sex (assuming that it induced passivity and that passivity were worth avoiding which are, of course, debatable points). (Note that the view discussed above that one has no duty to have sex at the cost of pregnancy contrasts with a traditional view that one has a duty to be pregnant and so cannot object to the activity which leads to it. The view that if sex is bad for a woman, she might avoid its consequences, contrasts with a traditional view that a woman's wanting to have sex is bad and so she must bear the consequences of it as a penalty.)

The conclusion seems to be that whether sex is worthwhile or to be avoided, we might be able to find a role for it in an argument justifying abortion. (From the legal, rather than moral, point of view, if opinion were divided regarding the worth and importance of sex, would it be permissible for the state to take one position rather than another and to pass laws on the basis of that position?)

Proving One Needn't Abstain

It has been argued that if sex is valuable or the cost of avoiding it is great, one need not avoid it on pain of being responsible for carriage if one becomes pregnant. But could one do more to show that abstinence, in particular, is a large enough sacrifice to have this effect, by considering other cases in which abstinence is not morally required to avoid responsibility for carriage? Suppose that once a child is conceived, a voluntary creator need not abstain or provide carriage to save its life. (We assume here, for argument's sake, that abstinence during pregnancy and long after birth will save a person's life. It is not enough to imagine that abstinence just during pregnancy would prevent miscarriage, as such abstinence would not last the length of one's reproductive years, although abstinence to avoid conception might.) Then, it might be thought, no one else need abstain from sex in order to avoid creating, on pain of having to provide carriage after creation. Such a conclusion would be too quick, however. For as we noted, having the good intention to create a nice life might help reduce the efforts, even foreseen ones, morally required to do so, and such an intention is not present if one creates unintentionally.

A second case worth thinking about is one in which abstinence would be physically required to avoid pregnancies that we foresee with certainty will unavoidably miscarry. That is, consider a woman who cannot tell in advance on which occasion of intercourse she will conceive, and she always miscarries whenever she does conceive. In her case total abstinence would be required to avoid pregnancies that will certainly miscarry. Suppose that she has no moral responsibility to abstain in order to prevent conceiving a fetus without minima coming about in *this* way. Then should she have to abstain to avoid becoming pregnant or else be required to provide carriage later if this will help the fetus gain the minima?

Even more farfetched, but also useful to consider, is a case in which a woman can avoid becoming pregnant, and thus having a miscarriage, only by providing carriage to a third party. Assume that she is not obligated to abstain or to provide carriage to a third party in order to prevent starting a pregnancy that would end in miscarriage. Should she then be obligated to provide carriage for a fetus that exists only because she did not abstain, if only by abstaining could she have prevented the pregnancy?

A possible problem with these two cases, however, is that it may be morally permissible to require lesser sacrifices in order to avoid creating a person than to save that person once it has been conceived. There are at least two separate reasons that this might be so: (1) The efforts made to avoid a pregnancy, unlike comparable efforts made after conception to save the fetus's life, do not result in a good life's being lived by a new person. (2) One cannot be sure that abstinence is in fact necessary on each occasion it is practiced to prevent a fetus without minima (that is, not all sex acts would result in pregnancy). Therefore, most of the sacrifice is probably wasted.

Suppose that the efforts that could be required to avoid creation were lower than those that could be required to save the resulting fetus. Then we could not automatically conclude that one need not provide carriage in order to save a life if one had failed to make prenatal efforts, just because one need not carry or abstain to prevent conceiving a fetus that could not possibly be saved once it was conceived. It would be consistent to say that a person had done nothing wrong in not abstaining to avoid a pregnancy that would certainly end in miscarriage, and yet, once pregnant as a result of a voluntary sex act, she is still obligated to carry the fetus.

The conclusion of our discussion so far is that we cannot automatically say that no woman is obligated to abstain (or provide carriage) to avoid pregnancy on pain of being required to carry during pregnancy, just because a voluntary creator is not obligated to abstain or carry if these actions would save her offspring's life. Nor can we say that she is not obligated to carry in order to save a fetus whose conception she caused but did not intend, just because she is not obligated to abstain (or carry) to prevent a pregnancy that will end in miscarriage.

Perhaps the correct way to show that abstinence is a large enough sacrifice that failing to make it will not result in responsibility for carrying a fetus is as follows: We cannot require a woman to abstain from sex during her childbearing years just to prevent a fetus existing that will not have minima, either by total abstinence when *all* sex leads to pregnancies that miscarry or to save an existing fetus that she did not create. The reason is that the fetus will be no worse(e) off living and dying than it would be if it had never lived, it should bear risks for the chance to gain the benefits of life and also because of the significant size of the sacrifices to the woman. Avoiding the existence of fetuses that will not have minima counts for something, per se, but it does not morally require abstinence or carriage.

Next we should decide what factors could add to the weight that preventing a life without minima would have in itself. Intentionally creating a fetus, given that we wish to avoid lives without minima, might add weight. But it will not if the intention to create a good new life has a tendency to reduce responsibility for sacrifices. Being in a position that requires carriage to save the fetus because abstinence was required to avoid this position adds possibly not saving (versus preventing) a life to the case where all sex would lead to miscarriage. But the chance of sex causing pregnancy is less than in that case and there is an excuse or justification for being pregnant.

In addition, the fact that abstaining is necessary to avoid becoming pregnant might relieve one of the responsibility to make the lesser efforts, cost m, once the fetus has been conceived. This is so even if these efforts are required of voluntary creators. This amounts to the claim that those who voluntarily create new persons have greater responsibilities for them than nonvoluntary creators do. If this is true, it would be wrong to think that we must not place any greater burdens on those who deliberately have fetuses than on those who do not, simply because people have a right to have children and pay a refraining cost if they do not try to exercise this right when uncertain that they will complete a pregnancy.

Proposal 5 for Unintentional Conception by Means of Voluntary Sex

Consider another (sterner) answer to this same question, what do those who conceive unintentionally, but as the result of a voluntary act, owe to their creations? Suppose that a woman would have been obligated to pay cost m to avoid producing a person who would not receive the minima. (Again, we imagine for the sake of argument that paying cost m could be efficacious in preventing pregnancy.) But cost m turned out to be insufficient, since abstinence was, in fact, necessary to prevent conception. Then, even though this woman did no wrong in not abstaining, she should pay cost m once she has conceived, to prevent the fetus's not receiving the minima.

A ground for this claim would be that even if one is blameless in getting into a situation that causes someone to exist who has a right to have cost m expended, if one actually confronts the person, one should pay cost m. (This assumes that one has not already expended certain strenuous efforts to avoid being in this situation, for such strenuous efforts might be deducted from cost m.) But, it could be counter argued, if one's desire to avoid paying cost m in pregnancy lead one to abstain, abstinence would, after all, be required.

Of whom can cost m be demanded? The stern argument says that cost m can be demanded of anyone to prevent his causing a person without minima. But does just any woman have to pay cost m (or its equivalent) to avoid becoming pregnant? It might be argued that she does not, on grounds of the uncertain usefulness of the sacrifice on any given occasion, no fetus will exist who is helped to live a better life because of such efforts, and because she is not in a voluntary bearer relationship to a fetus. Would just any woman (e.g., analogous to an innocent bystander) be morally obligated to pay cost m once she finds herself in a situation confronting a fetus who needs to have cost m expended in order to receive the minima? Presumably not. Has a woman who has conceived because of a blameless voluntary act thereby increased her responsibility to pay cost m for the sake of the fetus? It seems not. Would this conclusion be altered if we take very seriously the idea of agent regret? Agent regret is unlikely to yield an obligation to do as much as m. In the case of rape, not only is there no voluntary sex act by the pregnant person, but she also is not like just any bystander who sees a fetus in need. She is (often) a victim who has suffered. Therefore, she is probably less obligated to aid her fetus, having earned a right to even greater self-concern.

Two questions have been dealt with in this discussion. First, whether the aim of saving a fetus from dying without the minima, when it is no worse(e) for living and dying than if it had never existed, is, in itself, a sufficient reason for just anyone's being obligated to expend cost m (or its equivalent)? Second, if this is not a sufficient reason, could nonnegligently conceiving a fetus increase a woman's moral responsibilities so that she became obligated to expend cost m? I have suggested that it is reasonable to answer no to both these questions. Intentionally creating a person, however, might add enough weight to obligate a voluntary creator to pay cost m (if not carriage or abstinence). Suppose that, in itself, providing the minima is not worth enough to obligate just anyone (unrelated to the fetus) to pay cost m and that nonnegligently conceiving does not raise responsibilities as high as cost m. Then may we conclude that cost m could not be morally required in order to prevent the conception—on the hypothesis that this would be useful—of a fetus who we know will unavoidably receive no minima? The cost that is required to prevent causing a state of affairs could be higher than the cost someone would have to pay to help correct a state of affairs that she did not cause. That first cost cannot be set automatically by looking at the second cost. Instead, it must be determined by considering how serious it is that a fetus came to exist without the minima and so how serious it is to have conceived such a fetus as an unintended effect of a voluntary act. If not just any woman has to avoid even a certainly foreseen pregnancy at the price of cost m, then her responsibility for paying cost m should be tied (if it is tied to anything) to having performed a voluntary act which could easily have been avoided, if she foresaw that her act would create a fetus. Alternatively, paying cost m should be tied to having intentionally conceived a fetus when the cost of avoiding conception was not too high.

In sum, it seems that we should be able to distinguish between, on the one hand, efforts that can be required to avoid creating a fetus or can be required of those who produce a fetus despite reasonable efforts to avoid so doing and, on the other hand, efforts that can be required of voluntary bearers and parents and those who voluntarily have sex when the cost of avoidance is low.

Contraception

We have discussed avoiding unintended pregnancies by making efforts m, carriage, abstinence, or surgery (on the counterfactual hypothesis that these could prevent pregnancy). This helped us decide whether such efforts would be necessary to continue an unintended pregnancy begun by a voluntary act and to provide the fetus with minima. The use of contraceptive devices is a way of reducing both the chances of pregnancy and the cost of avoiding pregnancy. Nevertheless, contraception does not diminish the chances of avoiding pregnancy as much as abstinence does, and using contraception has its own cost. Our discussion of unintentional pregnancy resulting from voluntary acts should really be repeated considering whether refusal to pay the cost of contraception (rather than abstinence, m, or carriage) should make people responsible for providing carriage in order to ensure that their fetuses obtain the minima.

On the basis of the preceding discussion, is it reasonable to believe that we need not require someone to increase significantly her risk of a stroke or cancer if this were the effect on her of contraception, in order to avoid responsibility for providing carriage if she does become pregnant?

Suppose that contraception is relatively costless.[25] Then its use could well be required on pain of responsibility to carry the fetus if by not using it a woman became pregnant. If a woman does use contraceptives, then, it might be argued, this should be viewed not merely as reducing the number of occasions on which she might become pregnant, but also how much she owes to an unintended fetus. That is, it may be seen as a way of engaging in sex nonnegligently, in which case it should limit the size of the effort a woman would have to make if she became pregnant anyway. (This is on the assumption that she need not abstain to avoid becoming pregnant or provide carriage if she does not abstain, and that the chance of pregnancy is sufficiently small.)

Proposal 6 for Unintended Pregnancy Resulting from Voluntary Negligent Sex

Consider another type of case: Suppose that there is an unintended pregnancy as the result of a voluntary sex act and that the pregnancy could have been avoided at small cost. Suppose also the pregnant person never intended to continue with the pregnancy, although she knew that carrying the fetus to term would be necessary for it to have minima. Furthermore, there is a law entitling such a pregnant person to an abortion, and we wish to know whether this law is morally acceptable.

Assume that a new person is sometimes entitled to have minima at cost m from a voluntary creator. Some might suggest (as already noted) that such costs are also required to prevent one's own acts from leading to a new person with no significant chance of minima. Others (as also already noted) might argue for a lower level of cost to avoid pregnancy, on the ground that the participants' responsibilities will be greater if a voluntary act whose avoidance is relatively costless caused the conception of this fetus. Still, the pregnant woman in this example has certainly done something wrong if she failed to pay even a very small cost to avoid a pregnancy that will definitely end by killing a person whose existence without minima is to be avoided. Having failed to do what she should have done, might she then reasonably be made to provide carriage throughout the pregnancy? Furthermore, on evidence of such irresponsibility, should she be required to give up the new person for adoption at birth?

Perhaps the answer to both questions is yes, especially for repeated such offenses. (This assumes that the wrong behavior cannot be excused on the ground that the pregnant woman could not avoid being morally irresponsible. For example, some might argue that the type of behavior thought to be in keeping with a stereotype ideal of feminine personality itself militates against the frame of mind and type of will necessary for responsible behavior in sexual matters. For example, one reason given for not using contraception, even when it raises no health problems, is that some male partners do not want it to be used; they prefer that the woman be susceptible to becoming pregnant.[26] The woman's unwillingness to resist this preference of her male partner may be sanctioned by some models of appropriate female personality. If it is psychologically possible to violate the model, but the woman does not for fear of the cost that will be imposed on her, what is the cost? Is it a sufficiently high cost to excuse her failing to alter her conduct?)

The general idea here is that in itself, avoiding a life that will be without minima may be worth cost $m - x$ (for some value of x) to those who have not caused such a fetus's conception. Intending the pregnancy can change the required efforts to cost m. But not taking small precautions to prevent the pregnancy, in the absence of both the good intent to create a nice new life and a significant chance for the new person to gain such a benefit can raise the required efforts to cost $m + x =$ carriage. Therefore, the wrong of not taking simple precautions can raise the required efforts above even those required in an intentional pregnancy.

A counterargument to this conclusion might raise the following point: If what makes it wrong to engage in unprotected intercourse is a property that unprotected intercourse shares with pregnancy, then perhaps we should stop at the second stage what we failed to stop at the first. Let us place this point in context: There are at least two reasons for avoiding unprotected sex acts and intentional pregnancies that are frivolous. One reason is the fate of the fetus if abortions are permitted to end the pregnancies. The second reason is the condition of women if abortions are not permitted to end pregnancies. That is, women will frequently be pregnant, if birth control, abstinence, or abortion is not used. If the first reason weighs most with us, we will punish those who irresponsibly become pregnant, by not allowing them to have an abortion. By doing so, however, we thereby will be working against the second reason, in that more women will become pregnant. If we care that they not be pregnant, merely because it is a burden to them, then not having taken the proper precautions, it might behoove them to suffer the burden. If we care that women not be frequently pregnant because we thought it bad for their character or for the social equality of the sexes, then even failing to make small efforts to avoid sex might not lead to a requirement to carry. Even supposing these alternative grounds for wanting them not to be pregnant, if we give greater weight to the fate of the fetus, then the property that unprotected sex and pregnancy share will support a prohibition on abortion.

Some other points may help in considering this issue. It seems that responsible individuals are required to make efforts less than carriage in order to avoid pregnancy. Further, if they make the efforts that are required to avoid pregnancy but the pregnancy occurs nevertheless, the effort required to provide the minima will again be less than carriage. If all this is true, can it be that the efforts that an irresponsible person owes to her fetus are correctly set at carriage? If the efforts required as punishment should be set lower but carriage is the only effort that would do any good, it would still be wrong to require carriage. The male partner in the case of negligent sex will also be responsible for equally heavy burdens on behalf of the fetus. If, however, he is unable to be of use to the fetus, unavoidable sex inequality will result. This may be relevant in deciding what the woman should do. Contributions (e.g., financial) by the man to the woman may equalize some of the unequal burden.

Overall Summary

Let us summarize these six proposals for typical cases. A person is the sort of creature that has a right to have its voluntary creators try to provide minima for it even at cost m to themselves. These voluntary creators (or their substitutes) have a duty to pay cost m (if it is less than carriage, abstinence, or surgery). If this is so, then this type of creature has a right, at most, to have other potential causers of its existence pay cost m or less to avoid its living without the minima. The claims will be true if the creature is no worse(e) off without the minima than never living at all and also if it did have a significant chance to gain the benefits of life from voluntary creators. Alternatively, this significant chance can serve as compensation to it for ending up worse(e) off than never living. The responsibility of the potential creator includes efforts that she or he morally must make to prevent the creature's conception. Suppose that up to cost m efforts can be required but are useless to prevent conception, because only carriage, abstinence, or surgery would be sufficient. Then carriage, abstinence, or surgery cannot be required of a creator if the pregnancy occurs. Carriage, abstinence, or surgery can be required only if he or she has failed to do what he or she should have done to avoid conception. (Note that both sexes can be required to make efforts to avoid conception and to make postnatal sacrifices.)

Furthermore, it is really less than cost m that should be required of someone to prevent conception. One way to conclude this is to consider that before conception there is no voluntary bearer relationship in existence, there is no life that will be saved or benefited by paying cost m, only one that will be prevented, and the efforts may be wasted if conception would not have occurred each time the participants had sex. The problem here is to find out how much a potential creator, who is not involved in any voluntary bearer relation with a new person, is morally obligated to do in order to prevent that person from being conceived, when the new person ideally should not exist without minima, should be provided with minima at cost m from voluntary creators, but can itself be expected to bear risks.

The general direction of the proposals regarding particular cases is to acknowledge the responsibility for avoiding the conception of a life that will not have the minima. But because life is seen as a good thing to be born to, it is acceptable to impose risks on the fetus and even to reduce the responsibilities of those who intentionally try to produce a good new life. In some respects those who intentionally create a child have greater responsibilities than do those who try to avoid pregnancy but get pregnant anyway. And in some respects they have fewer responsibilities than do those who do not make sufficient efforts to avoid pregnancy. This view takes seriously whether there is a real chance for a new life with the goods of life and also which intentions caused such a chance. That is, it is concerned with whether the creators intended to produce a significant chance at a good life or, rather, produced a significant chance merely because there was uncertainty, caused by social conditions, as to whether they would be able to obtain an abortion.

If the more liberal of the proposals suggested are reasonable, abortions may be permissible to end many pregnancies, even if the fetus is a person, simply because the woman does not wish to share her body or undertake parental responsibilities that cannot be shifted to others. Keep in mind, however, that there are many claims on which this conclusion depends, and that the truth of many of them is difficult to determine (even, for example, what efforts we may kill to avoid), so it would be rash to be too confident about the conclusion. Additionally, in presenting the proposals as reasonable possibilities we have not said what all the alternative reasonable proposals are, and why we choose these rather than others. But it was the point of the section on "Liberalism, Equality, and the Theory of Value," to suggest that we need do no more than show that permissible abortion is one morally reasonable option.

Furthermore, this conclusion is subject to how Condition 5 should be understood in the light of a concern for providing the minima. The cutoff abortion argument permits a woman to refuse to make efforts that, considered individually, are greater than she would have to make in order to avoid having the fetus killed, given the other circumstances of abortion. But if there is great concern about providing the minima, then the differential standard may be more appropriate, that is, comparing the cost of the procedure resulting in death with the procedure preserving life and determining whether the difference required for the life-preserving procedure is greater than someone would have to undertake to avoid having the fetus killed. May the costs include the later consequences to her of that procedure? Yes. May the consequences include the later consequences to her of the success of that procedure (i.e., the consequences of someone's being alive)? No, with the following exception. It is permitted not to endure a procedure that itself is (alone or plus consequences of the procedure itself) differentially (i.e., in comparison with the alternatives) so large that the cost is greater than necessary in order to avoid having the fetus killed even if the desire not to endure the procedure stems from concern over what the success of the procedure involves. That is, she need not make a big effort to bring about an event she does not like; she may begin by not wanting an event to occur and wind up intending not to make a big effort to bring about an event she does not like. This differs from simply intending the nonexistence of the event itself (i.e., acting or refraining from action to acquire the nonexistence of the new person).

One significant limitation on requiring a procedure that is only a bit more burdensome than an abortion that kills the fetus is that there is always a straw that breaks the camel's back. That is, even when an additional burden is small, it may come in addition to so much that it simply cannot be demanded.

The Benefit–Burden Approach

Again, it may be best to understand this discussion of abortion, which builds on the cutoff abortion argument, as an attempt to explain the sort of reasons, or types of arguments, that someone who holds certain views about abortion could give for these views. It is not presented as a knock down argument for holding such views. Because the distinctive elements of the discussion are that a fetus should bear some risks for what is comparable to a benefit of life, and an emphasis on the burdens of abstaining from sex, refraining from having a child, and carriage, as well as benefits to the creator, I shall call this approach to abortion the *benefit–burden approach.*[27] Let us now describe the five conditions of the benefit–burden approach, corresponding to the conditions in the cutoff abortion argument, for three types of cases:

Rape

1a. Need for support in a woman's body does not by itself give a right to have such aid begun, or a duty to begin it, even for a person who may claim the minima from someone.

1b. Need alone does not give a right to have continuing aid, or a duty to provide it.

2a. No special obligations to begin aid.

2b. No special obligations to continue aid.

3. By being killed, the fetus loses only the life provided by the bodily support that is not justified by need or special obligation; it is not harmed(e) relative to prospects it (nonliterally) had before being conceived; and it does not lose anything that the woman is causally responsible for its having that it could retain independently of her.

According to the benefit–burden approach, and to the cutoff abortion argument, in cases of rape, many abortions may be permissible even if the fetus would be harmed(e) relative to its preconception prospects. Therefore, this condition is sufficient but not necessary.

　4. We kill in order to stop efforts significant enough to justify such killing, given the other conditions.

5. In this context, the difference in cost between killing the fetus and any other procedure that saves the fetus's life is excessively large, given the aim of not killing it.

Voluntary Pregnancy Forseeing the Need for Carriage

1a. Same as the preceding Condition 1a.

1b. Same as the preceding Condition 1b.

2a. No special obligation to begin carriage for a fetus outside the womb that she created if the refraining cost is sufficiently high, the fetus is not harmed(e) by living and dying relative to (nonliteral) preconception prospects, and/or the chance of receiving the "benefit" of life is sufficiently high that we may impose a risk of its not receiving it, even perhaps so high that we may impose a risk of its being harmed(e).

2b. No special obligation to continue carriage of a fetus begun in one's body for the reasons given in Condition 2a.

3. Same as the preceding Condition 3.
4. Same as the preceding Condition 4.
5. Same as the preceding Condition 5.

Voluntary Sex Forseeing (a Possibility of) Pregnancy, and Its Requirements

1a. Same as the preceding Condition 1a.
1b. Same as the preceding Condition 1b.
2a. No special obligation to provide carriage if the abstaining cost is sufficiently high and the fetus is not harmed(e) by living and dying relative to its preconception prospects.

We cannot here add, "and/or the probability of a pregnancy in which the fetus will be harmed(e) is sufficiently low." This is because the benefit–burden approach does not allow us to run risks unless there is expected benefit to the fetus, and we have assumed there is none in this type of pregnancy for an abortion will definitely be sought. We need the self- and assisted-defense argument to use a thesis concerning the permissibility of causing the risk of harm(e). That is, if it is permissible to cause a certain risk of harm, because it is costly to avoid being in the situation where one will harm then one need not do certain things to aid to prevent harm, and if one is already doing these things, one may stop.

2b. No special obligation to continue carriage, for the reasons given in Condition 2a.
3. Same as the preceding Condition 3.
4. Same as the preceding Condition 4.
5. Same as the preceding Condition 5.

Do the Numbers Count?

This entire discussion has proceeded as though we were talking about the moral permissibility of abortion in a single instance. This is true, even though when we considered the status costs of not permitting abortions, we included the effect of many pregnant women not having access to abortions. But do the numbers count; that is, if there would be many abortions do the arguments for permissibility become weaker? When considering this question, we must remember that if the fetus is the sort of creature that should not be created at will without the minima, the minima will have a structural role somewhat analogous to that had by being harmed(e) relative to prospects it had before attachment. That is, it is a reason to avoid creation.

First, if there are large numbers of rapes, does the fact that the fetus will not get the minima make a difference to permissibility? It seems unlikely that numbers count here, because even if many fetuses were harmed(e) relative to prior prospects, this would not mean that women who have been raped must bear the burden of preventing the fetuses prospects being so harmed(e).

Now consider intentional pregnancies. If the risk of not getting minima can be justified on a case-by-case basis from the point of view of the fetus's interests, by its chance of getting the "benefit of life," and the refraining cost is sufficiently large, then numbers of abortions sought in intentional pregnancies need not count either. (Of course, if we cannot justify terminating in a single such case, numbers are beside the point.)

What about numbers of abortions in cases of voluntary sex acts leading to pregnancies in which there was never any intention of continuing? Suppose that not getting minima is given a role in the argument similar to being harmed(e) relative to preconception prospects. If the number of killings that would occur is high, then even if the abstaining cost is also high, we might want to interfere with some abortions in these cases. That is, we might want to require abstaining costs from men and women until we reduce the number of occasions in which killings to detach are necessary. (For the same reasons, would we also want large numbers of women each of whom will certainly miscarry in her first pregnancy, to avoid such pregnancies, even if undertaken for the sake of a second successful pregnancy? Here the deaths would be foreseen, but no killings to detach would occur.)

This result is comparable to the one we got when we increased the numbers in the case in which car driving was imagined to lead to the attachment of a pedestrian and his detachment would harm him relative to his preattachment prospects. If not driving is costly to one person and to society and there is some moderate risk, then the driver would not be required to remain attached. But if the numbers of people in these types of cases increased and many pedestrians were put at risk, we might want to reduce the number of acts of driving allowed to each member of the society who might cause attachments. (In the case of pregnancy, both men and women cause attachments, and so they both would need to abstain, even though the fetus becomes attached only to a woman.)

Two disanalogies between pregnancy and the driver case should be considered. First, pedestrians who have no need to be attached may nevertheless, on some occasions, be drivers as well and so have an interest in a policy permitting the risk of attachment and detachment. In the case of abortions, must we also consider that fetuses have some probability of being adults with an interest in not abstaining on pain of carrying? In general, this may be true of fetuses, but not in cases in which there is no significant chance of their being carried to term, and that is what we are supposing is the case in merely foreseen pregnancy due to voluntary sex acts if abortion is permitted. Second, the fetus will not really be harmed(e) relative to its preattachment prospects (e.g., it will not lose out on goods of experience and activity it would otherwise have had or suffer pain). Is its failure not to get what it should have (minima) as well as the possibility that it is harmed(f), from a formal point of view, not so serious a concern when it occurs on a mass basis as the pedestrian's being killed when he would otherwise have been all right?

If the numbers become excessive in cases of voluntary sex and unintended pregnancy, and avoiding the cost of killing so many people is given first priority, there would still be room for disagreement over whether the abstaining cost or the cost of carriage is greater. For example, suppose that women place the carriage cost higher than the abstaining cost, but there is heavy social encouragement to have sexual relations. Such social encouragement transmits the message that it is right and good to have sexual relations, even when no pregnancy is intended. If women follow this message—but for them the cost of carriage is higher than the abstaining cost—abortions may once again be permissible in these cases, because something like moral coercion will have put women in the position of being pregnant. That is, given the cost to them of being pregnant if they may not have an abortion, it would not have been their duty to perform the good act (which social encouragement says sex is) at this cost. If they were convinced by society that they did have such a duty, and this made them faultless for being in a position in which duty did not require them to be, they would not be morally responsible for continuing carriage. If they really should have sex, but not at the cost of carriage, they should have sex and be relieved of carriage. If the costs of abstaining were made even greater by penalties imposed for not having sex, there may again be no duty to carry if pregnancy occurs.

A conflict over whether carriage or abstaining is the weightier loss, given that abortions will be limited, is, of course, only one type of conflict. We can describe six possible "value rankings" among the three possible outcomes, killing, carriage, or abstaining, on a scale of 1–3 which represents decreasing opposition to the forms of conduct.

	A	B	C	D	E	F
killing	1	3	2	1	3	2
carriage	2	1	3	3	2	1
abstaining	3	2	1	2	1	3

Position A could represent the situation we have been discussing in which society prohibits killing, and in response to this an individual may avoid sex rather than carry. Alternatively, it could represent an individual who above all wishes to avoid directing or doing a killing, but will avoid sex rather than carry.

Let us continue to take these as positions held by individuals. Then B represents an individual who above all wishes to avoid carriage, but not by abstaining, and so will direct or do a killing.

C represents someone who will not abstain and will carry rather than kill.

D represents someone who above all will not kill and would rather carry than abstain. Interestingly, the people represented by C and D, despite having a different internal structure to their values, wind up acting in the same way; they will not avoid sex for the sake of avoiding carriage that they will not end by killing.

E represents someone who will not give up sex but will do or direct a killing to end carriage. E and B, despite the differences in the internal structure of their values, windup killing to end carriage. If there were only two options, abstain or carry, then the difference between these two would show up. (The same is true of C and D.) B would abstain, and E would carry.

Finally, F represents someone who would abstain rather than kill, but if pregnant will kill rather than carry.

Two rather surprising conclusions we seem to have reached are, first, according to the benefit–burden approach, numbers of killings would not matter in the case of intentional pregnancies, and, second, that even if a defense of the permissibility of any individual abortion can be given for reason of abstaining costs, sufficiently large numbers of such acts by individuals might reduce the permissibility of abortion in cases of voluntary sex with pregnancy as a possible side effect. (One suggestion for lowering the numbers, which to some degree makes a principled distinction between cases, is to prohibit repeat abortions by the same individual in cases in which sex is voluntary and pregnancy a possible consequence. Another suggestion is insisting on the use of birth control.)

The Benefit–Burden Approach and the Failure to Have an Abortion

In concluding this presentation of the benefit–burden approach, I shall address two possible difficulties. First, it might be thought that because this approach places great weight on avoiding the creation of people without the minima, it implies that there is a moral obligation to have an abortion if a fetus is found to be so handicapped that it will not obtain the minima. If the approach recommended this, it would support the claims of some that women who do not abort deformed fetuses are liable for producing "wrongful life."

Suppose that the fetus is not a person at the time that abortion is possible and that there are no other real moral objections to destroying it. In that case, holding a woman responsible for "wrongful life" because she failed to have a safe abortion might have some merit. But holding her responsible for "wrongful life" will not necessarily be correct if the fetus is a person. That is, a woman may refuse to take advantage of the moral permissibility of abortion, on the grounds that it is in the interest of a person once conceived to remain alive as long as its life is no worse for it than nonexistence would be. It may be true that we should not begin creating a person without aiming for the minima. But this does not mean that once people actually have been conceived, we should not keep them alive even if they will not obtain the minima. If their lives are still not worse than not existing at all, perhaps they should be kept alive until they request not to be. (Recall that the minima provide more than enough to make a life no worse than not existing at all.) Analogously, we might argue for the moral obligation to use birth control in very poor countries where the minima cannot be obtained, but not for the moral obligation to kill people in such countries whose lives fall below the minima.

There is a second difficulty. We have argued on the assumption that the fetus is a person throughout pregnancy. We emphasize this, as it is not possible to automatically use either the cutoff abortion argument or the benefit–burden approach to justify aborting a fetus if there is a stage when it is a person if it is not a person throughout pregnancy. That is, if the fetus were a person from conception, there would be no time when it would be possible to abort a nonperson. Therefore, it matters less whether one has an early or late abortion, for one will be aborting a person whenever one aborts.

But, if the fetus develops into a person, then abortion would be possible at a time when we would not then be killing a person. If killing a nonperson (even one with the potential to become a person) is a far less serious issue than killing a person is, in failing to abort early we will have lost the opportunity to perform a morally less serious act.[28] Suppose that we want to have an abortion and the fetus has already developed into a person. We cannot simply argue for the permissibility of killing a person in the manner that we have done so far. Rather, we must argue for the permissibility of killing a person given that we failed to take advantage of the opportunity to end the pregnancy without killing a person. This may be harder to do than simply arguing for the permissibility of killing what was always a person. The reason is that it may be correct to penalize someone for failing to perform the morally less serious act by restricting permission to perform the more serious act. Likewise, suppose that the fetus develops in morally significant stages and that it is morally worse to kill it at a later stage rather than at an earlier one, even if it is never a person. Then arguments for the permissibility of killing a creature that had always had the properties of a later-stage creature need not necessarily justify killing it if we could have killed it when it had different properties.

I shall not consider in detail what restrictions should apply to later abortions if the fetus is considered to develop into a person. But it is worth noting that any penalties should be tempered by the reasons for delay.[29] Indeed, the general structure of one's thinking about this issue is a variant of the general question we have already considered, How much must someone do in order to avoid producing a person whom she will then kill? Having an abortion early then becomes analogous to avoiding the conception of a person, and we must consider the analogous questions: whether an early abortion was not undertaken because of coercion, because of the great efforts required, or intentionally. However, note that in regard to the development hypothesis, not having an early abortion (though analogous to not avoiding conception) is to fail on a second chance given to one to avoid harming a person. The first chance was to avoid a literal conception. If the fetus is a person from conception on, we have failed to avoid harming a person only once before the abortion. There can be any mix of reasons for not avoiding a literal conception and not having an early abortion. For example, one could voluntarily begin conception but be forced to delay terminating a pregnancy. How seriously we consider the reason for failing to have an early abortion may vary with why we did not avoid a literal conception. That is, there will be an interaction effect. For example, a voluntarily delayed abortion may follow either a forced pregnancy or a voluntary pregnancy. The need to have more time to consider the question is understandable in the first case but is not as understandable in the second.

It is ironic that those who take the so-called hard line, that a person exists from conception onward, provide a premise that could make later abortions more permissible than do those who work with a development premise. (On the other hand, those who follow a development premise make the justification for having conceived less crucial, given that it is a less serious matter if one conceives and aborts what is not immediately a person.)

Tribe's Discussion of Abortion

After presenting the argument for the permissibility of killing the violinist, we compared it with Judith Thomson's argument. Let us now briefly compare the benefit–burden approach with Lawrence Tribe's recent discussion of abortion even if the fetus is a person.[30] His discussion is only a small part of a wide-ranging historical and legal examination, and Tribe does not try to provide a detailed philosophical study. It thus would be unfair to assume that this is his aim. Nevertheless, I believe that some parts of the benefit–burden approach, as well as some points in the cutoff abortion argument, can be highlighted by seeing how their absence may account for a certain incompleteness in Tribe's discussion.

At first, at least, Tribe seems to concede that if the fetus were a person from conception onward, the implications for abortion would be significant. One reason is that a self-defense justification for killing the fetus would often be inappropriate: The fetus can hardly be portrayed as an aggressor. One could not use a self-defense justification if the pregnancy were voluntarily started. Our discussion tends to agree with the second point. But we also emphasized, contrary to what Tribe suggests, that innocent, nonactive threats—not just ordinary aggressors—can be killed in self-defense. Of course, the permissibility of a third party's assisting must be proved as well. Tribe also notes that we have no established calculus for balancing one life against another. Part of our aim in this and previous chapters has been to develop something like one.

Tribe also suggests that the fetus's personhood would have significant implications because the legal relation between it and the woman would be like that between Siamese twins. Each twin is an equal partner in the body they share, and one twin cannot do as he or she likes without giving equal weight to the interest of the other twin. This implies that a woman cannot abort a healthy fetus. By contrast, our discussion of various alternative natural orders, in which individuals bud inside others, suggests that the analogy with Siamese twins is incorrect. The case in which two parties have always shared the same body differs from the one in which a body is occupied by another party at a later time. Priority of ownership goes to the first occupant. This, of course, does not by itself show that killing the later occupant is permissible. It does, however, suggest a problem with using the Siamese twins as an analogous case.

The Control-of-Women Argument

Having first pointed to possible significant antiabortion implications of conceding the fetus's personhood, Tribe then relies on a Thomson-like argument to show that there would not necessarily be antiabortion results after all. It is not clear, to me anyway, whether he believes that the initial implications were improperly drawn. Perhaps he only wished to concede their initial plausibility. The point he emphasizes is that requiring a pregnancy to continue is to require more aid from the woman to the fetus than we would require from the father to the fetus or the child. This is one step to his conclusion that those who oppose abortions are truly concerned with the control of women rather than with the life of the fetus. That is, they impose a burden of aid on women that they would not impose on men.

The second step to Tribe's conclusion has two parts: (1) Many people are willing to allow abortions when pregnancy is the result of coerced sex rather than voluntary sex, even though the fetus is an innocent person in both cases. This suggests, Tribe thinks, that the objection to abortion is that women should bear the consequences of voluntary sex. This in turn implies that women should be burdened, in ways that men are not, for choosing to have sex. (2) When frozen fertilized eggs that could develop if implanted in a womb are outside anyone's womb, even prolife forces are undecided as to whether they have the rights of persons or whether they may be disposed of. But, when the fertilized egg is inside a woman, they agree that it may not be aborted. This again suggests that it is only when the control of a woman's life is at stake that there is greater concern about fetal rights. We can refer to this two-step (three-part) argument as the *control of women argument.*

Killing Versus Letting Die

Throughout his discussion, with rare exceptions, Tribe seems to move from the fact that one need not make certain efforts to save someone's life to the conclusion that one may also kill in order to stop making those efforts. But suppose that we have to make greater efforts in order not to kill someone (even when we want to kill him in order to end our efforts to save his life) than we have to make in order to save his life. Then the fact that we would not require someone to do x to save a fetus does not show that we could not permissibly require him to do x rather than to abort it. (Tribe is willing to accept that even detachment, which we foresee will—but do not intend to—lead to the fetus's death, counts as a killing.) That some would not permit abortion, therefore, does not necessarily mean that they would require a woman, anymore than a man, to put a fetus growing outside into her body if only that will save its life.

It should be clear that I ultimately disagree with placing too much emphasis in the abortion context on the distinction between not aiding and killing. Nevertheless, we must show, which I believe that Tribe does not, that we may kill to stop efforts that we need not make to save a fetus's life. Furthermore, because it is not obviously wrong to emphasize the distinction between killing and letting a fetus die, we need not attribute different motives to those who do emphasize the distinction.

Foreseen Versus Unforeseen Efforts

Tribe also fails to note the distinction between foreseen and unforeseen efforts. He notes that a court will not require even a voluntary father to give up a part of his body or even give a bone marrow transfusion to his child. How then can we require a woman to let her body be used for a fetus? Let us put aside the previous point, that she must kill in order to stop aid, whereas the father only does not aid. There is another difference: When the father has a child (in the sorts of cases that Tribe considers) he does not know for certain that the child will need the use of his body. But a woman does foresee the necessity of the use of her body. This might be a reason for requiring her to give bodily aid to the fetus, even though the father in the court case need not. Again, we may ultimately dispute this argument, by considering a case in which a father did know, before creating the child, that his bone marrow would be needed. But then we must think about this case in particular, not the one Tribe presents. I discount morally the further difference that we would have to interfere with a father to begin aid, but merely not interfere with the ongoing support of the fetus by the woman, if we require support. An imposition on her still occurs.

Voluntary Versus Coerced Sex

Does allowing abortion when sex has been coerced but not when it was voluntary, in itself, show a desire to control women's sexuality? Not clearly, I think, because it is not unreasonable, at least at first, to believe that in other contexts as well the difference between a coerced and a voluntary act makes a moral and legal difference. For example, if my car is forced by a remote control device to plow into someone, I will bear no responsibility for the disaster. But suppose that I am driving the car, even for good cause, and take reasonable precautions. In this era of strict liability, it might seem (again, at least at first) that I am not only causally responsible for the bad consequences but that I should also do something to compensate for them. Likewise, responsible use of birth control may be seen as a way of reducing occasions on which one needs to aid, but not responsibility for aid. At the very least, it requires some reasoning to explain why this would not be so.

I tried earlier to provide such reasoning. First I considered in more detail the analogy with driving. Second, the benefit–burden approach considered the cost of avoiding sexual conduct as diminishing the responsibility for correcting its consequences. If such reasoning is not obvious, however, one cannot conclude, as Tribe does, that those who emphasize the coerced–voluntary distinction are merely trying to control women's sexuality. They may simply think (perhaps incorrectly) that it is reasonable to require her to bear greater costs when she is morally responsible for the fetus's conception.

What of Tribe's point that men who perform the same type of voluntary sex act are not burdened as a consequence of it, but women are, and in addition, this leads to the subordination of women to men. First, suppose two people perform the same type of act in conjunction with each other to drown someone else. Suppose their joint victim can still be saved if they jump into the river and pull him out. Only one of the agents can swim, however. Could he argue that he be released from his duty to rescue his victim, on grounds that the other equally responsible agent will not be able to do likewise? Hardly. If the act which each committed would make him responsible for aiding, the fact that one person cannot aid does not diminish the other person's duty in this case. This suggests, that the mere fact that men cannot support the fetus is not enough to relieve women of the responsibility, even if what they do together is not criminal. Tribe also points to the fact that if women aid and men do not, this leads to the subordination of women. Here is an additional factor. The argument then is that this further effect might relieve someone of a duty that they would otherwise have. While we have not argued that independent of this equality factor, women would have no right to abort, it seems correct to make use of the possible effect of inequality between men and women that is, inequality is taken to be a cost on account of carriage. This can bring the cost of carriage up so high, that given what both men and women have done (e.g., had sex when refraining or abstaining costs were high) in the context of creation, women whould not be required to continue to support the fetus.

Finally, suppose that there is in fact less concern about the fate of unimplanted fertilized eggs than there is about even early abortion. (It is not clear that this is true.) Does this add weight to the control-of-women argument? It does not if the distinction between killing a fertilized egg versus not helping implant it provides an alternative account of the differential concern. (Of course, if this distinction is shown to be less than crucial in this context, then those who continue to exhibit a differential concern might well be exhibiting a bias against women.) Note that court decisions that do not permit the destruction of fertilized eggs, on the ground that they are persons, but also do not require that such eggs, if abandoned by their biological progenitors, be implanted in unrelated willing recipients, will, by their own reasoning, permit procreators to abandon their offspring and not require the search for adoptive parents. Not requiring a biological creator to put the egg in her womb (even if she should not destroy it) may be understandable, but not encouraging others to adopt seems unreasonable, given the court's premise that the fertilized eggs are persons. Decisions that do not permit the destruction of fertilized eggs on the ground that they are persons from conception onward should logically be committed to requiring adoption by willing strangers if biological parents do not want to use the eggs. They should not simply call for the continued storage of the fertilized eggs. If we do not, in fact, think that fertilized eggs should be put up for adoption, we may have to reject the grounds (i.e., the personhood of such eggs) for not permitting their destruction, and to permit destruction.

I conclude that the significant points Tribe makes would benefit from more argument, often of the sort provided in the discussion of the cutoff abortion argument and the benefit–burden approach.

The Immigration Argument

The benefit–burden approach emphasizes that creators may owe to their creations more than people ordinarily owe to other people. There is another approach to abortion, however, that I wish briefly to explore. I shall call this approach the *immigration argument*. It suggests that although creators have greater responsibilities than merely ensuring that their creations will be no worse(e) off than if they had never existed, abortion is permissible because creators owe to new persons still in the womb less than they owe to other people. (The immigration argument therefore may be combined with parts of the benefit–burden approach.)

Let me explain. Thomson's approach to abortion assumes that you are not obligated to share your body for a long period with the violinist in order to save his life. But suppose that we lived in a society in which people were entitled by law to share each other's bodies; there might be a social contract to this effect because it would maximize the number of lives saved. Would it follow then that in such a society a fetus (assumed to be a person) also had a right to use another person's body? It might not if we thought of the fetus as analogous to an immigrant who was on his way into the society rather than as someone already a member of the society. A person but not yet a citizen. Assume that we understood the right to get bodily support to save one's life not as a universal right of persons—that is, something to which persons have a right just because they are persons—but as a special right granted to members of the particular society in which the special contract was enforced. In addition, suppose that the members of the society were those who had already made the "immigration journey"—that is, the passage requiring assistance in someone's body that began with nonexistence. Then it might be that the immigration journey into the society and the need for support during it would not be covered by the rights enjoyed by people who had already made that journey.

When the immigration argument and parts of the benefit–burden approach are combined, they produce a society that is highly protective of its citizens and not quite so protective of its in-coming members. We are allowed to reject the assumption in Thomson's argument for abortion, in the cutoff abortion argument, and in the benefit–burden approach that we do not owe one another bodily support. Yet we can still construct an argument for abortion even if the fetus is considered to be a person.

One objection to the immigration argument is that even when a fetus is in the womb it is already here—in society. A response is that the immigration argument does not depend so much on mere physical presence in the society as we may think. In support of the immigration argument we can imagine the following analogy: Immigrants waiting in a room on Ellis Island, physically located in the United States, do not yet have rights equal to those granted to citizens of our society. It is not so much a question of their physical location as of how we think it right to conceive of their situation.

We can construct another analogy. This also denies the importance of physical location in the territory where full fledged citizens live: Suppose that once accepted for immigration to the United States, persons who reside in the U.S. embassy in Poland are granted all the rights of U.S. citizens and so have these rights while on the actual physical relocation move to the United States. If already being in the United States does not necessarily mean that one has all the rights of U.S. citizens, then not already being in this country does not necessarily mean that one does not have the rights of U.S. citizens.

Would it be morally unreasonable for citizens of the society to decide whether immigrants should have rights equal to established citizens' rights, based on factors such as the benefit–burden approach presents (i.e., based on how much their having such full-fledged rights would impose on the full-fledged citizens, how badly off the immigrants are in comparison to how they otherwise would have been if they are not fully protected, what risks for benefits we might expect them to bear, etc.)?

This response to the objection can be understood better if we consider another objection to the argument: If people come to our country to escape an undeserved threat of death, we do not send them back. They are allowed to stay. (An undeserved threat of death is not the same as an unjust threat of death. The fetus does not deserve to die, but we must not prejudge the permissibility of abortion by comparing its death with what is assumed to be an unjust killing of a refugee.) Is this not analogous to the case of the fetus who will die if it is not allowed to stay? Not entirely. The case of the fetus is, rather, analogous to a case in which the refugee escaping an undeserved death requires not mere residence in this country but residence in the body of one of its residents. Specifically, may the state require that a resident place the refugee in his body for nine months, as the alternative to sending him back, if citizens do this for each other?

Notes

1. If the cutoff abortion argument is not correct, is the output cutoff argument for the violinist case therefore incorrect as well? Not necessarily, because different factors may be present in each case. In particular, creation may make the difference.

2. Some conditions may be more resistant to historical change. For instance, producing a person who will have a great physical disability or who will live only a very short time might seem always to count strongly against reproducing. Even here, however, an element of relativism may creep in. If mutations changed us so that all we could reproduce were people who lived for only one year, we might nevertheless be justified in reproducing. That is, we would have radically changed our conception of our "normal" species. Economic and social hardships, unlike basic characteristics of the person, might have to be accepted at certain times in history. By associating itself with the call for "no unwanted children," the birth control movement is calling for a higher minimal standard for creating, insofar as it is concerned with not conceiving unwanted children,

for the children's sake. If we assume that the fetus is a person, however, it would be peculiar to think that aborting it because it is unwanted could be done for its sake—is it better for a person to die early than to live unwanted by its biological parents?

3. Derek Parfit, *Reasons and Persons* (Oxford, England: Oxford University Press, 1985).

4. This discussion is based on one in *Morality, Mortality,* and "Why Is Death Bad and Worse Than Pre-Natal Non-Existence?" *Pacific Philosophical Quarterly,* June 1988, pp. 161–4.

5. Parfit, *Reasons and Persons.* He also uses it about death.

6. I first drew such a distinction in an unpublished paper, "Death and Later Goods." I discuss it in greater detail in *Morality, Mortality.*

7. As described by Rawls in *A Theory of Justice.*

8. I discuss these issues in "Harming Some to Save Others," *Philosophical Studies* 57 (1989):227–60.

9. This is not to say that the absence of consent is not morally problematic. I am aware that some (e.g., S. Shiffrin) argue for its making all procreation immoral. Although I believe that the extreme versions of these views are wrong, I will not attempt to rebut them. Some remarks below (under f), however, bear on this issue.

10. Again, I realize that much needs to be said to defend this claim and also much might be said to oppose it. But I am concerned here with identifying certain factors that have some plausibility, to see what they would imply if they were true.

11. If human life were not worth living and were for this reason unlike a benefit, then we should not be depriving the fetus of much if we aborted it.

12. Notice that we have helped ourself to the idea of a quasi-obligation to participate in the human enterprise. Yet we have also claimed that choice as to whether to procreate saves someone from thinking of themselves as a mere part of nature. For these two approaches to be consistent, we would have to claim that once in existence a person may choose whether to participate in the ongoing human enterprise via biological reproduction, but there is no such requirement on choice for becoming a choosing person.

13. Shelly Kagan phrased this part of the summary.

14. Increasingly there is a call in Western societies for people to reproduce when they do not want to, in order to stop a falling birthrate and to preserve certain so-called desirable genes in the gene pool. Individuals who would not otherwise reproduce but who respond to this call voluntarily are, strictly speaking, voluntary creators. In fact, however, they can be compared with soldiers who respond to their nation's call: They believe that they are obligated to reproduce. The following discussion of voluntary creators does not necessarily apply to them, or to others who reproduce from duty.

15. An exception to this—the case in which someone can produce only a handicapped child—is discussed later.

16. *Unexpected* here means "not reasonably predictable at the time the pregnancy is initiated."

17. Thomas Scanlon's point about the significance of an objective rather than a subjective evaluation of burdens and benefits is relevant here. He considers someone who would sacrifice his food supply to build a monument to his god. Yet the fact that this person cares more for his god than for his food does not mean that we are obligated to help him build the monument rather than to provide him with food. The reason is that the food is recognized from an objective point of view as important, but the monument is not. See Scanlon, "Preference and Urgency," *Journal of Philosophy,* November 6, 1975, pp. 665–69.

18. In a conversation by Linda Emmanuel and Arthur Applbaum.

19. It may be worth distinguishing among the different efforts required by cost m. Suppose the activities typically carried out by mothers are not those they would engage in if they were not necessary for raising a family. Suppose the activities typically carried out by fathers (e.g., their jobs) are those they would probably do in any case, even if they had no family to support. This may suggest that the latter have some intrinsic value missing in the former.

20. This cost to refrain from deliberately creating a child should, obviously, be distinguished from the cost of abstaining from sexual intercourse.

21. The fact that there is a cost in not deliberately attempting to have a child is also relevent to a decision about the morality of creating a child when one cannot aim at the minima because it is impossible to obtain them. That is, consider someone who can only give birth to a handicapped child of limited intelligence who will not, however, suffer over its twenty-year lifetime. Would it be immoral for such a person to fulfill a desire to have a genetically related offspring? It might be argued that if the refraining cost is understandably high for such a person—that is, it is not irrational to want very much such a child—it is permissible for him to conceive it.

22. How this significant chance comes about may also be relevant. That is, the chance must be present because there is some intention to have the child rather than because we foresee that abortions may be difficult to obtain.

23. This account omits consideration of what Bernard Williams calls agent regret. With it an agent who has done nothing wrong but nevertheless causes harm (or puts someone in a situation in which he will be harmed unless something further is done) may feel that he should aid his victim more than any bystander should. See his "Moral Luck," in Bernard Williams, *Moral Luck* (Cambridge, England: Cambridge University Press, 1982).

24. Some feminist and psychoanalytic literature suggests this. As does some children's literature. One striking example is *The Stork Father,* complete with

separation from the mother, food deprivation, and stupefaction. I attend to such views as they make abortion harder to justify.

25. The safest way for a woman to avoid having a fetus is still a combination of IUD and abortion, not the pill. Still, it may be that the difference between the safest and less safe means of avoiding a fetus is a sacrifice sufficiently small that a woman should make it to avoid creating a life without minima. This reasoning assumes that it is the differential cost that is relevant.

26. According to a social worker at the abortion clinic, Brigham and Women's Hospital, Boston.

27. I first suggested an approach along these lines in 1972 in my "Abortion: A Philosophical Analysis," *Feminist Studies* 1 (Fall 1972):49–69.

28. I am assuming knowledge of the pregnancy and an opportunity to end it, from conception onward.

29. Apparently some women delay because they want their male partner to want to have a child. They want this because they see it as a sign of love for the woman. Once the women are given this sign, they are willing to abort the fetus (reported by a social worker at Brigham and Women's Hospital, Boston). It is the sign of love, not the child, that such women want. If such "reasoning" is morally irresponsible, we must then consider whether these women are truly permitted and encouraged to have the sorts of relationships with men that would provide no excuse for such bad conduct.

30. Lawrence Tribe, *A Clash of Absolutes* (New York: Norton, 1990).

6

Informed Consent, Responsibilities
in Pregnancy, and External Means
of Gestation

I have been considering arguments for the permissibility of abortion
even if the fetus is a person. Now, I wish to explore the implications of
the benefit–burden approach for a number of abortion-related topics: the
requirement that women seeking abortions be fully informed of the
fetus's status, responsibilities in pregnancy of those who do not abort,
and the use of external gestation devices. For purposes of these discussions, let us put to one side the difference that numbers of abortions
might make. If the benefit–burden approach were correct, what implications would it have for these issues?

Informed Consent

It has been proposed that even if abortion is not legally prohibited,
women should not be allowed to have abortions until they have been
fully informed about what they are doing. In particular, they should be
informed about the nature, the fate, and the status of the fetus. Apparently, it is assumed by the advocates of such legislation that this information might dissuade women from having abortions, for example, by
convincing them that the fetus is a person. What are the implications of
the benefit–burden approach for this issue?

The right to give informed consent is really the right to have full
information about the procedure to be undergone, and the right to refuse
or consent to the procedure on the basis of that information. This is a

right of any person who is to undergo a medical procedure. Patients, of course, may also have a right to be informed of their condition even if this information is unrelated to deciding on a procedure. There may be limits on such a right if there is a strong possibility of being harmed by its exercise or its exercise impeding cure. The right to full information can, presumably, be waived, unless it is also a duty to be fully informed before one acts. Perhaps in medical contexts we have come to the point where we will not allow people to act without being informed and so will not allow them to waive their right to give informed consent.[1] Thoughtful and informed decision making would then be not just a right but a duty. One reason that persons might have such a duty is to relieve doctors of the burden of making decisions for poorly informed patients, or just dealing with such patients. If we are tempted by the general idea of a duty to give informed consent, given the benefit–burden approach, would it be appropriate to require a woman to know physical facts about the fetus and its nature and status?

The benefit–burden approach tells us that the permissibility of abortion does not necessarily turn on physical details about the fetus or on the question of whether or not the fetus is a person. The physical facts about the fetus, which the proposal insists that the woman be told, may not determine, even in expert opinion, whether the fetus is a person. And even if the fetus is a person, according to the benefit–burden approach, in many cases abortion is permissible. Accordingly, if the benefit–burden approach were correct, providing or withholding information about the fetus could not make any difference to whether the woman does something permissible or impermissible, at least in many cases. In these cases, at least, the duty to act with full information could not be seen as arising from any danger of her doing something morally impermissible.

Further, it might be appropriate to require a woman's knowledge of her fetus's status only if it also were appropriate to require full knowledge in comparable cases. For example, should we require that a potential donor of a life-saving organ know in full detail what will happen to the potential beneficiary of his organ if he does not donate it? Should we require that a potential recipient of a scarce medical resource know in detail the fate of those who will die because he, and not they, receives the resource? Should these requirements apply, even though in these cases, as in many abortion cases if the benefit–burden approach is correct, someone acting without such information does not run the risk of doing something morally impermissible if he refuses to give the organ or uses the scarce resource?

It is important to see that requiring such informed states in these cases differs from ordinary informed consent. In the usual cases of informed consent, the patient is told the positives and negatives for him as an individual, from a medical point of view, of the procedure in question. In the abortion case, the woman would be required to consider the negatives of her act not for herself but for someone else, often without a recital of the benefits for her, in order that she not do anything wrong from the moral (rather than the medical) point of view. (The same would apply to the organ donor and scarce resource user.)

Although the fact that others are affected strengthens the claim that there is a moral duty to be informed, it makes it seem less like the sort of duty that a medical institution, in its medical role, should enforce. However, if we could cast the issue in terms of the woman's knowing possible negative medical consequences of her act for herself, perhaps we could argue more successfully for informed consent as it is ordinarily practiced medically. For example, some have argued that the woman should be informed of the possibility that she will have psychiatric problems because of her abortion. Then she could, perhaps, avoid an act that would impair her future mental health. Presumably the source of these problems would be guilt and regret over the abortion, perhaps because of the nature of the fetus.

Guilt and Regret

What can we say about this? First, there is a difference between telling people that they may have psychiatric problems and giving them information about the nature of their fetus. Let us consider the psychiatric problems first. If we warn women who are seeking abortions of possible psychiatric problems, for consistency's sake, should we not similarly warn people who refuse to donate a life-saving organ, or the users of scarce resources, as they might also feel guilt and regret? (We must, of course, be sure that we have data showing that guilt and regret reactions can in fact occur.) Also, should we not discuss the possibility of guilt or regret regarding opportunities lost or burdens encountered if a woman does not have an abortion?

In general, however, the argument based on avoiding guilt—putting regret to one side—is problematic if it treats guilt as though it were a physical pain. Whether or not one feels guilt is a function of whether one believes that one has done something wrong. Therefore, one can avoid guilt as much by believing that one has not acted wrongly, as by not acting. That is, according to the ordinary model of informed consent, in which we consider the positives and negatives for the agent herself, giving the woman information about the fetus should be a way of helping her avoid later guilt. It should do this by allowing her to make a moral decision with which she can live.

But the idea that one should inform oneself so that one may do what one thinks is right in order to avoid later guilt, as the medical model suggests, is itself peculiar. That one will feel guilty means that one will believe that one's act was wrong, and thus the reason to avoid such an act is simply that one does believe that it is wrong, not that the act will produce guilt. To say that we are concerned with people's acting correctly in accord with their beliefs only because we do not want them to feel guilty implies—perversely—that if we could give them a pill to erase their guilt, it would no longer matter how they acted. (Certainly it would get things backward to say that the act is wrong and should not be done because it will produce guilt.)

A misguided liberal would make the same sort of mistake if he suggested that we keep the woman in the dark about what she is doing, for if she acted in ignorance, she would not be able to blame herself and experience guilt. This argument fails to consider that the moral agent's primary desire should be to avoid acting wrongfully, not to avoid the knowledge of acting wrongfully, or the guilt that comes from acting wrongfully. For similar reasons, it is also misguided to warn someone of the regret she will feel at having missed opportunities if she does not have an abortion or to give her information whose purpose is to keep her from feeling such regret. It is the fact that she missed the opportunities, not whether or not she feels regret at this, that is usually important. If having a child produced chemicals that would eliminate regret for missed opportunities, this in itself would not imply that one had made the right decision in having a child. An error of a somewhat similar type is made by those who wish to give Jehovah's Witnesses blood transfusions without informing them. It has been argued that a Jehovah's Witness cares about not choosing to have a blood transfusion because choosing to have it would bring eternal punishment. It is said he does not care about being given the transfusion by others, as he cannot be punished for this. But presumably a true believer would not wish to carry the transfusion in him. It is for this reason that he will not give it to himself. That is, he will refuse to have it because he thinks it should not be in his body, not because he wishes to avoid guilt or even punishment. Therefore, it seems, he should not want others to put it in his body either, and others should not put it in his body.

Refusing to Give Information

Paternalistically trying to prevent guilt by refusing to give someone information when it is requested certainly seems unjustified, as such refusal conflicts with the right to give informed consent. For example, a technique used in late abortions is to induce miscarriage. Suppose a drug is used that induces miscarriage after several hours, rather than one that would induce it sooner, specifically in order that there be no chance that the fetus will come out alive. (Similarly, suppose women who appear for an abortion beyond a certain number of weeks are told to come back a few weeks later, even though this means aborting a more developed fetus. The reason being that the procedure used in earlier abortions might result in a live birth, but the procedure used in later abortions results in death. The purpose of delaying the abortion is to produce a dead fetus, not merely to remove it from the woman's body.) If the fetus did come out alive, would there be a conflict over whether to save it? A fetus at the stage of development of even late abortions cannot, at present, be saved. But the whole experience might be more traumatic for the woman and health personnel if it did come out alive.

Suppose that the woman asks the personnel performing the abortion why it is preferable that the miscarriage not occur sooner. It is inappropriately paternalistic not to tell her the true reason, namely, that the fetus might then come out alive. In this case the woman herself is requesting the information.[2]

Likewise, the use of an amnesia-inducing drug (which is common) to prevent the woman from remembering the abortion experience may be inappropriate. The woman should at least be able to choose whether the drug is used. (This would not defeat the aim of forgetfulness, should she choose the drug.)

The medical model that we have been examining should recommend either information or its absence, whichever is better to prevent guilt. Neither course of action justified in this way seems quite right.

Requiring Information

The most morally reasonable ground for requiring that someone—considering either having an abortion or refusing to donate a kidney—be fully informed of how such behavior will affect someone else is a non-paternalistic ground. (Does this diverge from the ordinary ground of informed consent when the agent's own costs and benefits are presented to him? Even here it does not seem correct to give a paternalistic justification for providing information.) That is our reason for thinking that someone should be informed is other than that it is in his best interest to be informed. It might be argued that such people should be informed because they have a responsibility as moral agents to act correctly as best they can determine. Knowing the facts about what they are doing is a means to that end. One does not stop being a moral agent simply because one enters a medical setting. Ordinarily, the duty to be informed may be even greater when others' lives are at stake than when one's own life alone is. (This implies that even if philosophers had proven the permissibility of some abortions, this need not necessarily relieve the individual having the abortion of having to think through the matter.)

If this is the best ground for requiring knowledge, it will not support requiring knowledge in order to avoid regret rather than guilt that may result from an abortion. The reason is that regret and what leads to it are not necessarily related to doing anything morally impermissible. A paternalistic motive would have to play a greater role in a justification for requiring information to prevent regret.

As we noted, however, it is not clear that it is medical practitioners who must see to it that moral agents carry out their moral responsibilities when the fates of others are at stake. Still, if a doctor must harm that other person, as the agent carrying out the patient's decision, it may be more understandable for him or her to urge the patient to consider the fate of that other person. This could be true even though it may conflict with the traditional idea that the doctor is supposed to focus all concern on the interests of one patient at a time.

The state, of course, rather than the doctor or medical institution, might enforce the duty to be fully informed, by means of laws requiring women to receive information about the fetus. The state should then enforce this duty in other cases in which a decision immediately affects someone else's welfare, say in regard to organ donation. (This presumes that abortion is a form of denying aid, even though it includes both creating a person and killing to stop aid.)

It might also be argued that being informed is important because individuals may wish to act on what they believe is a morally higher level than mere permissibility and adequate sensitivity. The fact that they would not be doing anything strictly impermissible regardless of how they act is, then, beside the point, given this other goal. (I suspect that some people might want to reinforce this point by arguing that there is no such thing as permissibility, only "permissibility for someone." That is, if a particular woman does not think it permissible to abort a person then it is "not permissible for her." Therefore, she should be informed of the status of the fetus, as she may be doing something "impermissible for her" if she has an abortion. My approach to ethical analysis rejects the idea that an act cannot be truly permissible for someone just because he thinks it is impermissible. A more objective way of determining permissibility has been employed here. Therefore I shall ignore this argument.)

Furthermore, if the benefit–burden approach to the permissibility of aborting persons is not clearly correct, the woman may be at risk of doing something truly impermissible, from anyone's point of view. This adds additional pressure for her to be informed about what she is doing.

The Unexamining Life

Having presented these arguments in favor of a rule requiring informed decision making, even when the negatives of someone's action fall totally on another person who is denied aid, let us now consider objections to such a rule and its associated duties. First, it is important to recognize that many of us typically avoid finding out information about the effect on others of our acts or omissions. One reason for this is that we believe that we have a right to act in a certain way; we know for certain that we will not alter our behavior no matter what information we get; and we want to avoid being upset by details that do not affect either the permissibility or the probability of what we do. If undetailed information about the fetus, and even the hypothesis that it is a person, is not enough to convince us that it is impermissible to have an abortion, we may wish to avoid finding out more detailed information that will not, in any case, alter our position regarding a duty or change our behavior.

Another reason for avoiding information is our belief that it might indeed change our behavior. In this case, we may think that we have a right to do something and do not want to be dissuaded from doing it. Therefore, we believe that we have a right to avoid learning information that might actually dissuade us. In particular, we often think that we have a right to protect ourselves from the greater degree of moral perfection of which we are in fact capable. We want to protect ourselves from supererogatory self-sacrifice (or even self-destruction) for the sake of the greater good. We may also be protecting ourselves from mere sentimentality, triggered by psychologically impressive experiences.

Therefore, by requiring that a pregnant woman have full information, we may be holding her to a higher standard than that to which we ordinarily hold ourselves. We ordinarily believe that it is permissible to live *the unexamining life.*[3]

The assumption behind both these points is that it is permissible not to aid. We are trying to avoid performing a supererogatory act, one beyond the call of duty, that we might be tempted to perform. This conclusion also assumes that the benefit–burden approach is correct and that it often cannot be our duty to refuse an abortion or to give up our organ, or refuse the scarce resource. But what if the benefit–burden approach is not correct?

Our Duty

Some have argued that our true duty is to maximize the overall good but that we do not easily recognize it, in part because we are not vividly exposed to facts about the needs of other people, our beliefs about them are mostly pale.[4] Such vivid exposure, it is claimed, would motivate us to act for the greatest good. (It is such vivid exposure to the fetus that is encouraged by pictures of it.) Of course, there should be vivid exposure to all the facts. This means that in the abortion context, vivid pictures should also be presented of pregnancy, delivery, and other consequences of continuing to carry, both good and bad. Furthermore, it has been argued, we know that we now are not motivated to act for the greater good because of our imperfect appreciation of the facts. This imperfect appreciation is a cognitive defect in us. Once we know how we would behave if we were more perfect cognizers having vivid knowledge, we become motivated to act as we would if we were perfect cognizers. This is true even if we still do not have vivid knowledge, on the analogy to our being motivated now to act according to the directives of a counselor who, we believe, is wiser than we are even though we cannot now follow his reasoning.

This argument is aimed at showing that we now are obligated to promote the greatest good, in part because we can be motivated to do it, even in the absence of vivid experiences, by the idea of what we would do if we were perfect, not defective, cognizers. The claim is not, however, that the capacity to be motivated is sufficient to prove an obligation. More must be done to show we are obliged besides showing we are capable of being moved.

My description of at least some people's behavior in regard to abortion is that they may be motivated not to have an abortion because of their vivid awareness of the fetus, but the fact that they could be so motivated does not indicate that they have an obligation not to have an abortion, even if this would promote the greatest good. (They also could be motivated by more pale propositional knowledge. I shall return to this later.) As I noted, both the cutoff abortion argument and the benefit–burden approach are nonconsequentialist. They assume the background view in normative ethics that we sometimes have a prerogative to do less than the greatest good but that in so acting we do not fail to do our duty. This is a view that most of us accept, or at least follow.[5]

Vivid exposure may not motivate us to act, but if vivid exposure (and not mere propositional knowledge of facts) does motivate us to act, this need not be because our current view of our duties is wrong. Evidence for the first point comes from the fact that if someone is dying at your feet and the only way to save him is to donate your right arm to make a serum, you most probably would not donate. Furthermore, the distinction you draw between your fate and his fate, giving greater weight to yours, does not depend on your having an even more vivid awareness of yourself than of him, as it may be that giving him what he needs from you will not truly harm you until some distant point in your future, and you have only pale, not vivid, knowledge of yourself at that distant point. Yet the idea that it is you, rather than someone else, who will suffer a significant loss in the future, may stop you from donating. The second point is that if we are motivated to donate, such motivation may only be a psychological phenomenon; that is, we are caused to act, but not for the sake of reasons that justify a duty. If we would not act with less vivid propositional knowledge of the same facts, this suggests that only psychological pressure is moving us to act when the facts are made vivid. Therefore, that being better observers of facts causes our action, may have no normative significance for determining the extent of our duties. We may then decide not to look at vividly presented facts, and not to act as if we had looked at them, because they would cause us to act in ways that we are not required to.

A vivid awareness of facts may be useful, however, in determining our duties, not because it magnifies facts or puts pressure on us, but because it makes us aware of new facts (sometimes best thought of as the components of an overarching fact, for example, what pain really consists of, in detail), or new interpretations of facts. Suppose a vivid knowledge of the fetus made possible such additional propositional knowledge, and it also could motivate us not to have an abortion, by convincing us that we had a duty not to have an abortion. Then we would not be caused to act by means of mere psychological pressure stemming from a vivid presentation of facts. The problem, however, may be that this new information is having this effect because an argument, such as the benefit–burden approach, is not also part of the information being given. Such information does not mention that some theories attempt to morally justify sometimes destroying persons. If these arguments were mentioned, the motivating effect of the facts about the fetus might be diminished. (Of course, they also might not.) Some may think that we need not mention the arguments supporting the permissibility of abortion, as the person coming for an abortion already knows them. But desiring to have an abortion—and responding to factors that lead to such a desire—is not the same as realizing that one may be justified in having the desire. Such justification is what an argument might provide.

To be informed of all facts and all arguments in propositional form, even if derived from a complete range of vivid presentations, seems a lot to require of ordinary people at the very time they come for an abortion, given that the law already permits abortion. Still, legal permissibility may be contingent on requiring some moral reflection, at least in those contexts in which there is no clearly convincing justification for the moral permissibility of abortion known to others. Then should we expect reflection also to be required in cases in which one is about to use a scarce resource or refuse a life-saving organ, or are these not comparable cases of moral uncertainty?

Suppose that all this additional knowledge, vivid or propositional, should not alter our conception of our duties from what the benefit–burden approach suggests. Should the ordinary person still be required to think through these things for herself? In matters as complex as abortion, may she rely on the opinions of others, if their arguments are judged convincing by experts? (Is it morally irresponsible for her as she votes to accept that there is a moral defense of democracy, even though she cannot figure it out or even understand it by herself?)

We may wish to avoid performing self-sacrificial acts beyond the call of duty and so wish to avoid what would tempt us to perform such acts. However, what if a person wanted to meet a higher standard than mere moral acceptability? It seems odd to think that she should be required to receive the information necessary to performing the supererogatory act if the act itself is not required and we are not sure that she would want to perform it. Presumably, the woman should be given further information only if she set herself this supererogatory task and asked for the data.

Finally, note that abortion laws in many European countries require that a woman be "counseled" as to the serious nature of an abortion. They may also require her to consult with the father of the fetus or with her parents (who have no veto) before acquiring an abortion. All this may take place even in the first trimester, in the absence of an assumption that the fetus is a person. The term *counseling* suggests a more directed, perhaps paternalistically motivated, procedure then does simple *informing*. No mention is made of counseling the woman regarding the risk of not having an abortion, that is, the physical, psychological, and life changes that will result if she continues the pregnancy, nor is mention made of counseling her concerning views on the permissibility of abortion. Subtle and interesting issues arise in connection with requiring consultation with others. (Similar issues arise in connection with having abortion procedures that a woman can use on herself versus those requiring involvement of others.) While many emphasize the right of a woman to decide about abortion on her own, guilt will probably be less if the decision (or act) is jointly made. Indeed, one hypothesis (subject to empirical confirmation) is that the dynamics of consultation are sometimes like those of the game of chicken: others who would have expressed disapproval had she made the decision to abort on her own, might encourage the abortion if she waits, thinking she will not have one. She has then called their bluff. Everyone wants to remain uninvolved unless they see the necessity for action forced upon them.[6]

Responsibilities in Pregnancy

Consider the Stewart case, in which a woman was said to have taken amphetamines and had sexual intercourse late in pregnancy, thereby causing damage to her fetus and finally its death.[7] She did these things, it was alleged, even though she had been warned by her doctor of their consequences for her pregnancy. Furthermore, when the fetus was born prematurely she failed to get assistance for it right away, and it died. Stewart was charged with parental neglect, but some people believed that she should have been put on trial for murder. (No attempt was made to prosecute the man who had sexual intercourse with Stewart. If he were aware of the consequences of his sex acts and if he performed as many as she did, any argument for prosecuting her on account of her sex acts should apply to him as well.) I shall consider this case, assuming the allegations are true, in the light of the benefit–burden approach.[8]

A short argument given for bringing the charges in the Stewart case is as follows: If a woman does not have an abortion, it means that she intends to go through with the pregnancy, and so she must do everything necessary to nurture her fetus.[9] This Stewart obviously did not do if the facts are as described. The position expressed by this brief argument can be held by those who think that early abortion is permissible because the fetus is then not a person and who wish to avoid the death of the fetus at a later stage when they believe that it is a person. It can also be held by those who seek to avoid delivering a newborn who will become a defective child as a result of events occurring at any time in a pregnancy, even if the fetus is never a person.

An Intention to Continue a Pregnancy

First let us examine this brief argument more closely. Contrary to what it states, not having an abortion does not signify an intention to continue a pregnancy. That one has not had an abortion by a certain point in pregnancy does not mean that one does not reserve the right (if it is granted by the benefit–burden approach) to have it later.

Furthermore, suppose that a woman who was raped does not have an abortion because she believes that killing the fetus is morally wrong. She may also believe that letting the fetus die because she does not want to make great efforts for it is acceptable. (This is close to the Roman Catholic position on all abortions, which maintains a strong distinction between killing with the aim of causing death and letting die only foreseeing death.) This woman may foresee that the fetus will become ill and require surgery, and she may fully intend to refuse to let her body be operated on for the fetus's sake. She therefore intends not to continue the pregnancy, even though she will not have an abortion. (The Supreme

Court's *Roe v. Wade* decision permitted states to limit abortions in the third trimester to threats to a woman's life and health. This implies that the states, unlike the benefit–burden approach, could hold that avoiding simple carriage (including delivery) is not a reason to terminate aid to the fetus by killing it. This need not, however, mean that the state can require women to provide carriage or equivalent assistance to save a fetus's life from natural disease or defect in the third trimester.[10]

In addition, suppose that a woman continues a pregnancy because she believes that abortion is morally wrong or because she thinks that once a person is conceived—assuming that the fetus is a person—it is better off alive, even without the minima, than dead. Continuing in these cases is not the same as voluntarily deciding to have a child, and so one's responsibilities to do things for the new person may be diminished from what they would be in a truly voluntary pregnancy.

An Obligation to Nurture

Suppose, however, that a woman refused to have an abortion because she chose to continue her pregnancy simply for the sake of having a child. According to the benefit–burden approach, even such voluntary creators need not do everything possible to nurture their fetus. In particular they need not carry, undergo surgery, or abstain during their entire reproductive years. ("Abstain" in the benefit–burden argument does not mean just short periods of abstaining.) This is true, even if they foresaw the need for these efforts before conceiving, if the possibility of no carriage, surgery, or abstinence is an acceptable risk to impose on the fetus in exchange for its having had a significant chance for a good life.

Furthermore, suppose that contrary to what I have been assuming, the fetus is not a person and remains at a nonperson, noninfant stage of development. It requires argument to explain why a woman who has not chosen abortion must avoid activities that will kill a nonperson or must not refuse use of her body for surgery in order to save its life. (Causing it damage that will show up in its later life is a different issue; for then the damage will affect a full-fledged person, even though the act that results in the damage occurs before the person exists.[11])

It may be true, however, that voluntary creators must ensure that their newly conceived persons have minima at the cost of efforts less than carriage, surgery, or abstinence or, during a grace period, make some of such lesser efforts. Assuming that not dying and not being a handicapped person are among the minima, the question in the Stewart case is whether the required parts of such lesser efforts include not smoking, not drinking, not taking drugs, and not having sexual intercourse for several months. Why should they not?

Responsibilities in Voluntary Pregnancy

Before addressing the question of responsibilities in voluntary pregnancy, and as a way of answering it, it is important to note the ways in which an argument from the premise of voluntary creation to the conclusion of greater responsibilities in pregnancy may go off course, and also how it can be made to stay on track.

First, we might state that the more freely that people are allowed to choose their pregnancies, the better care for the fetus and child we may require of them. For if we warn people in advance of these responsibilities, and which ones we will enforce, and they then consciously decide to create, they cannot complain when we hold them to those responsibilities, no matter how great they are. But this argument seems too strong. We may not raise responsibilities simply because people are forewarned, if the levels to which we raise them are unreasonable or if the cost of avoiding pregnancy is high. Still, as the approach described in Chapter 5 implies, I believe that there is merit in the strategy of increasing creators' responsibilities to some higher level if the creation is voluntary. Here, then, is a second argument for higher responsibilities in voluntary pregnancy. This argument goes beyond mere reliance on the idea of causal responsibility for a new person where there was a low refraining cost. Indeed this argument has a somewhat different role for *high* refraining costs than they had in Chapter 5. There high refraining costs led to lower responsibilities in pregnancy. In this argument, we try to connect high refraining costs to *increased* responsibilities.

Responsibilities and the Refraining Cost

The cost to someone of not having children who would have been healthy is presumably greater than the cost to someone of not having children who would have been unhealthy. The cost of not having children who would have been healthy increases as the desire to have them increases. A measure of the strength of the desire for the healthy children is how much one would do to have them. Thus the desire that makes it very costly to forego having healthy children should also increase one's willingness to make greater sacrifices so as to have them. (That is, if no children = cost x, one would pay $x - n$ to have them.) The truth of this is limited to some extent by the possibility of using multiple easy pregnancies rather than a single more difficult one to produce a healthy child. But if the fetus is a person, the idea of easily substituting one fetus for another would be peculiar, as well as morally inappropriate, for a person who wanted a child. Therefore, by legislating higher requirements for voluntary pregnancies we may discourage from voluntary pregnancy only those people for whom the refraining (from having children) cost is low.

Limiting Responsibilities

As we noted, someone who will not try to do much for a new person is probably someone for whom the cost of not having a child is low; the higher the cost of not having a child is for someone, the more he is likely to be willing to do for the new person. Yet we cannot demand everything for the new person, in part because it is possible for the cost of not having a child to be very high and yet still be lower than the cost of very great responsibilities for a new person. Therefore many people will prefer to pay the cost of not having a child, which is nevertheless truly painful. The problem is to set the cost of responsibilities at a level that does not dissuade from having children too many people who will thereby suffer a cost that is sufficiently high to be painful, assuming this would be morally permissible, when we consider the permissibility of imposing risks on the fetus, as well as the other creation factors emphasized in Chapter 5's discussion of the benefit–burden approach.

Avoiding Responsibilities

Another problem with increasing the responsibilities of voluntary creation is that so long as the bearer need not provide carriage, she may be more likely to have an abortion so as to avoid the other responsibilities, and as these other responsibilities of pregnancy become more onerous, she will withdraw carriage just as a way of avoiding them. That is, she refuses to make efforts she need not make, as a way of not helping produce a state of affairs she does not like (one in which she carried out her true responsibilities). The desire to avoid contributing in a large way to a state of affairs to which one objects is understandable. But it does not seem justified when the state of affairs to which one objects is merely the fulfillment of one's responsibilities. One way of dealing with this problem is to limit the right to withdraw carriage to cases in which the bearer objects to carriage itself or its associated nonrequired efforts, rather than to allow the withdrawal of carriage for the sake of avoiding other required efforts.

It is not clear, however, that it would be permissible to do this, because ordinarily a right to control something (e.g., one's body) gives one the right to decide what to do with it without having to pass a good-reasons test. I shall return to this point.

Enforcing Responsibilities

Freely choosing at some point in pregnancy not to have an abortion might also seem to support a third argument for enforced responsibilities in pregnancy. By deciding not to have an abortion and, specifically, by deciding to have a child, the woman has given the fetus (if a person) a specific right to be in her body. It is now an equal partner in it, a joint tenant, even if it has no right to be given such partnership.

This would imply that the fetus has a right to have the woman's body provide it with what it needs, when what is at stake for it is greater than the cost of such use to the woman. For example, her not drinking (alcohol) costs her less than her drinking costs the fetus, and so she should not drink. Notice that this specific right to the use of her body is not something that a parent has necessarily given to a child who is already out of the womb and who then needs to use his parent's body to survive. Therefore, according to this argument, we can distinguish between the parent who refuses to give a blood transfusion to a child who is outside her body and a voluntary bearer who refuses carriage to a fetus who is still inside her body.

The objection to this argument (which the benefit–burden approach suggests) is that by deciding not to abort at time t_1, because she intends to have a child, a bearer does not give a fetus a joint and equal right to her body. Rather, she allows it to stay until such time, perhaps t_2, as she decides that she does not want it to stay, given that the considerations that give her permission to abort, according to the benefit–burden approach, may still hold at t_2. As we noted earlier, one problem is that among the things that might lead a woman to want to abort, perhaps illegitimately, at t_2 is the fetus's presence interfering with what she may do to her body, such as drinking or smoking.

At this stage in the argument, we are left with the view that it is reasonable to require more for the fetus from voluntary bearers than from others, but with the possibility that they will withdraw carriage in order to avoid making any, or any part of, lesser efforts. A possible solution to this problem begins by recalling how the right to discontinue a voluntary pregnancy was derived in the benefit–burden approach: Creation factors such as the cost of not having a child, the imposition of carriage, the permissibility of not protecting a new person from all risks, and a significant chance for it to have minima together helped argue for a right to withdraw carriage. If making part of the lesser efforts is at stake, not carriage or the whole lesser efforts (cost m), permission to stop part of the lesser efforts might not be generated in the same way. If it were predicted that the threat of ending carriage would be used as a mere excuse for not making part of the lesser efforts, thereby increasing the number of dead or damaged persons, the argument could restrict the withdrawal of carriage. In particular, an examination of reasons for withdrawing would, theoretically, be appropriate. (In practice, of course, it would be difficult to enforce such an examination-of-reasons requirement.)

Suppose that it would be theoretically consistent with the benefit–burden approach to limit the withdrawal of carriage so that one could not escape making some part of the lesser efforts in voluntary pregnancy. The remaining question is the one with which we began: Is doing or not doing certain things to one's own body, such as not smoking and not drinking (if it is foreseen before pregnancy that not doing them are necessary to produce minima), a part of the lesser efforts that can be required of a voluntary bearer?

Take the issue of smoking cigarettes. Some people (e.g., George Annas)[12] have argued that a pregnant woman need not stop smoking, even though her smoking may damage the fetus. His reason is that parents do not have to stop smoking to prevent damage to their children once they are out of the womb. But suppose that we know that smoking in the presence of a child who is outside the womb had a high probability of causing it serious brain damage. I believe that it would then be impermissible for a parent, or anyone else, to smoke in the child's presence, even if there were nowhere else to go to smoke except where the child was. If we suppose that a pregnant woman endangers the fetus in this same direct manner by smoking, why should she not be obligated to stop?

The Distinction Between Harming and Not Aiding

Perhaps there is a difference between the case of a person inside a woman's body and a person outside her body. In the course of living her life, a pregnant woman (isolated, suppose, from everyone but the fetus inside her) does certain things to her body. For example, she smokes. These activities affect another person (assuming the fetus is a person) only because they affect what might metaphorically be called her private territory (the inside of her body). That other person is in her private territory. By contrast, a child on the outside can be seen to reside either in its own private territory or in public territory in which it has an equal right to be. Getting smoke to the child by pouring it into his own or public territory, even as a result of doing something to one's own body first, may be prohibited.

Refusing to give up the sort of act that smoking in private is—where no smoke spills over into public territory or into territory owned by another person—even seems different from refusing to do certain acts specifically directed toward fetal welfare. That is, it might be suggested, a parent or voluntary bearer need not avoid doing certain things to her body for her offspring's sake, if these things in themselves are necessary to help the offspring. Still, he may have to avoid doing the same sort of thing if this is a mere means to fulfilling some other duty of aid or noninterference. For example, he may have to give up smoking in order to save money to buy milk, if he has a duty to provide milk.

Perhaps only whatever behaviors regarding his own body that a voluntary creator would be obligated to refrain from (or to undertake) for the sake of *saving* his externally situated offspring are the behaviors that the pregnant woman is obligated to refrain from in order to avoid harming the internally situated offspring. Harms involve crossings of personal, protected boundaries between people that make the person harmed worse off. But when someone is inside another's private territory, without an equal claim to be there, perhaps not doing something that harms him should be treated in the same way as doing something that would aid someone who is either in public or his own territory, especially when he is in need of aid through no fault of the person whose aid he needs? Annas proposes that harming a fetal person should be compared with harming a child outside the body. Our present proposal, by contrast, suggests that harming a fetus should be compared with not aiding a fetus outside the body.

For example, suppose that a creator's fetus, who is growing in a lab, is stricken by nature with a fatal disease. Miraculously enough, what will cure the disease is the creator's not smoking in his own private space. Is he required to do so? If he is, perhaps we could conclude that a pregnant woman should also be obligated to stop smoking in order to avoid killing her internally situated fetus. On the other hand, if the creator need not stop smoking in his private space to help his external fetus, then the pregnant woman need not stop smoking either. Further, we have suggested that according to the benefit—burden approach if she were obligated to stop smoking, she could not threaten to stop letting the fetus use her body merely because she wanted to smoke.

But can we even conclude that she should stop smoking if the creator who does not carry his fetus should stop smoking? The woman who is already giving the fetus more than she must might have to be indulged; if she must give up other things, in addition to her bodily autonomy, the effort of pregnancy may become too burdensome. It is possible that nothing more should be demanded of her. When someone is receiving an extraordinary form of aid (bodily carriage) then he might have to tolerate serious risks that come from the refusal to make smaller additional sacrifices, such as not smoking, because these sacrifices are not demandable in addition to the larger sacrifices which are already being made.

This proposal has some peculiar implications. Suppose that someone is in my one-room house and the alternative is that he will die if he leaves. Suppose further that I am not obligated to keep him in my house (perhaps because he has a disease that might harm me), even given the alternative he would face if I evicted him. Nevertheless I let him stay. I am used to doing target practice every evening in my house. This is perfectly permissible when I am alone, and it would be a sacrifice for me not to do my target practice. However, if I do it when someone is in my house, I run the risk of killing him. Suppose we take my refraining from practice as an instance of a further sacrifice undertaken for my guest's sake. If the argument just given for the case of the fetus were correct, would it not imply the following: It is certainly permissible for me to do target practice even if this may kill my guest, if I do not have to stop it in order to save his life if he were outside my house. Furthermore, given that this sacrifice comes on top of a larger one, the weight it has is greater than if it were made on its own. This would imply that I might do practice when someone is in the house even if I had to stop to save the life outside. This conclusion, which, at the very least, equates harming an insider with not aiding an outsider, seems difficult to accept. That is, the added weight of not shooting, when it comes on top of the guest's residence, should not make us forget that it is also harming and not merely not aiding. Certainly in some cases the harming and simple not aiding will be morally different: If I had to do target practice to save my life, I would have a good excuse for not stopping to save the person outside. On the other hand, it would at least be harder to justify doing target practice to save my life if it would kill someone occupying my house. But our current question is whether, when there is no such pressing reason for me to do target practice, I am equally obligated to abandon it to save someone outside or to not kill someone inside. Perhaps in this particular case, saving and not killing are equal, and likewise for the case of not smoking. This is because we ought to save at these costs, and not doing target practice or not smoking coming on top of residence still does not justify engaging in them. But we must be aware that as costs rise, there may be a separating of the ways: For example, we may not have to aid the external person at such higher costs, but we may still have to pay the cost not to kill the internal person.

It may be true that refraining from target practice or refraining from smoking is a part of helping someone, rather than merely not harming him, only when this person is on the inside. Yet all the same, perhaps we cannot engage in the practice because it also will harm someone. Here aiding takes the form of not harming, and not harming takes the form of aiding. Given the significance to the woman of having her body used, removing the fetus may be permissible at any time. But if she keeps the fetus, does it not seem that she may be obligated to make smaller sacrifices for its sake, when not making these sacrifices would result in her harming her fetus, even if these smaller sacrifices would not be necessary as aid alone, and even if these sacrifices count for more because they come on top of residence in her.

It is important to distinguish this argument from one that claims that anyone who avoids harming someone is thereby aiding him, for example, that someone always owes his life to the person who does not kill him. It is when refraining from the harmful act occurs in a situation in which the person is already dependent in the ordinary sense, and the act would be innocent enough to another if not for the dependence, that refraining from harm is also another sacrifice of freedom that aids.

Any conclusion that a woman is obligated to make the smaller sacrifices of not acting in certain ways, rather than to act and thus harm, does not necessarily support large-scale invasions of privacy to monitor the behavior of pregnant women. The reason is that such monitoring and invasions would greatly raise the cost of the sacrifice that women must make for their fetus, and this could rule it out as a requirement. Nevertheless, if one non-intrusively discovered that the requirement had been evaded, punitive measures might be recommended.

One objection to this argument depends on the adequacy of the analogous case it uses. Has the analogy been constructed properly? It was constructed so that it too pertained to an activity that is innocent when done in a certain environment until someone else is admitted to that environment. Target practice becomes a danger to someone in the house, just as smoking becomes a danger to someone in the womb, even if smoking does not become a danger to someone in the house. But should we instead construct the example so that drinking Coke or smoking or having sex in one's own one-room house risks disturbing the visitor, with fatal effect? Would one have to eliminate these activities if one keeps the visitor in the house for nine months? Perhaps not. But perhaps this is only because sensitivity to such activities is abnormal in an adult human being. What this case might show is that if a fetus were abnormal (i.e., very different from other fetuses) in being sensitive to smoking or sex or drugs, then the pregnant woman might not be morally obligated to avoid such activities. But the fetus is not abnormal in this respect.

Although it is not abnormal to be killed by a bullet in target practice, perhaps it is the violent nature of target practice that makes it wrong to engage in. What if it were normal for someone cooped up in a house for many months to be driven mad by the repeated playing of a Beethoven violin sonata? This activity is not in any way a violent activity in itself, nor is smoking or drinking Coke. Should the person in whose house the visitor resides to avoid death, give up playing his favorite sonata?

Regardless of how we decide this case, we must remember to determine how difficult it is for someone to make what seem like intrinsically small sacrifices by considering how weighty such sacrifices are to a person who is already undergoing another greater burden (e.g., carrying someone in her body). If certain activities are all that make the experience bearable, in part, perhaps, because they help the person retain a sense of equality, that she is not cut off from doing many things non-pregnant people do, then giving them up will have greater weight.

This analysis takes seriously any harmful activities whose avoidance is not a great sacrifice alone or in combination with support. Nevertheless, it still suggests that those outside the woman's womb whose smoke enters her and immediately endangers her fetus may often be more liable to being stopped from smoking than she is. The reason is that others pour smoke into her territory so they are not being called on to refrain from an activity that affects their own body space, as she is. If inequality in enforcement of responsibilities is not to arise, those others who knowingly endanger the fetus should be prosecuted if the pregnant woman is.

Harming, Not Aiding, and a Fetus That Is Not a Person

Let us assume that the fetus is not yet a person. There seem to be some situations that we have not yet considered in which the pregnant woman's engaging in a life-style that makes the fetus worse off than it would otherwise have been is more completely akin to not aiding (rather than to harming) a person who is outside the womb. Suppose, for example, that smoking during pregnancy would produce a child with an IQ of 140, whereas not smoking in pregnancy would produce a child with an IQ of 180. Because the 180 IQ was not already the person's IQ—there being no person yet—not giving up smoking could be understood as failing to help it obtain forty more IQ points. This seems like a case in which the woman makes the person worse off than he might otherwise have been, but she does not harm him. By contrast, suppose that a child outside the womb already had an IQ of 180, and my smoking in his vicinity lowered his IQ to 140. My smoking would be taking something away from him that was already his, something that he had a right to keep. (Recall the contentious proposal made earlier, that not refraining from harming a person in the womb is akin to not aiding someone outside the womb. If the fetus in the womb were already a person with an IQ of 180, then according to that proposal, not smoking helps him retain his gifts rather than helping him obtain them. If we reject that proposal, we are saying that not smoking is indeed a further sacrifice to help the fetus retain his IQ, but it nevertheless is also a way of not harming him.)

Application of this analysis to the Stewart case is complicated by at

least three real-world factors. First, what Stewart was (supposedly) doing to her body was not something that she would be legally permitted to
do even if she were not pregnant; that is, she was (supposedly) taking
amphetamines. Second, although the benefit–burden approach would
often allow abortions late into pregnancy simply because a woman did
not want to let her body be used, state laws are often not so liberal. It is
open to states to confer the right to have an abortion in later stages of
pregnancy only if the pregnant woman's life or health is threatened. This
might be interpreted to mean that at that point the fetus has as much right
to the woman's body as she has, except when her life and health is at
stake. This would imply that she is not refraining from doing something
to her privately held territory. Furthermore, because her smoking has
more disutility for the fetus than her smoking has utility for her, she may
not pour smoke into the jointly held territory. This conclusion can be
avoided only if the right to remain in the body rather than to be aborted is
a specific right, one that does not imply joint ownership or disposition of
the body according to the stronger of the two interests.

The third point is that Stewart did not aid the fetus at small expense
once it was out of the womb. That is, she did not immediately call for
medical help for the premature birth. There is a difference between not
altering one's life-style for a guest who needs a rather extraordinary type
of residence and not calling for the police to aid a person on one's
doorstep, especially when the need for aid is caused by one's life-style.

External Means of Gestation

Means of gestation external to the womb that eliminate the need for the
creator's carriage present interesting problems for both the benefit–
burden approach and the cutoff abortion argument.[13]

First, what method of external gestation is desirable? I believe that
ideally the use of mechanical means is preferable to the use of surrogate
humans. If the technology is good, the humans are probably less efficient, themselves possibly threatening to abort. Also, human surrogates
may come to constitute an underclass who earn their living by this use of
their bodies. Barring the appearance of wombs in men, this will also
reinforce the social differences between males and females. In addition,
human surrogates may develop emotional attachments that compete with
those of the proposed parents. (This did happen in the case of Baby
M.)[14]

One objection to mechanical external gestation (MEG for short), however, is that it is bad for a woman never to experience pregnancy. Although this is a debatable point, I shall assume for the moment that MEG would be used primarily by those women who have already had the experience of pregnancy and who want additional children but not additional pregnancies. The objection that I wish to consider is the view that carrying the fetus in her womb is a necessary prerequisite for motherhood (in every instance of a new child). What does this view mean? Pregnancy certainly does not seem necessary if women are allowed to be only as good mothers as fathers are good fathers or as adoptive parents are good adoptive parents. And should they not be allowed this?

Good Enough Parents

Perhaps what is meant, however, is that the willingness to carry a fetus in one's body is necessary in order to be a good parent. A father or adoptive parents may be willing and eager but unable. A woman who is able to carry a fetus but prefers a MEG pregnancy is said to be unwilling. What can we say about these observations? First, willingness may be necessary for ideal parenthood, but must we require such an ideal from everyone on pain of not being parents? May we not propose a theory of acceptable (rather than ideal) parenthood? In Chapter 5 we considered a theory of acceptable and responsible parenthood, entailing definite responsibilities for voluntary creators but (within limits) excluding certain types of sacrifices as obligatory. We emphasized that the best interests of the offspring must be weighed against the best interests, as well as the desire for a child, of the creators.

Second, it is not true that a woman who is able to carry a fetus but chooses a MEG pregnancy is thereby shown to be unwilling to carry a child in her body. First, MEG would replace the woman only during the period when she could be merely a voluntary bearer, rather than an involved parent. That is, she may not yet be involved in the committed interactive relationship that provides a greater impetus to sacrifice. She may be willing to carry as a parent but not as a voluntary bearer. (Of course, if she is interested in becoming a committed parent and carriage helped that come about, she has a reason to do it. But again, only if becoming as good a parent as a good father is were not sufficient.)

Second, preferring to change the world so that humans need not provide carriage is consistent with the willingness to carry if it is necessary. Consider an analogy: Suppose that fathers had in their blood the needed chemicals to cure their children of childhood diseases, but extracting these chemicals would require nine months of transfusions to the child. Suppose that we thought a father should be willing to do this if it were necessary. Would we, therefore, think it wrong to give the children drugs made in a laboratory instead of transfusions over the nine-month period? Would we think that fathers who used the available drugs thereby showed themselves unwilling to give their blood if this were necessary?

As things are now, the children of fathers and adoptive parents have been in someone's womb. Perhaps the fear is that with MEG the fetus would suffer because of the absence of some particular stimulation available in women's wombs. But this sort of stimulation perhaps could be provided in a mechanical environment. If it cannot, the old question returns: How much must people (men or women) who want to be acceptable parents do to produce perfectly stimulated fetuses?

Finally, the concern may be that pregnancy creates a special bond between a woman and her fetus, even hormonal changes that make women especially sensitive and responsive to their children after birth, and that this bond, with its benefits for child and woman, will be lost with MEG. To consider this worry, let us return to our previous analogy: It may be true that a parent who spends nine months transferring his blood to his sick child may have a closer, more meaningful relationship with that child than a parent who does not. But would we deem this a sufficient reason for not developing and giving the child a laboratory drug instead? The degree of benefit here is important. If pathological conditions resulted in children or mothers who used MEG, the argument would be stronger for its not being used. And of course those who placed a superlatively sensitive bond above the other goods of life might opt for natural pregnancy.

MEG and Equality

We should also recall that the special bonding that pregnancy (and later breast feeding) may develop between women and children is probably one source of the inequality in later child-raising responsibilities between men and women. For example, fairness alone might dictate that if women assume greater responsibility in the gestation period, men should assume greater responsibility for child care in the nine months following birth. (In this case, paternity leave might be even more important than maternity leave.) But the bonds formed in pregnancy may stand in the way of such a distribution of labor.

To highlight the cost of the special bond between mother and offspring, consider yet another analogy: Suppose that a group of platypuses who had offspring by laying eggs held a convention to vote as to whether to switch to internal gestation. The plan is that certain members of this community of equals would become special caretakers for the offspring and be provided with chemicals to make them enjoy the caring role. Child care would improve over what it is now in some respects, but only in some respects. For it may be that unequally valuable personality structures in men and women stem from the fact that the mother is the initial love object of both sexes. Even those who become caretakers benefit from any improvement, as they too began as children.

I believe that we could understand if the platypuses rejected the plan. The group might be concerned that social and political inequality might result and prefer to retain their original equality rather than have child care improved in certain respects. The fact that chemicals would make those who become caretakers happy in their position would not be seen as a solution to the inequality. Quite apart from inequality, the caretakers might oppose internal gestation for its burdensomeness and effects on personal independence, even if these effects were equally distributed.

On the other side, it could be argued that this is an incomplete picture: If the relationship in the internal gestation role is truly valuable, such a role for some platypuses would not introduce unequally valuable lives, for it might introduce a better life. Further, if chemical mechanisms are already present before pregnancy that result in depression when people do not become pregnant, or if significant pathology will result in children not maternally gestated, this will speak strongly in favor of non-MEG reproduction.

MEG and Power

Furthermore, some people may regard MEG as a threat to whatever power women do have in society, seeing reproduction as a source of power. This argument is worth exploring a bit. It is sometimes said that it is odd that women are handicapped in many ways by society because of the special "talent" they have to bear children, in addition to the other talents they share with men. But it is not at all odd that people with more than one "talent" end up being less successful, in a certain sense, than someone who has only one talent. If someone has a talent for computers and painting and leaves his job to paint pictures, his talent for painting may well interfere with his success at computing.

If, however, this extra activity is socially very useful, we may think it best not to penalize this person at work for his absences (insofar as this is possible). Therefore, men and women who have the ability to fight in wars to defend their country—a socially useful activity—may have their jobs protected. (And this will be true even if they enjoy fighting in wars and would do it even if it were not socially useful.) Likewise, if child-bearing were a socially useful "talent" and we encouraged women to exercise it, we might consider protecting their jobs as we do those of veterans, even if they enjoyed the reproductive labor and would do it anyway.[15] This protection would counteract, to some extent, the "natural" effects (described earlier) of exercising a talent that took one away from one's other work. It could not, of course, compensate for any drop in capacity caused by one's energies' being directed elsewhere.

If MEG were available, exercising one's reproductive talent would no longer be as socially useful, and so society's interest in compensating for it would be much less. This could hurt some women who wanted to continue to reproduce biologically. On the other hand, if becoming pregnant were a strong and unavoidable need, perhaps an argument for such benefits as job protection could be based on the justice of social support for "satisfying unavoidable needs," as distinct from mere developed tastes.[16] In this respect, consider another analogy: Suppose that a particular group of humans needed no sleep and could perform much more efficiently at jobs than we ordinary humans, who do have a biological need for sleep, can. Should we allow an economic underclass of "sleepers" to develop, or should we introduce some job protections? (Would it matter how many people would be affected?) Perhaps, more generally, preventing a means of reproduction totally external to women may be necessary to maintain any sort of power for them, on the grounds that being indispensable in such an important respect is bound to affect anyone's bargaining position or attractiveness.

Although it is not clear how strong an argument against MEG can be made by the considerations presented so far, I do not wish to deny that there may be both advantages and disadvantages to MEG. My only purpose has been to suggest some advantages, not to present a conclusive argument for MEG. If MEG offers certain benefits, what problem will it raise for the benefit–burden approach to abortion in particular?

Partial External Gestation (PEG) and Viability

Assume that there are at least two different types of mechanical external gestation devices: a partial (PEG) one and a total (TEG) one. A PEG essentially provides early viability for a fetus who can be removed from the woman's womb, but a PEG pregnancy must begin in the womb. Both the benefit–burden approach and the cutoff abortion argument are in certain ways connected to the view that the fetus would be no worse off if it were killed than if it had never been in the woman's body. Of course this is far from being a sufficient—and in the benefit–burden approach not even a necessary—condition for the permissibility of abortion. (That is, we allowed that the risk of being worse(e) off than if one had never existed might be worth the chance of a life with minima, or at least be acceptable given the chance for minima and the other factors moving in the direction of reduced costs for creation.)

If it is possible to move a fetus to a machine, another relevant comparison is introduced: The fetus will be worse off if it is aborted than it would be in a machine, where it does not need to impose on the woman in order to continue living. If there is a better alternative for the fetus than death by abortion, which also removes it from a woman's body, why should a woman be permitted to have an abortion? Perhaps she should be morally obligated either to go through with the pregnancy or to transfer the fetus safely. (This point was already raised when we discussed viability in connection with the cutoff abortion argument and in discussing Condition 5 in the abortion argument and in the benefit–burden approach.)

Suppose also that the fetus would have a safer gestation in a machine than in a woman who is willing to carry it. Then the woman's body, which it does not need, would stand in the way of the fetus's better prospects. What right has she then to continue the pregnancy rather than to transfer the fetus to a PEG? (Of course, if the fetus benefited from being in her in terms of bonding and the like, that would be a reason from the point of view of its interests for her continuing the pregnancy.)

These arguments help explain the significance of viability for the abortion discussion, independently of identifying viability with a crucial stage in fetal development. Consideration of a PEG method also reveals the possibility of a dilemma for those who are both concerned for the fetus's welfare and intent on having women be gestating mothers. The reason is that removing a fetus from a woman's womb might often improve its welfare. That is, the interests of fetuses may coincide with the interests of women if avoiding pregnancy is in the interest of both, or their interests may conflict if it is only in the woman's interest to continue pregnancy.

The Removal Procedure

What can we say about these arguments? First, they may depend on its being true that the procedure to remove the fetus from the woman itself requires no greater sacrifice than the woman would have to make in order to save the fetus's life or to avoid having it killed. If this were so, and removal did require a greater sacrifice, a woman need not make it. There would then be no morally relevant alternative to abortion that promised a better existence for the fetus that could be used for comparative purposes: The fetus may be worse off if killed than if transferred to PEG, but not worse off than it had a right to be.

We have already noted that the benefit–burden approach may have a result different from that of the cutoff abortion argument on the issue of whether we consider burdens comparatively or noncomparatively. That is, given the approach's concern for achieving the minima, what is crucial is whether the difference in burden between removal to a machine and abortion is greater than the woman would have to endure in order to ensure that the fetus obtained the minima. If concern for the minima were the sole determining factor, the same should be true of carrying through a pregnancy: We should see whether the difference in physical cost between transferring the fetus to a machine and continuing the pregnancy is greater than the woman would have to pay in order to avoid imposing the risks that come from being in her womb on the fetus. (It is unlikely, however, that seeking the minima is the only determining factor, as we shall see.)

What if the abortion procedure or live birth involves more or equal risk for the woman than does the fetus's removal to the machine, but the latter effort is still greater than required in order to avoid killing it? Should its removal, which is better for the fetus, then be required?

To prefer running a big risk in abortion so as not to produce a person whose mere existence would be a disturbance to oneself seems morally suspect (even though the alternative would be to have surgery, a cost that one need not pay to bring about an end that one does not like). Given how the benefit–burden approach derives a right not to continue with carriage, it would not endorse this abortion. That is, it takes seriously that a person should not be created without the minima, but it concedes on aborting, in part because of the significance of carriage. Especially if creating is voluntary, objecting to the existence of the new person and aborting it only for this reason is not in keeping with the spirit of the benefit–burden approach. But even if creation is not the result of a voluntary act or is the unintended consequence of a voluntary act whose avoidance would have been costly, the desire not to produce the new person seems inadequate to justify having an abortion when carriage is not necessary as an alternative.

This is also the conclusion of the benefit–burden approach when PEG is not available and carriage is necessary to avoid an abortion that is even more risky than carriage. Then the woman's not wanting to contribute great efforts to produce an outcome that will be burdensome to her on account of the fetus's existence is not an acceptable reason for having an abortion, because the differential cost is what is relevant. Furthermore, in the case of voluntary creation, in which one conceives because of the desire to produce a new person, changing one's mind and paying a higher price than carriage to avoid this result would not be permitted. These restrictions on avoiding great efforts which are nevertheless comparatively smaller stem from the concern for what is owed to a new person. It is only if differential effort necessary to save the fetus is itself greater than what the woman would need to do to save the fetus that she is not required to make the effort.

Arguments for requiring the fetus's removal to a PEG even if a woman wants to continue carrying it depend on the assumption that if someone or something is available to do more for the fetus than its current bearer would have do, the current bearer who chooses to continue must do as much for the fetus as the alternative would, or lose it. As noted when discussing the creation factors, this is not a standard to which we hold even voluntary parents, although it is a standard to which we often hold other caretakers. That is, we sometimes know even before pregnancy that potential adoptive parents would do much more for the new person than its natural parents would. But we still do not raise the requirements of acceptable parenthood for the natural parents. We do not expect them to do what the adoptive parents would have done, on pain of losing their children. Likewise, if a parent refuses to rush into a burning building to save his newborn infant, the fact that someone else is willing to rush in does not mean that the parent will lose custody of the infant, so long as running into burning buildings has not been established as a parental duty.

This noncomparative determination of parental duties might help explain why a person who wanted to be pregnant would not be obligated to give up the fetus to a PEG. The interests of voluntary bearers and parents in keeping their children, not only the minima interests of offspring, must be considered when these interests conflict. The psychological cost to the pregnant person who wants to be pregnant of making the fetus better off by not going through with the pregnancy herself is, perhaps, greater than she must endure. The noncomparative determination of duties is also relevant to the view[17] that someone whose fetus survives an abortion has lost any right to it, as she abandoned it in trying to have an abortion. If having an abortion is a way of refusing residence in one's body and the erstwhile bearer has no obligation to provide such residence, then she will be refusing nothing she was required to give. Legal abandonment means only a refusal to give what one is required to give. Therefore, a woman might still have a claim to her fetus if it survived abortion.

Total External Gestation

Now suppose that TEG (total external gestation) became available. How would this affect the benefit–burden approach? The effect of PEG was limited in part by the possibility that the removal procedure might itself be an impermissible imposition on the woman for the fetus's sake. But TEG does not include such a procedure. Rather, in a voluntary pregnancy it means choosing between beginning the pregnancy in an external device and beginning it in one's body. Suppose that a woman chooses to have the pregnancy in her body, even if it were predicted that a machine would gestate the fetus safely. It might be argued that she should be prohibited from having an abortion on any ground at all. The reason is that she would then deprive the fetus of a safe environment, which it could have without imposing on her. This may result in her being obligated, on pain of making the fetus worse off than it would have been without her assistance, to provide it with just as good a gestation. (The same problem would arise for someone who started a pregnancy in a machine and then decided to implant it in her body rather than keep it in the machine.)

As we noted, in pregnancy as it is now possible, we foresee that a fetus will be dependent. However, the creator does not make it dependent when it could have been independent. If TEG were available and a woman did not use it, she would be choosing to make a fetus dependent on her when it could exist without being dependent on her. (The problems that stem from voluntarily creating dependencies that can be avoided will increase if we are ever able to decide whether people begin life as fully developed adults or as infants.)

The claim that technology that may help increase the freedom of women should not have bad consequences for them seems an inappropriate response to the conclusion that a woman who does not use TEG may not have an abortion. The argument uses ordinary reasoning. For example, it could apply as well to the following case: Suppose that men had special capacities to help dying violinists and sometimes voluntarily let their bodies be so used. Then an artificial device was developed to help the violinists. If a man still insisted on helping, there is good reason to believe he must meet the standard of the machine.

The fact that men would be less free is bad, but is this more important than preventing their making in this way the violinists worse off than they might have been? Should we insist that machines not be built to save violinists because of the possible effects on men's freedom? Should we build the machines only on the condition that the previous arrangements concerning men not be disturbed? Should we, as a society, care less about saving the lives of some people by inventing means that by themselves do not require great sacrifices from others, because doing so might interfere with the freedom of men to attach and detach violinists? This seems especially questionable if exercising this freedom is not a matter of men's life or death.

In this case, there will be conflicts between, on the one hand, the group that includes both men who want the machines built so they need not support violinists and those concerned with better care for violinists and, on the other hand, the group that includes men who want to continue helping violinists but do not want more responsibilities associated with this.

The Value of Pregnancy

Let us return to TEG for fetuses. The loss to at least some women of not carrying a fetus in their own bodies may be so great—even though with TEG this no longer means not having a genetically related child—that they would rather not have children than have them in TEG. But by not having children they will suffer a large personal cost and also prevent the existence of a new life. The violinist will be plugged into the machine if not into the man, but there will be no fetus to plug into a machine if the woman refuses the options of using a TEG or being committed to an uninterruptable pregnancy. Given these costs (no fetus, unhappy woman), should we refuse to raise the requirements of pregnancy so as to ensure the same outcome as we could achieve by using a machine?

Unless there is a shortage of children, the threat of not having a child is not very effective, especially because there is no person who is literally deprived by not being created. We therefore are left with the costs to the woman as the dominant consideration.

We need to decide in regard to machine substitutes, whether there is a morally crucial difference between pregnancy and the case of the violinist. This difference may be that once again, the standard to which parents and bearers are held when we decide what they are obligated to do for their offspring is not set by the best that would be done for the offspring by others. Why is this? Both the desire of some people to bear children in their bodies and the cost to them of not having children in this way are so significant that they compete with the interests of the fetus. This may account for the permissibility of not having to sacrifice a womb pregnancy and of our not raising the amount of risk that women must take during that pregnancy in order to match the good outcome of a machine. (What may have been left out of this discussion is the concern about who will gain control over children not bonded early on to women. If this is a dangerous prospect, there will be another reason not to hold women to the standard of the machine.)

Notes

1. In fact, the procedures for providing patients with enough information to give an informed consent are probably inadequate. The failure to give data

pertinent to the particular category into which one falls, rather than to the general category, is one such problem. For example, one may be told the risks of a procedure averaged over all patient populations, rather than given the available figure on the risks for one's own age group. This problem can easily be corrected. Others may be more difficult to correct.

2. Not giving full information for fear that an agent will not evaluate it correctly and so act against his own interests also seems to be unacceptably paternalistic, at least if the agent is competent. (A competent agent is not necessarily one who makes only self-interested rational or morally responsible choices.)

3. I owe this phrase to Jonathan Bennett.

4. Shelly Kagan, *The Limits of Morality* (Oxford: Oxford University Press, 1989). Also see my review in *Philosophy and Phenomenological Research,* December 1991.

5. I discuss these issues and an attempt to justify nonconsequentialist morality elsewhere.

6. See Mary Ann Glendon, *Abortion and Divorce in Western Law* (Cambridge, MA: Harvard University Press, 1989).

7. People of the State of California v. Pamela Rae Stewart, Municipal Court of the State of California, County of San Diego, Case #508197. Stewart is also known as Monson.

8. According to the ACLU lawyer who handled the case, Lynn Paltrow, there is a dispute over whether the allegations accurately represent the facts.

9. Such a view can be found in John Robertson, "The Right to Procreate and in Utero Therapy," in John Arras and Nancy Rhoden, eds., *Ethical Issues in Modern Medicine* (Mountain View, Calif.: Mayfield, 1989).

10. Nancy Rhoden makes this point in "Caesarians and Samaritans," in John Arras and Nancy Rhoden, eds., *Ethical Issues in Modern Medicine* (Mountain View, Calif: Mayfield, 1989).

11. The Supreme Court in *Roe v. Wade* claimed that in regard to abortion, the state had no compelling interest in fetal life until viability. But it is possible that even if the state should have no interest in the ending of fetal life before viability, it should have a compelling interest in fetal life before viability if the life will not be ended. This is because handicaps of later persons-to-be can develop early in pregnancy. Suppose that one causes someone to be worse off than he might otherwise have been by doing something in the course of living one's life that affects him in the womb or before he is a person. It is worth noting that this may be, in certain ways, more like not aiding a person who is outside the womb than like harming such an outside person. This point is discussed below.

12. George Annas, "Pregnant Women as Fetal Containers," *Hastings Center Report,* April 1986, pp. 13–14.

13. The material in this section (along with shorter versions of earlier sec-

tions) was first presented as the conclusion of two public lectures: a Silver Lecture in Law, Science and Technology at Columbia Law School in January 1987, and a Faculty Colloquium public lecture at New York University Law School in April 1987.

14. Some people, of course, are opposed to human surrogates just because they do not form emotional attachments. That is, they object to the surrogate's deliberately entering into reproduction without an interest in keeping the eventual child and to her being able to leave it after bearing it. But if the child will have a caring parent, should it matter that its bearer is not that parent? And if in fact bearing a child or being genetically related to it does not create strong bonds in itself, why should we pretend that it does? The children involved will simply have to understand that genetic ties/bearing relations may not automatically produce lasting concern. Those who want genetic offspring, therefore, may desire simply that and not to have emotional bonds to the offspring. This is consistent with there being people who want a child because they want to be emotionally bonded only to a genetically related child.

15. Although the following question can always be raised: Why pay (by protecting jobs) for reproductive or warrior services that most women and men would perform for free?

16. See Thomas Scanlon, "Preference and Urgency," *Journal of Philosophy,* November 6, 1975, pp. 665–69.

17. Argued by Raymond M. Herbenick in "Remarks on Abortion, Abandonment, and Adoption Opportunities," *Philosophy and Public Affairs,* Fall 1975, pp. 98–104.

Index